Reconsidering Canadian Curriculum Studies

Curriculum Studies Worldwide

This series supports the internationalization of curriculum studies worldwide. At this historical moment, curriculum inquiry occurs within national borders. Like the founders of the International Association for the Advancement of Curriculum Studies, we do not envision a worldwide field of curriculum studies mirroring the standardization the larger phenomenon of globalization threatens. In establishing this series, our commitment is to provide support for complicated conversation within and across national and regional borders regarding the content, context, and process of education, the organizational and intellectual center of which is the curriculum.

Reconsidering Canadian Curriculum Studies: Provoking Historical, Present, and Future Perspectives
Edited By Nicholas Ng-A-Fook and Jennifer Rottmann

Reconsidering Canadian Curriculum Studies

Provoking historical, present, and future perspectives

Edited by
Nicholas Ng-A-Fook
and
Jennifer Rottmann

palgrave
macmillan

RECONSIDERING CANADIAN CURRICULUM STUDIES

First published in 2012 by
PALGRAVE MACMILLAN®
in the United States—a division of St. Martin's Press LLC,
175 Fifth Avenue, New York, NY 10010.

Where this book is distributed in the UK, Europe and the rest of the world,
this is by Palgrave Macmillan, a division of Macmillan Publishers Limited,
registered in England, company number 785998, of Houndmills,
Basingstoke, Hampshire RG21 6XS.

Palgrave Macmillan is the global academic imprint of the above companies
and has companies and representatives throughout the world.

Palgrave® and Macmillan® are registered trademarks in the United States,
the United Kingdom, Europe and other countries.

ISBN: 978–1–137–00896–1

Library of Congress Cataloging-in-Publication Data

Reconsidering Canadian curriculum studies : provoking historical, present,
and future perspectives / edited by Nicholas Ng-A-Fook and Jennifer
Rottmann.
    p. cm.—(Curriculum studies worldwide)
    ISBN 978–1–137–00896–1 (hardback)
    1. Education—Curricula—Social aspects—Canada. 2. Curriculum
change—Canada. 3. Education—Curricula—Social aspects. 4. Curriculum
change. I. Ng-A-Fook, Nicholas. II. Rottmann, Jennifer.

LB1564.C2R44 2012
375'.0010971—dc23   2012015246

A catalogue record of the book is available from the British Library.

Design by Newgen Imaging Systems (P) Ltd., Chennai, India.

First edition: October 2012

10 9 8 7 6 5 4 3 2 1

CONTENTS

Part 3 Curriculum, Intertexts, and Wisdom Traditions

FIGURES

ACKNOWLEDGMENTS

WE WOULD LIKE TO THANK PAST AND PRESENT CURRICULUM scholars either here in Canada or abroad who continue to ensure the intellectual vibrancy of our field of study and ongoing capacity to contribute to the worldliness of complicated conversations taking place among policy makers, curriculum scholars, educational administrators, teachers, and students.

Most of the chapters included in this collection were first presented as shorter drafts at the 4th Biennial Provoking Curriculum Studies conference held at the University of Ottawa in the spring of 2009. We would like to thank Ingrid Johnston, who at the time was the acting President of the Canadian Association for Curriculum Studies, for her support both in terms of the conference theme and advice on its logistical organization. In that vein, we would also like to thank Hans Smits as past conference chair for his invaluable advice on how to structure the program, making this biennial gathering a continued success for international curriculum scholars to experiment with the aesthetics of their research and conference presentations.

For their exceptional editorial assistance, we extend our heartfelt thanks to Tasha Ausman, Tanya Howard, Brian Kom, and Shenin Yazdanian, who read each manuscript from start to finish and offered invaluable editorial suggestions to each author. Our sincerest gratitude goes out to the authors for contributing their work, openness toward making difficult editorial decisions, and patiently waiting for us to find our collection a publication home. To this end, the book could not have been brought to its final completion without the oversight and editorial commitment of both Burke Gerstenschlager and Kaylan Connally at Palgrave Macmillan.

Finally, we are internally indebted to William F. Pinar and Janet Miller for welcoming this collection into their series Curriculum Studies Worldwide. Bill and Janet continue to be two of the most ardent and caring supporters of our work as curriculum scholars, and without their compassionate public service to our field of study, this book would not be possible. For his dedication to the internationalization of curriculum studies, his close reading and respective thought-provoking editorial advice, as well as his intellectual contributions in the "Afterward," we cannot thank Bill enough.

Series Editors' Introduction

"Provisional Modes of Connectivity Amid Difference: Canadian Curriculum Studies"

"Provisions"
What should we have taken
with us? We never could decide
on that, or what to wear,
or at what time of
year we should make the journey
So here we are in thin
raincoats and rubber boots
On the disastrous ice, the wind rising
Nothing in our pockets
But a pencil stub, two oranges
Four Toronto streetcar tickets
and an elastic band holding a bundle
of small white filing cards
printed with important facts.

Margaret Atwood

THIS SERIES' INAUGURAL BOOK, *Reconsidering Canadian Curriculum Studies: Provoking Historical, Present, and Future Perspectives*, vividly illustrates how complicated curricular conversations within national borders indeed may inspire nonidentical exchanges within and across national perimeters worldwide. I believe that this volume could stir such interactions through its specific focus on the intellectual advancement of Canadian curriculum studies in ways that gesture toward generative and crosscutting modes of complicated conversational engagement. While traversing the sweeping expanses of Canada's territories, its mountains, Great Plains, Prairies, and indigenous lands, authors specifically point to that which has been dismissed as excess or as easily excluded from Canadian versions of those "small white filing cards printed with important facts" about what and whose knowledges are of the most worth. Such conditions currently characterize education, in general, and by extension, curriculum studies worldwide.

In this challenging and evocative collection, then, coeditors Nicholas Ng-A-Fook and Jennifer Rottmann have drawn together Canadian and American scholars who collectively, and yet from differing curricular and methodological emphases, identify often dire consequences of never thinking beyond or "asking more" from official versions of those "important facts." For example, even in light of a formal Canadian stance of embracing cultural and national heterogeneity, these authors variously interrogate bundled-together "facts" that heretofore have comprised a colonized version of "one national Canadian history." This version of a history has left no room for the life-sustaining and generative "provisions" for any "journey" that the multiple peoples, lands, languages, and wisdom traditions located within Canadian borders could offer. Such provisions, if not in the past, certainly in the present and into the future, can act not only as buffers against the "disastrous ice"—the gouges of massacres, famines, commodifications of nature, subjugations of certain peoples and not others—but also as crucial resources for the re-thinking of living and learning as interrelated and intertwined.

Those twined aspects support a notion of curriculum as created, embodied, and read within particular and contingent places and settings, filled with individuals inflected with the past as it evidences in the present and in any envisioned international futures. Grappling with such intersections as well as disruptions of time, place, subjectivity, and culture, these authors construe varied approaches to examining crucial issues of Canadian life that frame any versions of its curriculum studies and school curriculum. Throughout their work, all contributors to this volume thus gesture toward not just examination and preservation of the past, but of the lands and its resources and histories of its people. They also conceptualize various versions of reconstructions of selves and others against and within present manifestations of that past, writ large—reconsiderations that now resist essentialized sameness or reified and therefore immutable difference.

This collection, then—an outgrowth of elongated and ongoing conversations among its authors and other Canadian curriculum scholars—presents readers with an array of topics and research journeys that, while distinctly located within and across Canada's borders, also portray each author's connections to and ethical concerns for all peoples situated within particular places of living and learning. Even as these authors insist on examining the unique particularities of Canadian lived lives—"a pencil stub, two oranges, four Toronto streetcar tickets," as it were—readers might extrapolate their own versions of curriculum studies and inquiries as always contextualized within analyses and theorizings of specific histories, politics, discourses, cultures, places, and subjectivities.

At the same time, these book chapter authors work from, and thus represent, a variety of intellectual traditions, reading, and writing practices, and even curricular conceptions that are situated within Canadian contexts and histories. Through their variances, however, they also demonstrate emergent possibilities that may indeed provoke others to conceive and create versions of curriculum studies that might both attend to and transcend artificial limits of a field formulated only as forever bound within and to specific constructed borders and demarcations.

For, while attending in deep, unique, and provocative ways to the human and nonhuman particularities of education and curriculum studies within Canada as nation, the authors in this text simultaneously have created an international meeting place of sorts here, a locus from which to reconsider what curriculum studies might look like at work in a multitude of worldwide contexts. In so doing, they also demonstrate a variety of ways in which we all might work differently, within our human collectivity as well as our various national uniquenesses, toward the internationalization of curriculum studies worldwide.

For instance, the conceptualization of *métissage* as both a research approach and a literary praxis provides a sophisticated theorization and exquisitely crafted form of life writing, a prominent mode of inquiry represented in this text. The curriculum theorists working within this mode who appear in this collection braid strands of their own writing and imagework with those of others. In that braiding, they offer to the field of curriculum studies not only a distinctive form of narrative curriculum inquiry but also complex means of highlighting paradoxes, contradictions, muddles, surprises and messy complexities of life stories that refuse to be spoken and written as familiar and comfortable.

These and the other authors in this text thus create new iterations and provocations that foreground their interconnections across differing cultures, ethnicities and races, in particular. They do so, not only through *métissage* but also through hermeneutic and auto/ethno/graphical as well as multicultural, complexity, and ecojustice theorizings, for example, thus providing examples of curriculum inquiries that are productive of possibly new and unanticipated constructions of selves and histories. By extension, further and differing national and international efforts, provoked by the work contained in this first book to appear in the *Curriculum Studies Worldwide* Series, may wish to focus on intricately knotted examinations, readings and analyses of particular social and cultural histories as means by which to both restore and create anew the unique "provisions" provided by and through situated peoples, lands, languages, and wisdom traditions.

For indeed, the works gathered together in this textual meeting place collectively command our worldly commitments to *refusing* singular, unitary and exclusionary versions of what and whose knowledges are deemed of the most worth. These primary curricular questions and these authors' foregroundings of their currency within and without national borders indeed open up a field of questions that reject boundaries and fixities, which historically have inevitably produced a domain of outsiders. Rather, these authors emphasize both the profoundly situational nature of life-supporting "provisions" that are social, historical, political and aesthetic manifestations of particular lands and peoples *and* ways in which such provisions too might be moving, crossing, and interweaving with/in other worldly manifestations. Thus, these authors collectively provoke and inspire complicated curriculum inquiries and conversations that could gesture toward further ways in which to work for the possible internationalization of curriculum studies.

As series co-editor William Pinar further details in his "Afterword," this volume indeed represents a remarkable collective achievement. We are delighted to present *Reconsidering Canadian Curriculum Studies: Provoking Historical, Present, and Future Perspectives* as the first book in this series, for indeed this volume pries open questions that make multiple, resistant *and* collective readings possible. These juxtaposed readings may enable those of us situated within and across the worldwide field of curriculum studies to reconsider how we might make associations—provisions, if you will—across variegated categorical, discursive, historical, social and cultural contexts. Indeed, we might, after reading this volume, set into motion further readings and inquiries of the curriculum studies field as both self- and cross-interrogating. By extension, then, the authors here may be providing "provisions" for such provisional moves toward connectivity amidst difference—toward the internationalization of curriculum studies worldwide.

JANET L. MILLER
Teachers College,
Columbia University

INTRODUCTION: AN UNCOMMON COUNTENANCE

NICHOLAS NG-A-FOOK AND JENNIFER ROTTMANN

> *To understand one's own situation requires close attention to history...In so doing, we might discern passages to a future worthy of those who have gone before us and those who have yet to come.*
>
> Pinar 2008, xvii

> *There is, however, a conspicuous lack of attention being paid to the meaning of curriculum theory in a Canadian context.*
>
> Osborne 1982, 95

> *And here in Canada, I ponder the word "nation" in "the founding nations," "the first nations," "the Canadian nation." I am pulled into the tensionality of differences of meaning. I ask more.*
>
> Aoki [1991] 2005, 383

EVENTS PROVOKE US TO RECONSIDER OUR ATTENTION to the world. How then, might an event like a conference call us to attend to our professional duties, to ask more of our historical present and future circumstances, whether we are attending to the worldliness of education as administrators, teachers, or curriculum scholars? How can such reconsiderations of our attendance to the world shift us away from disciplining bodies of knowledge through teachers and students marked as present or absent? Instead, how might we retrace our reconceptualization of attendance, its genealogy, reflectively and recursively, through its curricular roots (routes) to the etymological praxis of being present, presenting one's self, while stretching our minds toward something...like reconsidering an uncommon countenance of Canadian curriculum studies.[1] This book is a provocation, a calling forth, an invitation if you will, to experienced and burgeoning curriculum scholars, administrators, teachers, and graduate students to stretch their minds toward historical, present, and future reconceptualizations of Canadian curriculum studies. Like Aoki ([1991] 2005), in this book we provoke you to ask more...to feel the worldliness of education tremble when we utter words like "Canadian," "nation," and "land."

This collection is not the first to ask us to reconsider our professional duties and attendance to the field of Canadian curriculum studies. More than 40 years ago, Robin Barrow provoked curriculum scholars to reconsider the "common sense" of curriculum theorizing taking place (or not) within the different faculties of education across Canada. At the time, Barrow (1979) provided a personal view that provoked Canadian curriculum theorists to think things through, to suspect and question our personal and professional stances in relation to what he called a "Western industrialized state" (20). An admitted outsider from Britain, Barrow told us then

> the fact that I am approaching the matter from the outside will allow me to be less bound by cultural assumptions, less inclined to let sleeping dogs lie, less respectful and more candidate in my criticism than the insider is prone to be...There is not yet a very clear or long standing tradition of educational theory in Canada. So, encouraged by the generous reception accorded to other outsiders, I humbly submit this essay, which for the most part consists of arguments, proposals and suggestions that are essentially supra-cultural and supra-national, being derived from reflection on what schooling and education ought ideally to be. (20–21)

Indeed, his call for a "common core curriculum" that moved beyond the rhetoric of progressive and radical education movements provoked Canadian curriculum scholars, like Antoinette Oberg (1980a) and later Ken Osborne (1982), to pay attention, to ponder, and to ask more. "An essay in curriculum theory," as Barrow (1979) stressed then, "involves an attempt to think curriculum matters through from the beginning in a systematic way" (16). Although there was a sense during the 1970s and 1980s of "a conspicuous lack of attention being paid to the meaning of curriculum theory in a Canadian context" (Osborne 1982, 95), many curriculum scholars (like Ted Aoki [1980] 2005; Deborah Britzman, 1998, 2006, 2009; Jacques Daignault 1983; van Manen 1979, 1982; Antoinette Oberg 1980b; George Beauchamps 1972; William F. Pinar [1975] 2000); Madeleine Grumet 1980,

1981; Janet Miller 1979, 1980, 1982) both here in Canada and the United States were reconsidering their professional obligations to the field of curriculum studies in terms of theorizing differences of possible international meanings for curriculum theory . . . stretching our minds toward curriculum inquiry in a new key.

The year prior to Barrow's publication, Aoki ([1980] 2005) was busy provoking curriculum studies at the University of Alberta, to go beyond its apparent common sense. "Increasingly," he tells us then, "we have come to give [Canadian curriculum studies] a phenomenological emphasis" (109). And yet, at times, during their reconsiderations of the field, Aoki and his colleagues felt "suspended as in brackets," wondering whether or not they were constructing a "mystified dream world, in the process of estranging themselves from the mainstream flow of educational researchers" (109–110). Catching glimpses through their theoretical passageways to the future, Aoki and his colleagues became more "sensitive to the urgency of coming to know how to communicate cross-paradigmatically at the level of deep structure" (110) to theorize within the uncommon countenance of Canadian curriculum studies and commit their professional duties toward cocreating research paths upon which we contemporary scholars now tread.

During the 1980s, scholars like George Tomkins working outside the field of Canadian curriculum studies (within the field of Canadian Studies) published what remains the most comprehensive historiography on Canadian curriculum studies. *Common Countenance: Stability in and Change in the Canadian Curriculum* traces (and not without interpretive limitations) a history of preindustrial and public curriculum from the 1840s to the 1980s. As Canadians, we owe our thanks to yet another international scholar William F. Pinar (2008a, 2008b) now working at the University of British Columbia for provoking the republication of *A Common Countenance*, and reminding us to ask more of our intellectual histories. Working as a cosmopolitan scholar with a long history of disrupting axiological voids within the worldliness of curriculum studies, Pinar (2003, 2009, 2010, 2011a, 2011b, 2012) has been committed for more than 20 years to the intellectual and international advancement of curriculum studies. "While Tomkins' study is not primarily intellectual history," as Pinar (2008a) makes clear, "it provides a structure of such a history" . . . and, "what we are missing are intellectual histories of Canadian curriculum studies . . . and of the Canadian school curriculum after 1980" (xi–xii). Since the 1980s, Canadian curriculum theorists, and perhaps most notably Cynthia Chambers (1999, 2003, 2004a, 2004b), have sought to advance different interpretive meanings of and for Canadian curriculum theory.

Twenty years after Barrow's provocative call, Chambers (1999) published "A Topography for Canadian Curriculum Theory." Our challenge as curriculum theorists, Chambers (1999) reminded us then, "will be to write a topography for curriculum theory, one that begins at home but journeys elsewhere" (148). In this initial intellectual study of our field, Chambers speculates about some common topographic characteristics found within the Canadian territories of curriculum theorizing including issues of survival, of being an alienated outsider, of the impact of colonialism and our tenuous relations to the land. Today this essay continues to ask more, to pay attention, to stretch our minds toward such provocative questions: (1) How are we experimenting with tools from different Canadian intellectual traditions and incorporating them into our theorizing? (2) What kinds of languages and interpretive tools have we created to study what we know and where we want to go? And (3), In what ways have, and are, curriculum theorists writing in a detailed way the topos—the particular places and regions where we live and work—and how are these places inscribed in our theorizing, as either presence or absence, whether we want them there or not?

While mapping out part of that intellectual topography for the first *Internationalization Handbook of Curriculum Research*, Chambers (2003) emphasized that indigenous education remains particularly contentious and underrepresented in (mainstream or contemporary) Canadian curriculum scholarship. Since then, several Canadian curriculum scholars have sought to address such present absences in both provocative and productive ways (Chambers 2008; Cole 2006; Donald 2004, 2009a, 2009b; Haig-Brown 2008; Hasebe-Ludt, Chambers & Leggo 2009; Kanu 2011; Nahachewsky & Johnston, 2009; Stanley & Young 2011). In this collection, we continue to reconsider the uncommon countenance of Canadian curriculum studies and respective tensioned differences of meanings in response to Chambers' provocations at the turn of the last century. How might we Canadians, or those abroad, then learn from our pasts to discern passages toward a future topography worthy of those who have gone before us and those who have yet to come?

Since its inception, "The Canadian Association for Curriculum Studies" and its respective journal (thanks to the past, as well as the current editors Karen Krasny and Chloe Brushwood) continue to play a prominent role in supporting the ongoing intellectual advancement of curriculum studies. In fact, we can trace the fruition of this book back to the first Canadian Association for Curriculum Studies co-sponsored Provoking Curriculum Studies conference at the University of British Columbia. In 2003, this conference asked curriculum scholars to stretch their minds toward the theme of "Provoking Curriculum," with a subtheme of narrative experimentation. Initially, this conference was created to encourage creative presentations and conversations around interpretive and critical approaches to curriculum theorizing. This first conference celebrated the illustrious career of Dr. Ted Aoki, and the publication of his writings (see Aoki 2003; Pinar & Irwin 2005).

Since then, four other conference proceedings have taken place. In 2005, the University of Victoria hosted the second of such gatherings, which focused on "Trans/forming Narratives." In 2007, the University of Calgary sponsored the third meeting of this conference in Banff, where scholars provoked our curricular narratives with themes of "Shifting Borders and Spaces."

In 2009, the University of Ottawa would become the next site for this biennial pro/vocation to take place. In an effort to eliminate traveling to Ottawa twice within the same year, the conference was rescheduled to take place at the end of May 2009, rather than in February, as previously planned, to coincide with the arrival of the curriculum scholars who were also attending the Canadian Society for the Study of Education at Carleton University. This was the first time that the "Provoking Curriculum Studies Conference" would take place outside the western territories of Canada. Furthermore, hosting the conference at our national capital university provided a unique occasion to provoke a multilingual and multicultural rendition of this conference despite its colonial limits at an officially sanctioned bilingual university.

Past conference organizers, like Hans Smits (2008), expressed the difficulties he and others previously had faced in soliciting francophone participation. Although scholars from Quebec, New Brunswick, and Ontario did participate, francophone representation remained fairly limited. Nonetheless, our hope was that our gathering within this capital institution would afford international, immigrant, indigenous, multilingual curriculum scholars a common time and place to share our uncommon countenance of lived experiences both within and outside the field of Canadian curriculum studies. This collection of essays represents the experimentation of different international and national scholars who sought to attend to our conference theme of *An Uncommon Countenance: Provoking Historical, Present, and Future Perspectives within Canadian Curriculum Studies* (Ng-A-Fook 2011). Our most recent conference gathering in 2011 returned in many ways to its beginnings at the University of Alberta, where Aoki improvised, like jazz, theorizing curriculum in a new key, provoking curriculum studies as an aesthetics of vulnerability.

Therefore, the thematic thrust of the book evokes both historical and intellectual pro/vocations of a Canadian topography within curriculum studies, where scholars experiment with various theoretical and methodological ways to find an uncommon common place and begin the difficult work of reaching into and across our interdisciplinary territories of difference, both here in Canada and abroad (Chambers 1999, 2008; Pinar 2008b). The chapters in the book provide a historical overview of the various educational movements and intellectual trends that have informed the field of curriculum studies. And, as Chambers warned in 2003, this book is by no means representational of the diverse array of innovative curriculum theorizing—historical or contemporary—taking place across Canada (for other examples see work of Daignault 1983, 1992; Gidney [1999] 2002; Farley 2008, 2009, 2010; Ibrahim 2005; Irwin 2003, 2004, 2006; Leggo 2007, 2010; Lloyd 2011, 2012; Matthews 2009; Mishra Tarc 2011a, 2011b; Nellis 2005; Snowber 1999, 2002; Snowber & Wiebe 2011; Smith 2009; Sumara, Davis & Laidlaw 2001); but rather, represents a potential starting point to ponder, and then to ask more.[2]

Nonetheless, our collective work in this book shares examples of narrative experimentations with curriculum theorizing in relation to such historical movements and intellectual trends. The different chapters address educational issues such as, but not limited to indigenous studies, environmental education, intersectional, transnational, and comparative conceptualizations of antiracist education, multicultural education, internationalization, semiotic readings of urban landscapes, book clubs, as well as hermeneutic and auto/ethnographic interpretations of children's books inspiriting different provocations of curriculum theorizing.

This unique collection of essays provides an opportunity for its readers to engage in a "complicated conversation" if you will (Pinar 2006), a starting point to take up the different educational issues that these Canadian scholars put forth. As part of this conversation, the book attends to (methodologically and theoretically) what Chambers (1999) and Pinar (2007) call the vertical and horizontal topographies of the particular places and regions we both live and work within as curriculum scholars. Here *verticality* is, as Pinar (2007) explains, the historical and intellectual topography of a discipline. Whereas *horizontality*, he suggests, refers to analyses of present circumstances, both in terms of internal intellectual trends, as well as in terms of the external social and political milieus influencing the international field of curriculum studies. Studying the verticality and horizontality of such interdisciplinary topographies, as Pinar (2007) makes clear, affords us a unique opportunity to understand a series of scholarly moves both outside and within (as a form of wayfinding) what Chambers (1999, 2006) has called the topos of Canadian curriculum studies.

Established professors, junior scholars, and graduate students have written the essays in this collection. Consequently, the book provides a sampling of the diversity of lived experiences afforded to all who participate within the broader international field of curriculum studies. Each author invokes life writing and/or intertextual analysis as a mode of inquiry to narrate the tensionality of differences of meaning. Moreover, the authors provide provoking and innovative insights on how future Canadian curriculum scholarship might advance educational knowledge across interdisciplinary topographies that work to disrupt, blur, and complicate traditional modes of engaging the concept of "curriculum." Therefore, we invite readers to stretch your minds as you travel across the passageways of following three sections of the book: (1) Curriculum, Place, and Indigenousness; (2) Curriculum, Culture, and Language; and (3) Curriculum, Intertexts, and Wisdom Traditions.

CURRICULUM, PLACE, AND INDIGENOUSNESS

> [W]e take métissage as a counternarrative to the grand narratives of our times, a site for writing and surviving in the interval between different cultures and languages, particularly in colonial contexts; a way of merging and blurring genres, texts and identities; an active literary stance, political strategy, and pedagogical praxis.
>
> Hasebe-Ludt, Chambers, and Leggo 2009, 9

The ways in which we reread and live the intellectual history and present material realities of curriculum policies, here in Canada or in the United States, often continue to narrate national creation stories that disinherit indigenous histories, knowledge, and language by ignoring the potential pedagogical value they might bring to our contemporary educational contexts (Battiste 2011). Therefore, the concept of "indigenousness" and its respective teachings provide a potential passageway toward the future, for us to recursively and reflectively ask more of our national narratives, of narrating alter/native visions of living a Canadian post/colonial curriculum (Kanu 2009). A curriculum of the "postcolony" identifies a given historical trajectory of societies recently emerging, as Mbembe (2001) maintains,

> from the experience of colonization and violence which the colonial relationship involves. To be sure, the postcolony is chaotically pluralistic; it has nonetheless an internal coherence. It is a specific system of signs, a particular way of fabricating simulacra or re-forming stereotypes...The postcolony is characterized by a distinctive style of improvisation, by a tendency to excess and lack of proportion, as well as by distinctive ways identities are multiplied, transformed, and put into circulation. (102)

Reconsidering the worldliness of educational possibilities within and beyond our narrative imaginations of a Canadian postcolony, this section provides provocative examples of life writing and ecojustice research that take up indigenousness as an aesthetic form of theorizing our historical, present, and future relations to the uncommon countenances of curriculum, indigenousness, and place.

We start Part 1 with an invitation from Cynthia Chambers to reconsider the ambivalence many Canadians have with their relations to the past. She provokes us to learn from our life histories as passageways for how we might retrace our individual and collective genealogies as treaty people here in Canada. In turn, we are invited to disrupt the commonness of our national narrative descriptions of living as commoners on the uncommon territorial and political grounds of a cosmopolitan commons. She stresses that we are all treaty people. As curriculum scholars then, we are asked to attune ourselves toward reconsidering the negotiated contexts of our historical and contemporary relationships to treaties as a Canadian common countenance.

In chapter 2, Donald provokes curriculum scholars to ask more of the ways in which we narrate Aboriginal-Canadian relations. He suggests that future Aboriginal-Canadian relations must begin with a thoughtful account of the present state of affairs in order to reveal the very deep linkages to our past. Applying Barthes's (1972) semiotic notions of the sign, signifier and the signified, Donald provides a passageway for us to reconsider the image of the fort as "naturally" situated on the frontier, and the ongoing assumption that First Nation, Métis, and Inuit peoples remain outside accepted narrative visions of nationality. Holding different philosophies and worldviews in an organic tension creates, as Donald tells us in this chapter, a possibility for more meaningful talk on shared educational interests and initiatives that can be simultaneously life-giving and life sustaining for us all.

In chapter 3, the authors work with the concept of *métissage* as a critical point of departure. Building on this innovative curricular form of life writing, *métissage* asks us to reconsider how personal and family stories can be braided within the larger narratives of nation and nationality. Inspired by the Blackfoot concept *aoksisowaato'p*, which refers to the ethical importance of visiting a place as an act of relational renewal, Narcisse Blood tells prophetic tales that both honor and acknowledge the relationship to oneself, one's family, community, animals, dwellings, and land. Whereas Ramona Big Head shares her experiences of creating a play portraying the "untold" story of the 1870 Baker Massacre woven together with the personal trauma of destruction and loss. Cynthia Chambers parallels cautionary tales of magpies and buffalo, reminding us of how quickly things can go terribly wrong and of how hard it is for us to make them right again. Dwayne Donald revisits Edmonton and evokes the tumultuous relationship that the Cree and the Métis had with the Canadian government. Erika Hasebe-Ludt walks us through the streets of Vancouver's Downtown Eastside (DTES) articulating her thoughts and reflections about the tragic disappearance and deaths of many women, as well as of the diasporas of the Japanese community who are part of the legacy of a troubled national history of deprivation, expulsion, and racism. These stories ask us to reconsider our ethical relations to place, and what happens, whence we might forget. The chapter ends with a cautionary reminder of our obligation to take care of our stories and to take care of the land where such stories unravel, as a matter of physical and spiritual survival, as part of the webs of responsibilities that bind all living and nonliving things.

In chapter 4, the authors investigate different theoretical approaches that respond to the emerging ecojustice movement in Canada. Nicholas Ng-A-Fook traces the ways in which his intellectual studies within the international field of curriculum studies have helped him to reconsider concepts like environmental sustainability, greenwashing, and ecojustice. Darren Stanley draws on transdisciplinarity and complexity theories to address the kinds of conditions that underlie the emergence of healthy living and learning organizations. Andrejs Kulnieks works from an ecojustice framework to contemplate how a deep analysis of language can foster a greater awareness of life histories in relation to place. Kelly Young ends the chapter and this section by reconsidering how an ecojustice education framework can illuminate metaphors that perpetuate antiecological habits of mind in the development of identity formation. Indeed, the authors in this section draw upon life writing and ecojustice research to provoke us to ask more of our relations to curriculum, place, and indigenousness.

CURRICULUM, CULTURE, AND LANGUAGE

Now, I am beginning to understand the landscape of multiculturalism in the language of AND...AND...AND..., each AND allowing lines of movement to grow in the middle. Within such an understanding, Canadian multiculturalism is a polyphony of lines of movement that grow in the abundance of middles, the "betweens" and "AND" that populate our landscape.

Aoki [1992] 2005, 271

In 1971, Canada sought to confirm its place in the world as a cosmopolitan society by establishing a multicultural policy in federal legislation. Our national government has since built upon this first policy by integrating its initial tenants into the Canadian Human Rights Act (1977), the Charter of Rights of Freedoms (1982), and the Multicultural Act (1988). In fact, Canada was the first country, as Ghosh and Abdi (2004) remind us, to create and implement a multicultural policy at the federal level of government. It is not surprising then, that during 1990s curriculum scholars like Ted Aoki were invited to events like the Designing Japanese Canadian Curriculum conference hosted at the Novotel Hotel in North York Ontario. At this historical event, Aoki ([1992] 2005) told the audience,

I am supportive of the understanding of Canada as a multiplicity of cultures, particularly as a counterpoint whenever the dominant majority cultures

become indifferent to Canada's minorities. I suppose I reflect a minority
voice that asks that minorities not be erased. (268)

And yet, during this talk, drawing on the work of Deleuze, Aoki provokes minority scholars to ask more of our theorizing in relation to concepts like multiculturalism. He invites us to stretch our understandings of
multiculturalism beyond the striated linearity of its conceptualizations as a
noun—as a curriculum of historical dates to remember and celebration of
their respective multicultural festivities. To do so, he asks us to reconsider
Canadian multiculturalism as a polyphony of lines of movement that grow
in the abundance of conjunctive middles, the "betweens" and "AND," that
populate the international landscape we call curriculum studies. In Part 2,
the authors provoke us to pay attention to the historical and contemporary
ways in which we might begin to stretch the curricular lines of movement
leading toward minority children's language rights, the historical and present racialization of Asian Canadians, multicultural education, and the provocative curriculum of marginalized women smoking on the streets.

In chapter 5, for example, Egéa-Kuehne invites us to reconsider the lack
of rights afforded to those who speak languages other than English or French
in countries like Algeria, Canada, France, and/or the United States. She calls
for the right to be educated in one's mother tongue. She introduces us to
the curricular "interdicts" placed upon minority languages, which arguably
threaten their very existence. A first interdict is the deliberate refusal to
provide education to a child in their mother tongue. Consequently, the only
viable option for students who speak minority languages is often offered as
taking that language as a "foreign" language subject within the contexts of
public schooling. Her chapter calls upon curriculum scholars to pay more
attention to the disappearance of minority languages. Such loss, she warns,
would constitute an interdict to a child's capacity to articulate their human
rights.

In chapter 6, Coloma illustrates the ways in which Asian identities have
been and are racialized through the four following interpretive frameworks:
(1) *pan-ethnic*; (2) *intersectional*; (3) *transnational*; and (4) *comparative*. A
pan-ethnic framework, Coloma tells us, remains a contentious category.
This racializing framework works to both include and exclude those
who have been racialized and/or have been identified as Asian Canadian.
Reconsidering Canadian history through *intersectional and transnational*
frameworks, Coloma provokes us to reread its curriculum for the existing
narrative absences of Asian Canadians. Drawing upon a comparative interpretive framework, Coloma ends the chapter by asking us to provoke the
pedagogical ways in which the history curriculum works to create our collective public memory of who are included or excluded from the narratives
about Canada that we teach children. Collectively these frameworks invite

us to produce a more nuanced conceptualization of the processes of racialization as well as researching their respective historical lines of movement within the broader international field of curriculum studies.

Questioning what role curriculum studies might play in the promise of an equitable education for all, in chapter 7 Egéa-Kuehne addresses the complicated and conflicting layers of multicultural education. Educators arguably face a dual exigency of simultaneously responding to the necessity of respecting the particularities of individual differences and singularities, *and* the universality of majority norms and/or laws, such as citizenship (as a form of assimilation). In this chapter, she asks us to recognize that different kinds of cultures carry language and tradition differences. Therefore, all minority children face unique difficulties negotiating the processes of social adjustment and academic performance in school. In this chapter, Egéa-Kuehne urges educators to take risks in their leaning, and discover the unfamiliar that migrates beyond themselves and the striated boundaries of their immediate sociopolitical contexts.

In chapter 8, Sharon Cook rereads the smokescreens of curriculum for what we might learn from marginalized women performing their identities, cigarettes in hand, while surviving a curriculum of the streets. Cook invites us to consider her gendered document analysis of four historical black and white photographs taken by Lincoln Charles, of women smoking. For most of its history smoking, as Cook makes clear, has been a countercultural practice used by women. Like Hasebe-Ludt in Part 1, she provokes us to more pay attention to the vicissitudes of women living in on the streets of Vancouver's notorious Lower East Side (aka Skid Row) and in Toronto. Narrating the story of each photograph, paying particular attention to how the cigarette is used to control and empower, Cook asks us to reconsider the formal and hidden curricula of the streets, and the many social challenges of being an adolescent, urban woman in Canada.

In many ways, the authors in this section invite us to reconsider narrative constructions where English and French "cultures" and "languages" dominate Canadian history or contemporary policies in relation to racialized and gendered marginalized communities and their respective minority languages. These authors ask us to pay more attention to the historical landscape of multiculturalism, where each AND affords us new lines of movement to grow somewhere within an abundance of middles that populate the conjunctive curricular spaces among curriculum, culture, and language.

CURRICULUM, INTERTEXTS, AND WISDOM TRADITIONS

the word curriculum is yearning for new meanings... wherever teachers and students gather in the name of inspirited education.

Aoki [1996] 2005, 423

I have found the writing of certain existentialists extremely thought-provoking.

Huebner [1959] 1999

Wisdom can never be an enclave against the world but an invitation to live fully in the world in a healthy, life giving way.

Smith 2011, 172

Yearning for new meanings during the 1950s and 1960s, south of our national border Dwayne Huebner provoked us to ask more of our wisdom traditions, to attend to our capacity to wonder in awe of an inspirited education. "I have been reading casually, unsystematically, and perhaps without real comprehension," he told us then, "some of the writings of Gabriel Marcel, Buber, Berdyaev, Kierkegaard, Jasper, and Heidegger" (Huebner 1959, 3). He invited curriculum theorists, as Chambers was to do here 40 years later, to reconsider our theoretical tools for reinterpreting the existential dimensions of our lives together in schools—at that time, a thought-provoking pro/vocation for contemporary curriculum scholars. "Here is a channel of information about human being," he suggested in 1959, "to which we as professional educators have not been attuned by producers and users of educational knowledge" (3). A year prior to Tomkins's ([1986] 2008) first publication of *A Common Countenance*, Huebner (1985) called upon us to ask more of words like "spirit" and "spiritual." He invited us to reconsider curriculum studies through interpretive tools like phenomenology and hermeneutics to critique instrumental language (of the Tyler rationale, teachers do and then think, theory and practice, outcomes, standardize testing, etc.) and its rhetoric of accountability that even today dominates the worldliness of education. Other scholars in the United States and in Canada took up his pro/vocation, to pay attention, to ask more of "how the teacher's work influences the teacher's life" in extremely thought-provoking ways (Huebner [1987] 1999, 379). The authors in this collection much like Huebner, are inhabited by wisdom traditions (existential or otherwise) received from a (intellectual Father/Mother) homeland both here and elsewhere (Chambers 2003).

Chambers first traced an intellectual history of such Canadian phenomenological and hermeneutical poetics in *"As Canadian as Possible under the Circumstances": A View of Contemporary Discourses in Canada*, and its intertextual passageways offers us thought-provoking practical wisdom of both their limitations and possibilities. During the 1980s Canadian scholars, as Chambers (2003) tells us, like Ted Aoki, Max van Manen, Kenneth Jacknicke, Terrence Carson, David Smith, Margaret Hunsberger, and Dennis Sumara took up the study of phenomenological and hermeneutic research—inspiriting the worldliness of Canadian curriculum studies both at home and abroad. These Canadian scholars asked us to reconsider our curriculum theorizing as a form of poeticizing the world and its ordinary particulars, reminding us of our love for poetry and our poets, where such "poetry shows us what we cannot see and love, and yet always did, about each other and the words" (Chambers 2003, 227). In this collection then, we must remind ourselves of the cosmopolitan poetics of an intellectual history, while reading the ways in which these international contemporary authors invite us to reconsider what we cannot see, and love through their provocations of curriculum theorizing intertexts as an aesthetic of wisdom traditions, inspiriting education, venturing beyond prescriptive enclaves— yearning to live life fully in a life-giving way.

In chapter 9, William Doll Jr. begins with recursively and reflectively retracing pivotal writers and poets like Aoki, Bateson, Dewey, and Whitehead who have inspired his playful improvisations with curriculum theorizing. He asks us to reconsider Aoki's visions of inspiriting multiplicity within our reflections on reflections, while yearning for new curricular meanings, poetically, in what Smith (2011) calls "the most creative senses" (255). Doll draws our attention to a multiple perspectives framework; what he calls the 3 S's (Science, Story and Spirit). Each has its own mode of thought: analytic, interpretive, and intuitive. Reconsidering Aoki's (1990) essay "Inspiriting the Curriculum", William Doll Jr. posits the need for a curriculum to be inspirited, to bring life to it, to infuse it with a soul—to open it up to a fullness of possibilities.

Jardine and Seidel open up their hermeneutic pro/vocations in chapter 10, with a picture book named *Wabi Sabi* (Reibstein & Young 1982). Written in ten sections separated by roman numerals like a scroll, this chapter dances among and within intertextual experiences that are in their words, hard to explain. While retracing Wabi Sabi's world-venturing journey to open up the simplicity and complexity of a name, the authors invite us to reconsider the curricular etymology of words, while flirting with the slippages between names and things, putting back into motion that which has atrophied, opening up what was a closed case, helping us to remember something that was forgotten, and awakening life in something that seemed dead and lost from the intergenerational places we are a/kin to inhabit with others. In turn, we are called upon to attend to the hermeneutic venture of *experiencing* any word as a worldly, intertextual, and interpretative adventure.

In chapter 11, working with Aoki's (2003) notion of the slope [/], Palulis creates a forward sloping auto/ethno/graphy of a teaching life drifting like driftwork among post-structural geo/graphies. She invites us in to the intertexts of *Lulie the Iceberg* (Takamado 2008), where her travels bricolage recollections of lived experiences juxtaposed with intertextual artifacts of a/r/tography. These stories are traced across the theoretical landscapes of eco-literacy and geo-literacy, giving life to a living, breathing among pedagogical slopes of diffractions. Diffraction patterns, as Palulis contends, open spaces for, and the recording of, differences and interactions with intertexts. Threaded through the poetics of this chapter is how a children's storybook can act as driftwork to open up environmental issues and concerns, a space to hear the silence of Northern voices in Southern classrooms, and a way in which to ask more of how we are interconnected to texts, teaching, and nature—like driftwork, like icebergs, shifting, drifting, and swerving.

In chapter 12, Lewkowich invites us to stretch our minds toward the ways in which reading leaks interminably across the porous boundaries of disciplines and curricula: and more specifically, across the margins of medicine and literature. We are introduced to the difficult conversations that ensue in a reading group, spawned out of Memorial University's faculty of medicine in St. John's, Newfoundland. Emerging out of a larger study[3], Lewkowich observes the interpretive reading practices of HAM; the group's title born out of nostalgic memories of Dr. Seuss and the humorous tendency toward "hamming it up." Lewkowich frames his analysis of the collective's readings experiences through two key thought-provoking metaphorical concepts. The first is Michel de Certeau's notion of reading as a curriculum of poaching, where readers claim meaning and gamble with the precariousness interpretations of intertexts. The second is the concept of landwash: the phenomena of tidal flow where the seashore is in between high and low tide. The space of HAM, Lewkowich tells us, is a landwash site, a poetic *tour* of inquiry and pedagogy. This interstitial site provides a unique place, a middle way, a yearning to provoke change and progress, while remaining murky and marginal. In turn, this murky space creates the potentiality for multiple interpretations, poaching of meaning, and the much needed blurring of a medicated curriculum.

As teachers venturing into graduate work, in chapter 13 Lapthorne and Barrett offer their intersecting stories and historicity of two women's struggles to compose themselves as both teachers and intellectual scholars, which they see as an uncommon possibility for new teachers within Canadian curriculum studies. Using the Gadamerian notion of *bildung*—the work of becoming—this piece pulls together their ideas, voices and questions that provoke, compel and afford these authors what Smith (2011) calls a new pedagogical hermeneutics to reconsider the life they need to teach and study, to live life more fully in a life-giving way. Woven together as *métissage*, these two authors use life writing as an intertextual opportunity to study wisdom traditions, while reconsidering one's teaching identity. In the interest of self-understanding, these two teachers deem *currere* a necessary praxis, to explore the relationship between intellectual study and one's life history as women and as teachers. From this vantage point, as new teachers, as graduate students, as women, their conversations provoke us to ponder, to ask more of our interpretive pedagogical models, to pay attention to other voices, and reconsider the possibilities of being otherwise.

These scholars in this section provoke us to ask more of Canadian curriculum studies, to reconsider the wisdom traditions and languages we speak anew, infinitely recreating our lived experiences with intertexts in relation to the tensionality of differences of meaning, paying attention to curriculum that yearns for new passageways to the future, which seem to refuse any easy definitions—instead improvising with the worldliness of education, in a healthy life giving way.

PROVOKING PASSAGEWAYS TO THE FUTURE

When we come together from such diverse backgrounds, with international histories that involved colonization, occupation, political ignorance, and arrogance, how can we speak with each other in such a way that the past does not overshadow the present encounter?

Trueit 2000, ix

This is difficult work, and yet, the need has never been greater.

Chambers 2003, 246

Reconsidering Canadian curriculum studies invites us to ponder, pay attention to, to ask more, as we study the tensionality of differences of meaning in relation to the worldliness of education. This collection of essays invites us to study their historical topographies, their lines of movement, while stretching our understandings of contemporary circumstances either here in Canada or abroad. And, during such intellectual study we must be nonetheless suspicious, as Derrida ([1991] 1992) makes clear, "of *both* repetitive memory *and* the completely other of the absolutely new; of *both* anamnestic capitalization *and* the amnesic exposure to what would be no longer identifiable at all" (19). Indeed, this suspicious space of study is a psychic place where we can stretch our minds and share in each other's intellectual otherness in such a way that the past does not overshadow our present encounter.

Our sense then, is that the chapters put forth in this book and their respective overall themes would serve as an excellent introductory text for professors and students to study, suspiciously, in courses like an *Introduction to Curriculum Studies, Internationalization of Curriculum Studies,* or *Contemporary Issues in Curriculum Studies* at the undergraduate and graduate levels here in Canada. Or, for educators and educational researchers in other countries who teach an internationalization of curriculum studies and are interested in including a text on some of the different types of curriculum research taking place here in Canada. As such, the chapters in this book series seek to provoke readers to imagine alter/native ways in which we might learn from reconsidering Canadian curriculum studies to advance knowledge within the broader international field of curriculum studies as one of the polyphonic passageways to the future.

ENDNOTES

1. Taken from the *Shorter Oxford English Dictionary: On Historical Principles* (5th ed), Oxford, England: Oxford University Press, 145.
2. After the 2009 conference, a call for essays was sent out to those who attended the conference. The essays were then sent out for peer review. The following collection represents the essays that made it through our peer review process and whose authors gave us copyright permission to publish their submissions.
3. Lewkowich's study emerged out of Judith P. Robertson's (2003) SSHRC funded study entitled 2003. *Saltwater Chronicles: Understanding Reading in the Regional Book Club of Newfoundland and Labrador.* SSHRC Grant # 040121303.

REFERENCES

Aoki, T. 2003. "Ted T. Aoki's Speech." *Educational Insights* 8 (2): 1–4. Available at http://www.ccfi.educ.ubc.ca/publication/insights/v08n02/celebrate/index.html. Acessed on May 31, 2012.

———. (1992) 2005. "Taiko Drums and Sushi, Perogies and Sauerkraut: Mirroring a Half-Life in Multicultural Education." In *Curriculum in a New Key*, edited by William F. Pinar & Rita Irwin, 377–387. New Jersey: Lawrence Erlbaum Associates.

———. (1980) 2005. "Toward Curriculum in a New Key." In *Curriculum in a New Key*, edited by William F. Pinar and Rita Irwin, 89–110. New Jersey: Lawrence Erlbaum Associates.

———. (1990) 2005. "Inspiriting and the Curriculum." In *Curriculum in a New Key*, edited by William F. Pinar and Rita Irwin, 357–365. New Jersey: Lawrence Erlbaum Associates.

Barrow, R. 1979. *The Canadian Curriculum: A Personal View.* London, Ontario: University of Western Ontario.

Battiste, M. 2011. "Curriculum Reform through Constitutional Reconciliation of Indigenous Knowledge." In *Contemporary Studies in Canadian Curriculum: Principles, Portraits, & Practices, edited by* Darren Stanley & Kelly Young, 287–312. Calgary, AB: Detselig Enterprises LTD.

Beauchamps, G. 1972. "Basic Components of a Curriculum Theory." *Curriculum Theory Network* 10: 16–22.

Britzman, D. 1998. *Lost Subjects, Contested Objects*. New York, New York: State University of New York Press.

———. 2006. *Novel Education*. New York, New York: Peter Lang.

———. 2009. *The Very Thought of Education*. New York, New York: State University of New York Press.

Chambers, C. 1999. "A Topography for Canadian Curriculum Theory." *Canadian Journal of Education* 24 (2): 137–150.

———. 2003. "'As Canadian as Possible Under the Circumstances': A View of Contemporary Curriculum Discourses in Canada." In *The Internationalization Handbook of Curriculum Research*, edited by William F. Pinar, 221–252. Mahwah, NJ: Lawrence Erlbaum Associated.

———. 2004a. "Antoinette Oberg: A Real Teacher…and An Organic but not so Public Intellectual…" *Journal of the Canadian Association for Curriculum Studies* 2 (1): 245–260.

———. 2004b. "Research that matters: Finding a Path with Heart." *Journal of the Canadian Association for Curriculum Studies* 2 (1): 1–19.

———. 2006. "'Where do I belong?' Canadian Curriculum as Passport Home." *Journal of the American Association for the Advancement of Curriculum Studies* 2: 1–18.

———. 2008. "Where are we? Finding Common Ground in a Curriculum of Place." *Journal of the Canadian Association for Curriculum Studies* 6 (2): 113–128.

Cole, P. 2006. *Coyote Raven Go Canoeing: Coming Home to the Village*. Montreal, QC: McGill-Queen's Press.

Daignault, J. 1983. "Curriculum and Action-research: An Artistic Activity in a Perverse Way." *Journal of Curriculum Theorizing* 5 (3): 4–28.

———. 1992. "Traces of Work from Different Places." In *Understanding curriculum as phenomenological and deconstructed text*, edited by William F. Pinar & William Reynolds, 195–215. New York: Teachers College Press.

Derrida, J. (1991) 1992. *The Other Heading: Reflections on Today's Europe*, (trans.) P. A. Brault and M. B. Naas. Bloomington: Indiana University Press.

Donald, D. 2004. "Edmonton Pentimento: Re-Reading History in the Case of the Papaschase Cree." *Journal of Canadian Curriculum Studies* 2 (1): 21–54.

———. 2009a. "The Curricular Problem of Indigenousness: Colonial Frontier Logics, Teacher Resistances, and the Acknowledgement of Ethical Space." In *Beyond "Presentism": Re-imagining the Historical, Personal, and Social Places of Curriculum*, edited by J. Nhachewsky & I. Johnston, 23–39. Rotterdam, Netherlands: Sense Publishers.

———. 2009b. "Forts, Curriculum, and Indigenous Métissage: Imagining Decolonization of Aboriginal-Canadian Relations in Educational Contexts. First Nations Perspectives." *The Journal of the Manitoba First Nations Education Resource Centre* 2 (1): 1–24.

Farley, L. 2008. "An Oedipus for Our Time: On the Un-Discipline of Historical Relations." *Journal of Curriculum Theorizing* 24 (1): 20–31.

———. 2009. "Radical Hope: On the Problem of Uncertainty in History Education." *Curriculum Inquiry* 39 (4): 537–554.

Farley, L. 2010. "The Reluctant Pilgrim: Questioning Belief After Historical Loss." *Journal of the Canadian Association of Curriculum Studies* 8 (1): 6–40.

Ghosh, R. & Abdi, A., eds. 2004. *Education and the Politics of Difference*. Toronto: Canadian Scholar's Press.

Gidney, R. (1999) 2002. *From Hope to Harris: The Reshaping of Ontario Schools*. Toronto: University of Toronto Press.

Grumet, M. 1980. "Autobiography and Reconceptualization." *Journal of Curriculum Theorizing* 2 (2): 155–158.

———. 1981. "Restitution and Reconstructions of Educational Experience: An Autobiographical Method for Curriculum Theory." In *Rethinking Curriculum Studies*, edited by M. Lawn & L. Barton, 115–130. London, England: Croom Helm.

Haig-Brown, C. 2008. "Taking Indigenous Thought Seriously: A Rant on Globalization with Some Cautionary Notes." *Journal of Canadian Curriculum Studies* 6 (2): 8–24.

Hasebe-Ludt, E., C. Chambers & Leggo, C., 2009. *Life Writing and Literary Métissage as an Ethos for Our Times*. New York: Peter Lang Publishing, Inc.

Huebner, D. 1959. "The Capacity for Wonder and Education." In *The Lure of the Transcendent*, edited by Vicki Hillis, 1–9. Mahwah, New Jersey: Lawrence Erlbaum Associates.

———. 1985. "Spirituality and Knowing." In *The Lure of the Transcendent*, edited by Vicki Hillis, 340–352. Mahwah, New Jersey: Lawrence Erlbaum Associates.

———. (1987) 1999. "Teaching as a Vocation." In *The Lure of the Transcendent*, edited by Vicki Hillis, 379–387. Mahwah, New Jersey: Lawrence Erlbaum Associates.

Ibrahim, A. 2005. "The Question of the Question is the Foreigner: Towards an Economy of Hospitality." *Journal of Curriculum Theorizing* 21 (2): 149–162.

Irwin, Rita L. 2003. "Toward an Aesthetic of Unfolding In/Sights through Curriculum." *Journal of the Canadian Association for Curriculum Studies* 1 (2): 63–78.

———. 2004. "A/r/tography: A Metonymic Métissage." In *A/r/tography: Rendering Self Through Arts-based Living Inquiry*, edited by R. L. Irwin & A. de Cosson, 27–38. Vancouver, BC: Pacific Educational Press.

———. 2006. "Walking to Create an Aesthetic and Spiritual Currere." *Visual Arts Research,* 32 (1): 75–82.

Kanu, Y., ed. 2009. *Curriculum as Cultural Practice: Postcolonial Imaginations*. Toronto: University of Toronto Press.

———. 2011. *Integrating Aboriginal Perspectives into the School Curriculum*. Toronto: University of Toronto Press.

Leggo, C. 2007. "The Syntax of Silence." *Journal of Canadian Association for Curriculum Studies* 5 (1): 94–101.

———. 2010. "Life Writing Across Traditions." *Transnational Curriculum Inquiry* 7 (2): 47–61.

Lloyd, R. J. 2011. "Running With and Like my Dog: An Animate Curriculum for Living Life beyond the Track." *Journal of Curriculum Theorizing,* 27 (3): 117–133.

————. 2012. "Breastfeeding Mothers and Lovers: An Ebbing and Flowing Curriculum of the Fluid Embrace." In *Mothering a Bodied Curriculum: Emplacement, Desire, Affect*, edited by Stephanie Springgay's & Debra Freedman, 270–293. Toronto, ON: University of Toronto Press.

Oberg, A. A. 1980a. Untitled Book Review. *Canadian Journal of Education* 5 (1): 93–97.

————. 1980b. "Implications of Curriculum Decisions by Teachers for Curriculum Making." In *Curriculum Canada II*, edited by J. J. Bernier & G. Tomkins. Vancouver, BC: University of British Columbia, Centre for the Study of Curriculum and Instruction.

Osborne, K. 1982. " 'The Canadian Curriculum': A Response to Barrow." *Canadian Journal of Education* 7 (2): 94–109.

Mathews, S. 2009. "To Placate or Provoke? A Critical Review of the Disciplines Approach to History Curriculum." *Journal of the Canadian Association for Curriculum Studies* 7 (2): 86–109.

Mbembe, A. 2001. *On the Postcolony*. Los Angeles: University of California Press.

Mishra Tarc, A. 2011a. "Curriculum as Difficult Inheritance." *Journal of Curriculum and Pedagogy* 8 (1): 15–18.

Mishra Tarc, A. 2011b. "Reparative Curriculum." *Curriculum Inquiry* 40: 350–372.

Miller, J. 1979. "Curriculum Theory: A Recent History." *Journal of Curriculum Theorizing* 1 (1): 28–43.

————. 1980. "Women: The Evolving Educational Consciousness." *Journal of Curriculum Theorizing* 2 (1): 238–247.

————. 1982. "The Sound of Silence Breaking: Feminist Pedagogy and Curriculum Theory." *Journal of Curriculum Theorizing* 4 (1): 5–11.

Nahachewsky, J. & Ingrid Johnston., eds. 2009. *Beyond "Presentism": Re-Imagining the Historical, Personal, and Social Places of Curriculum*. Rotterdam: Sense Publishers.

Ng-A-Fook, N. 2011. "Provoking A Canadian Curriculum Theory Project: A Question of/for *Currere*, Denkbild and Aesthetics." *Media: Culture: Pedagogy*, 15 (2): n.p.

Nellis, R. 2005. "Trans/formational Spectral Narrative: Not Giving up the Ghost!" Journal of the Canadian Association for Curriculum Studies 3 (1): 41–49.

Pinar, W. F. (1975) 2000. *Curriculum Studies: The Reconceptualization*. Troy, New York: Educator's International Press, Inc.

————. ed. 2003. *The Internationalization Handbook of Curriculum Research*. Mahwah, NJ: Lawrence Erlbaum Associated.

————. 2006. "Complicated Conversation." In *The Synoptic Text Today and other Essays*, edited by William Pinar, 163–178. New York: Peter Lang Publishing, Inc.

————. 2007. *Intellectual Advancement Through Disciplinarity: Verticality and Horizontality in Curriculum Studies*. Rotterdam: Sense Publishing.

————. 2008a. "Introduction." In *A Common Countenance: Stability and Change in the Canadian Curriculum*, edited by George Tomkins, xi–xxiv. Vancouver, BC: Pacific Educational Press.

20   N. NG-A-FOOK AND J. ROTTMANN

Pinar, W. F. 2008b. "Introduction to a Common Countenance." *Journal of the Canadian Association for Curriculum Studies* 6 (2): 129–155.

———. 2009. *The Worldliness of a Cosmopolitan Education.* New York: Routledge.

———. 2010. *Curriculum Studies in South Africa.* New York: Palgrave Macmillan.

———. 2011a. *Curriculum Studies in Brazil.* New York: Palgrave Macmillan.

———. 2011b. *Curriculum Studies in Mexico.* New York: Palgrave Macmillan.

———. 2012. *What is Curriculum Theory?* Second Edition. New York: Routledge.

Pinar, W. F. & Irwin, R., eds. 2005. *Curriculum in a New Key.* New Jersey: Lawrence Erlbaum Associates.

Reibstein, Mark, & Ed Young (Illus.). 2008. *Wabi Sabi.* New York: Little, Brown and Company.

Smith, D. 2011. "Can Wisdom Trump the Market as a Basis for Education?" In *Contemporary Studies in Canadian Curriculum: Principles, Portraits, & Practices,* edited by Darren Stanley & Kelly Young, 153–187. Calgary, Alberta: Detselig.

Smith, D. 2009. "Postcolonialism and Globalization: Thoughts towards a New Hermeneutic Pedagogy." In *Curriculum as Cultural Practice: Postcolonial Imaginations,* edited by Yatta Kanu, 251–259. Toronto: University of Toronto Press.

Smits, H. 2008. "Is a Canadian Curriculum Studies Possible? (What Are the Conditions of Possibility?): Some Preliminary Notes for Further Inquiry." *Journal of the Canadian Association for Curriculum Studies* 6 (2): 97–112.

Snowber, C. N. 2002. "A Curriculum of Beauty." *Teacher Educational Quarterly* 29 (4): 119–123.

———. 1999. "The Eros of Listening: Dancing into presence." *Journal of Curriculum Theorizing* 15 (3): 17–25.

Snowber, C. & S. Wiebe. 2011. "The Visceral Imagination: A Fertile for Non-Textual Knowing." *Journal of Curriculum Theorizing* 27 (2): 101–113.

Stanley, D. & Young, K. eds. 2011. *Contemporary Studies in Canadian Curriculum: Principles, Portraits, & Practices.* Calgary, AB: Detselig Enterprises LTD.

Sumara, D., B. Davis & L. Laidlaw. 2001. "Canadian Identity and Curriculum Theory: An Ecological, Postmodern Perspective." *Canadian Journal of Education* 26 (2): 144–163.

Takamado, Hisako. 1998. *Lulie the Iceberg.* New York, Tokyo and London: Kodansha.

Tomkins, G. (1986) 2008. *A Common Countenance: Stability and Change in the Canadian Curriculum.* Vancouver, BC: Pacific Educational Press.

van Manen, M. 1979. "Objective Inquiry in the Structures of Subjectivity." *Journal of Curriculum Theorizing* 1 (1): 44–64.

———. 1982. "Phenomenological Pedagogy." *Curriculum Inquiry* 12 (3): 283–299.

PART 1

CURRICULUM, PLACE, AND INDIGENOUSNESS

"WE ARE ALL TREATY PEOPLE":[1] THE CONTEMPORARY COUNTENANCE OF CANADIAN CURRICULUM STUDIES

CYNTHIA CHAMBERS

I'M A COMMONER BY BIRTH, WITH NO INHERITED rights of property or privilege other than race (color white) and language (English): Irish peasants on my mother's side, landless Scots on my father's side. My mother cursed my father: "You, son of a coal miner!" The men in my father's family went underground to mine shale, not coal, (AAPG n.d.), a distinction that my father was careful to point out, and which my mother was careful to ignore. My father's retort was to call my mother "Irish," with all the disdain of a curse, one that accounted for her various shortcomings: a voice too loud, a tongue too quick, and manners too coarse. One March 17th, long after my mother had died, my father phoned from Vancouver to wish me a happy St. Patrick's Day, adding, "Well, you ARE Irish!" A quick reminder of what is uncommon between us. Although, both my 90-year-old father and I know that lowland Scots and northern Irish have bonked back and forth across Irish Channel since the Battle of the Boyne. Such national leapfrogging makes purity of identity based solely on nationality fictional and hard to defend, though defend, my ancestors did. While my father's father, Thomas Chambers, was born in Scotland, his father was born in County Antrim, Ireland. However, Thomas Chambers would become enraged at the mere insinuation that he was Irish. He also referred to my mother as Irish, which didn't bode well for my parents' marital relations. Thomas Chambers called my mother Irish even though her family had immigrated to Canada a century before his family even stepped off the boat. And, although his wife, Agnes Chambers, was born near Edinburgh in 1888, she went on to celebrate her birthday—March 17th, St. Patrick's Day— till she was 105 years old. Just missing steerage on *The Titanic*, so the story goes, my grandparents, Thomas and Agnes Chambers, left the shale mines of Broxburn, near Edinburgh, Scotland for the Alberta coal branch, where they raised my father and his siblings in a small miner's shack. Blackballed from the Scottish shale mines for his union activity, Thomas Chambers swore that his sons would not go underground. And they didn't.

"A man's a man for a' that," sayeth Robbie Burns (Robertson 1904/1963, 326), words repeated each year, on the bard's birthday, as the haggis was piped into the small dining room of my grandparent's home on Grant Street in East Vancouver. These words are more likely to be heard at family funerals these days.

While my father came from landless Scottish miners, my mother's people did have land back in the old country, centuries ago in County Clare and Tipperary, land that had been confiscated from Catholics and bestowed upon the good soldiers of Cromwell's army, as just reward for their defeat of the Irish on behalf of the commonwealth, the first one, that is (Elliot 2004). My mother's family, the Clarkes, left the United "Kingdom" for the colonies, just so many anonymous characters in a mass migration of Irish to Ontario. Family oral tradition picks up the story when they land in Manitock, near Ottawa, to work on the Rideau Canal. After soldiering for the British in the Boer War, my great-grandfather William Nicholas Clarke left Ottawa for Vancouver Island. He carried his silver teapot, inscribed by the Orange Order, across the country to the place where his children would be born but where he would die, late one July night in an automobile accident: the crash of a Model T Ford in 1911. The first traffic fatality on the Vancouver Island, family legend goes. After a night at the pub, so the inquiry transcripts go.

And while my great-grandfather died young, so did his son, George William Clarke. My grandfather, George William Clarke, lived his entire short life on the West Coast of Canada, and then he died at age 42, of *melanoma carcinoma* which began on his bare back, on his strong shoulders that had stroked the one mile from Kitsalino Beach out to sea and home again, every day, rain or shine. A butcher by trade, he died unaware of August Jack (*Khatsahlano, Xats'alanexw*), the great storyteller, healer, and *Swxwú7mesh* (Squamish) leader after whom Kitsalino Beach is named. Died ignorant, I imagine, of the removal of August Jack and his people from that now trendy neighborhood where my mother had spent much of her girlhood.

My mother's mother, Alice Clarke, was English. Second generation English with their colonial longing for a homeland never seen and forever lost, with their blindness to a past not their own. For the immigrants of my grandmother's generation it was as if their adopted country had no story, or at least not one worth learning about or remembering. They acted as if the story of their new home only began with their arrival on its shores. Alice Clarke, my grandmother, believed her station to be above all that Scots-Irish rabble: she cared not for Scottish bards, secret Masonic handshakes, or bearers of the Cross. A devout atheist, a one-time communist, longtime welder, and a believer in women's rights, she walked away from her middle-class home in Kitsalino, Vancouver; she abandoned her teenaged children to the streets of Vancouver, and with her new lover, a handsome rogue, better known for congeniality than industriousness, she headed to the Yukon. My grandmother walked away from the South. She left a life of curling tongs, permanent hair waves, and white gloves for a life in the North, where she could carry a rifle and wear red lipstick, where she could swing a prospector's axe and chain-smoke Rothman's cigarettes, where she could begin or end the day with rye and ginger neat, if she fancied, and she often did.

In the North, expatriates from the South didn't ask each other where they came from or why they'd come. The North was a place where southerners could reimagine and reinvent themselves. Just as Ontario had been such a place for the Clarkes, and the Alberta coal branch for the Chambers. Such reinvention might have been necessary for those who fled Vancouver for the boom in Whitehorse brought on by World War II. Those addicts and dealers, prostitutes and rounders might have needed a change in identity, but my grandmother, Alice Clarke, looked no further than the blue blood in her veins to know who she was. While she may have been a card-carrying communist when she welded in the Vancouver shipyards during World War II, and "what tho' on hamely fare" (Robertson 1904/1963, 328) we dined, a part of her still held to our British ancestors and the prince that "mak a belted knight / A marquis, duke and a' that" (Robertson 1904/1963, 326). My grandmother was what Robbie Burns would have called a "fool" for silk and a "knave" for wine (Robertson 1904/1963, 326). She warned me against commoners, which, in spite of our circumstances, of "honest poverty" (ibid.) she insisted that we were not. Like the old George Gershwin tune, "Let's Call the Whole Thing Off," my grandmother repeatedly told me that while "They say to*may*toes! We say to*mah*toes!" She admonished me about the dangers of exceeding the bounds of civility. "Never say the bum is drunk," she would tell me. "Always say, 'The gentleman is inebriated!'" Her nicotine-stained fingers held a Melmac mug of instant coffee as if it were Ceylon tea in fine bone china. Her stories were mythical tales of freedom, lyrical narratives of a heroine with a royal English past who had journeyed to the North, where she could be the unapologetic atheist and freethinker that she believed herself to be. In the North, Alice Clarke's hope for freedom lay, not with class struggle, a man's a man for a' that (Robertson 1904/1963, 326), but with modernity.

Because in Canada, as well as in Australia, the settlers believed that to be modern they had to break with the past, they and their descendants are deeply ambivalent about the past (David Malouf in Rabinovitch & Wachtel 2009). In many ways, Alice Clarke did her best to divorce the past. She was a tradeswoman who laid a fine bead of solder, wielded a hammer and an axe, and tightened the screws to the floor, all with equal skill. She sewed silk pajamas, linen drapes and muskrat fur coats with equal agility on her industrial sewing machine, the long ash of her cigarette rarely in peril. She sang an unending hymn of praise for the seemingly infinite glory of technological innovation. Many decades later, her speech garbled by a stroke, she still tried to operate her microwave oven and satellite television.

When I entered grade one in Whitehorse, Yukon, I encountered an entire curriculum that backed the currency of my grandmother's ambivalence about the past, her faith in modernism, and her restless confusion about the present. We show our children what to believe and how to believe when they are very young. We show our children how to have faith, says Ted Chamberlin (2003), "how to believe properly" (131) in their culture or way of life. We learn *how to believe* scientists and mathematicians, teachers and the curriculum, just as we learn how to believe singers, poets, artists, and storytellers. We learn to believe with our imaginations (Chamberlin 2003).

Perhaps my family, and our adopted country, is more Irish than we acknowledge. As Jonathan Swift (1711) said of his people: "We have just enough religion to make us hate, but not enough to make us love one another" (cited in Chamberlin 2003, 202). My mother and father fought their last battle the year before Sputnik was launched. This battle forever ruptured the domesticity of my mother's life and tore asunder her dream of a secure place in the middle class. With me in tow, my mother fled suburbia and followed her mother, and her rogue of a new husband, to the North.

The national narrative goes that by the twentieth century, the Dominion of Canada had evolved "peacefully" into "an autonomous nation" united with other countries by a "common allegiance" to the British Crown. Although allegiance was required, the North had nothing in common with the provinces, or with the autonomy and rights that the *British North America Act* (1867) afforded them. Instead, the North became Canada's "colony within" as the leftist political scientist and economist Mel Watkins (1977) called it. Never underestimate the capacity of the colonized for imperial rule. (The common countenance of the Canadian school, as well as university, curricula—past and present—provide ample exemplars of this.)

Like most colonies around the globe, the Canadian North was expendable. It was to be the first point of defense in a possible nuclear attack from the then, and apparently still, evil Russian empire on the true democracies of the world, that is, the United States and the "real" Canada, that mile-wide strip of civilization along the American-Canadian border (Jockel 1987).

And, the North is still expendable. For example, Canada is littered with abandoned mines; however, in the Northwest Territories (NWT) alone (that is not including the Yukon, Nunavut, or the northern half of the Western and Central provinces), there are over 600 deserted mine sites, all of them contaminated. Like all colonies, the North was, and is, vital to the economy of the colonial home office—a jeweled chest overflowing, in this case, with silver and uranium, lead and zinc, and of course, gold, and then that other gold, oil. And natural gas. And now, there are diamonds. Moreover, like all colonies, this one bore, and continues to bear, the troublesome burden of people living and laboring there, long before the corporations or Corpus Christi, long before the schools and their version of history and modernity and what ought to be the stake of humanity in the world.

In 1899, following the Klondike Gold Rush, the Crown pursued a treaty with the northern Dene. Like most creation stories, treaties are riddled with contradictions (Chamberlin 2003), and the numbered treaties between the Crown and the indigenous peoples of Canada are no exception. The Crown only bothered with treaties when they wanted title to the land, that is, when they wanted enclosure of the commons. And by 1899, the British had had plenty of experience with this.

Early covenants, such as the *Charter of the Forest* in 1217, protected the traditional rights of British serfs and vassals to forage in forests owned by royalty. However, over time, acts of enclosure ended the ancient practice of communal access to land. In England, the commons was slowly relegated to rough pasture in mountainous areas and a few parts of the lowlands. Over the centuries, enclosure of the commons for the creation of commodities gave rise to a landless working class: men and boys who went to the mines, women and girls who went to the mills. The British honed their skills for enacting enclosure of the commons at home. But as their empire grew, so did their practice of removing indigenous peoples from land held in common so that it could be put to "good" use, John Locke's sacred work of creating capital. And this is the story at the heart of colonialism: the people whose land was taken weren't using it anyways. Well, they were not using it *productively*. "For I aske," John Locke (1689), the seventeenth century political philosopher, queried

whether in the wild woods and uncultivated wast of America left to Nature, without any improvement, tillage or husbandry, a thousand acres will yeild

the needy and wretched inhabitants as many conveniencies of life as ten acres
of equally fertile land doe in Devonshire where they are well cultivated?
(Kurland & Lerner 2000, Chap. 16, doc. 03)

With the empire came British sensibilities about "being civilized"
(Herzfeld 2006, 135), and with that came a program to rationalize and order
the emptiness and dishabille of uncivilized space, and the uncivilized people
living there (Shiva 1997). These ideas might be dismissed as ancient relics of
a bygone intellectual dark age, if only they did not remain everyday utter-
ances on the prairies and in the North. "That Indian land is just wasted;
laying there doing nothing!"

This is the legacy of colonialism, the story of the enclosure of the commons, a commons unproductive in the hands of those without the brains,
industry, or culture to realize what they had. This is the heart of the treaty
story in Canada. In the language of the Crown, the indigenous peoples... "DO HEREBY CEDE, RELEASE, SURRENDER AND YIELD
UP to the Government of the Dominion of Canada, for Her Majesty the
Queen and Her Successors forever, all their rights, titles, and privileges
whatsoever, to the lands included" (AANDC 2010; Fumoleau 1973, 75)
within the bounds of the treaty. In the language of the commoner: Hand
over your valuable land and resources in exchange for a flag, a suit, a silver
medal, annual annuities of five dollars per year, and one square mile of land
per family of five. "As long as the sun shines and the rivers flow" (ibid.) is
the poetry of the treaties, the poetry of that solemn and binding covenant
kept alive in the stories. Poetry, conspicuously absent from the written agreement.[2] The trick of the treaties is that they both recognize Aboriginal title
and extinguish it in a single sleight of hand. Like a writ of marriage and a
decree nisi absolute rolled into one.

For the northern Dene, like southern First Nations such as the Blackfoot,
the treaties were conversation starters, rather than conversation stoppers.
The treaty negotiations, signings, and annual payments were "ceremonies
of belief" in a never ending, constantly unfolding narrative about what it
means for *newcomer* and *old-timer* to live together in these lands.[3] In the
old stories of the Dene and the Blackfoot, human beings are the "newcomers," and the animals are the "old-timers," who receive the newcomers with
compassion. In the old stories, the animals and humans understood and
spoke each other's language. That was the time, the Inuit say, when the
animals "took their hoods off" to speak to human beings (Chambers 2010,
13). In the new stories, the Dene and the Blackfoot are the old-timers, and
my ancestors, the newcomers. For the Dene and the Blackfoot, the treaty
negotiations are part of a very old tradition of speaking on behalf of the
commons. At the negotiations, the Dene and the Blackfoot spoke to their

people's need to make a livelihood. They spoke as if their lives depended upon it, because they did.

Even without You-tube and Facebook, stories travel; some have legs. And, as far north as their land was, by 1899, the Dene had already heard the stories from the South—the ones about how destitute the people were after the demise of the bison. They had heard the ones about the beaver trapped to the brink of extinction. They had heard the stories about the Cree and the Blackfoot enclosed on reserves, divorced from their livelihood, exiled from the places that had sustained them. In the North, people pay attention to stories, and wise people pay careful attention to certain stories, like the ones that tell about times of want, stories about times when the land cannot or does not provide, stories of famine.

As stories about the starvation that followed the demise of the buffalo herds made their way north, the Dene foresaw the danger to be unleashed if they relinquished responsibility to the land, to a people who had no stories, no songs, and no memories of their land. Perhaps for the Dene, and the Blackfoot, the treaties, the initial negotiations as well as the annual celebrations, were ceremonies that sanctified the land for everyone who lived on it: human and other-than human. The treaties certainly were, and continue to be, an invitation—an invitation to meet again: same time, same place, next year.

And, like other First Nations in Canada, the Dene had creation stories that predated the treaties. Like the one about Yamozha, who broke into the giant beaver's lodge, and chased the mother and her young to the fork of the DehCho (the Mackenzie River) and the Bear River, near present-day Tulita. At the confluence of these two great rivers, Yamozha killed and skinned the massive beaver, pinning their hides to the nearby cliffs, roasting their juicy flesh over an open fire. Where the delicious and precious grease dripped off the roasting beavers and soaked the earth, the ground ignited and has smoldered ever since. In 1920, Imperial Oil struck oil where the beavers gave up their fat, and then the Dominion of Canada wanted another treaty, number 11 (Chambers 1989; Chambers, Hasebe-Ludt, & Donald 2002).

The treaties are a story that we share. I say "we" because when I got married 40 years ago, I acquired treaty status through marriage. But, even without that marriage, even without the status of being both Dene and not-Dene, the treaties would still be my story, and my family's story. It is *our* story: the one about the commons, what was shared and what was lost. It is an elegy to what remains to be lost if we refuse to listen to each other's stories no matter how strange they may sound, if we refuse to learn from each other's stories, songs, and poems, from each other's knowledge about this world and how to make our way in it. Old-timers and newcomers alike, "we are all treaty people" (Epp 2008). "The treaties are for you, too" Frank Weasel

Head, Blackfoot spiritual leader and holder of many transferred rights, told a group of young non-Aboriginal student teachers at the southern prairie university where I teach (personal communication 2005).

"As long as the sun shines and the rivers flow" is the covenant of the treaties in Canada, a lyrical phrase that is what Chamberlin (2003) calls "a testament to the power of tales" (144). "As long as the sun shines and the rivers flow" is like John Milton's "bright countenance of truth," the true face of the commons that we share, indigenous and newcomer, men and women, southerner and northerner, human and other-than-human. The commons is what sustains us all: it is the true curriculum, the one that calls us to renew our relationships with one another, that calls us to renew our commitment to what we have in common, to our stake in the world and its survival, upon which our own depends.

> In the words of the bard, Robbie Burns,
> Then let us pray that come it may,
> As come it will for a' that;
> That Sense and Worth, o'er a' the earth,
> May bear the gree, and a' that.
> For a' that, and a' that,
> It's coming yet, for a' that,
> That man to man the warld o'er
> Shall brothers be for a' that. (Robertson 1904/1963, 329)

My ancestor didn't know the old stories, the ones that were here, in what is now Canada, before they arrived. They didn't know and they didn't ask. My ancestors were under the spell of a different story, the classic European emigration story: The Pied Piper of Hamelin. They were charmed by sweet promises of progress and adventure because they wanted to believe those things were possible, particularly for *them*. They wanted to believe in those ideas of the North that were rampant in the South, in the imaginations of southern Canadians: that it is a cold and empty landscape, amenable to transformation through civilization and history; that it is a frozen terra heaving with permafrost, waiting for the orderly press of modernity—roads, airstrips, utilidors, plywood houses and diesel fuel; that it is a dangerous hinterland, where "nature" is a cunning enemy that can be outsmarted, if not caged, by technology.

My family believed and lived out this immigration fairy tale, a different story than the one told by their Aboriginal neighbors and coworkers. What my family, and immigrants like them, shared with indigenous northerners was the need to make a living, to earn a livelihood. The Dene, the Métis, and the Inuvialuit needed diesel fuel, matches, shells, batteries, flour, sugar, and tea, especially when living out on their traplines or at their fish camps.

My father, and later, my stepfather flew the planes that carried such supplies South to North, from town to bush. My uncle and my step-grandfather, that handsome rogue who ran off with Alice, flew the planes that carried the sick and the wounded from bush camp to hospital. The bush pilots of my family and others like them carried children from home and hearth to "hostel," that Northern euphemism for the residential schools.

In the North, as in the South, the tale of the treaties does not begin in 1876 or 1899; nor does it end with the last of the numbered treaties in 1921. Instead, the treaty tale laid the path for other stories: the ones about Imperial Oil and Eldorado, Cominco and Giant Mines, Diavik and De Beers. The one about the people from the small village of Deline, formerly called Fort Franklin. The men and women packed out raw uranium in burlap sacks from the nearby mine at Port Radium on Great Bear Lake. Packed out raw uranium for three dollars a day—only to learn that their labor had helped build the bombs dropped on Hiroshima and Nagasaki, only to suffer twice as many illnesses as any other aboriginal community. Only to live with the two tonnes of radioactive tailings left behind. Deline is the kind of hot spot that no place wants to be.

Or, the story about Giant Mine five miles north of downtown Yellowknife, Northwest Territories that went broke after 64 years of mining gold, leaving a toxic legacy of 237,000 tons of arsenic trioxide stored in 15 underground chambers "a stone's throw from Great Slave Lake." So much arsenic trioxide that it could fill an 11-story office building and there would still be tons left over. And you don't need much—like that catchy Brylcreem pomade jingle from the 1950s, "A l'il dab'll do ya"—kill you, that is. With global warming, the permafrost is melting, and groundwater is leaking into these chambers. The federal government is left holding the bag, because Royal Oak, the company that last owned the mine, went broke. The Canadian government's latest plan, the "Frozen Block Alternative," is to freeze the chambers and keep them frozen, like your local hockey arena (AANDC 2011). Sounds more precariously perched than the ash on my grandmother's cigarette. And a lot more dangerous. It is a bit ironic that in the North, of all places, survival might depend on our capacity to keep toxic waste frozen, artificially.

There may be as many as ten thousand such abandoned mines in Canada most of which are most likely hazardous to public health and the environment: 5,700 hundred in Ontario, 45 in Quebec and 75 in the northern Saskatchewan, including the "dreaded uranium mines." There are over 600 contaminated sites in the Northwest Territories, and the worst of these are old gold mines (McLearn 2009).

Like all stories, the one about the treaties, and the land arrangements that followed in their wake, hold some Northerners together and keep others apart, hold some Canadians together and keep others apart (Chamberlin 2003). And no story tells the truth, the whole truth and nothing but the truth; each is a bargain between what can be told and what cannot, or will not, be spoken. Between what has been forgotten, intentionally or otherwise, and what is remembered, in whole or in part. The stories of the treaties "like all narratives, tell one story in place of another" (Cixous & Calle-Gruber 1997, 178). Dante (cited in Hanrahan 2006, 184) writes:

> In order to tell a certain story, sometimes we must tell another story, and go so far as to burn it.

The treaty story does not include the Inuvialuit of the Western Arctic, the Inuinnait of the Central Arctic or the Inuit of the Eastern Arctic. Without a treaty the Western Inuvialuit sought a comprehensive land claim agreement that gave them ownership over 35,000 square miles of their traditional territory and protected their rights to harvest throughout that territory. It gave them the right as well as the responsibility to protect and preserve the living beings in the Arctic on which the survival of those who live there depends, which then later evolved into "co-management" of arctic wildlife, fisheries and environment. Signed in 1984, the *Inuvialuit Final Agreement (IFA)* was one of the first of its kind, and was hailed as a model for joint "management" of resources. Often idealized, the *IFA* is fraught with problems, not the least of which is the metaphor of "management"—as if the critical question was how to "manage" the animals, birds, fish, plants, oceans, and rivers. And in the Eastern Arctic, Inuit fought for their own territory, and 1999, Nunavut (which translates as "our land") came into being.

"In all our conflicts," says Ted Chamberlin (2003) "we need to find a ceremony that will sanctify the land for everyone who lives on it" (227). Or, perhaps for *everything* and *everyone* who lives *within* it.

Eventually my mother moved to the South. This time my grandmother followed her. By then Al Boles, Alice's handsome rogue, was gone. He flew away with a doctor he was flying around on her medical rounds to northern communities. Eventually, I left the North, too, first for graduate school, and then the academy. I became a doctor, instead of eloping with one. While all that glitters may not be gold, it could be. That is the power of the imagination and of what we learn to believe.

I still have family and friends in the North: my oldest son, Kris Erasmus and his family, live in Yellowknife, on top of the highly toxic arsenic trioxide left behind after the gold was gone. And for the past five years I've had the gift of returning North to work with the people of Ulukhaktok (formerly called "Holman Island"), a predominantly Inuinnait community in the Inuvialuit Settlement Region, the only Inuinnait community that chose to remain in the Northwest Territories after Nunavut was formed. As a research team, we have puzzled over the curriculum question: What are the living literacies of this place? And the pedagogical question: How do the people of Ulukhaktok collectively remember (Connerton 1989) what needs to be remembered? And how do the people teach the young to remember? What is it children must learn so that they earn a livelihood in, and be committed to, the place that they live in? To be educated so that they may act on that commitment in ways that works on behalf of all of those who inhabit that place? We recorded Elders' life histories, and then struggled with translations from Inuinnaqtun to English, and back again (Chambers & Balanoff 2009; Chambers 2010). In their stories, the Inuinnait Elders speak of a different kind of commons, one of a shared past, a past that is still present. But like the Avalon of my ancestors, the past of the Inuinnait Elders, and all the knowledge and wisdom it holds, is slowly being shrouded in mists of fog, not from the Welsh marshes of my ancestral home, but from the rapidly melting sea ice. Like the constellations on a clear night, the past of which Ulukhaktok Elders speak may help us find our way through these times, when the commons continues to be enclosed and what remains is endangered (Chambers & Balanoff 2009). For Ulukhaktokmiut, the people of Ulukhaktok, the countenance of the commons lives on in the language, stories, dances, and songs, in clothing and art, in tools and what must be made from them. It lives on: in *nunakput*, our land; and in *hila*, which encompasses all of the cosmos, atmosphere, oceans, and living beings who dwell in these realms. It is in dwelling on the land with all those other beings, where the past becomes present: for Innuinait dwelling and wayfinding within *nunakput* is impossible without the commons, without the collective wisdom of those who had come before, without the smarts and the skills to live in this place (Chambers 2010). What we have in common, the Ulukhaktokmiut Elders tell us, is our need to live, to make a livelihood that does no harm. What we have in common is our need for a curriculum that can help us to do *just* that.

Perhaps what the commons needs most—at the moment—is some good old-fashioned common sense. Growing up in the North, I witnessed the common sense that I hear the Elders in Ulukhaktok speak of—a knowledge of the world; not the entire world but the world where they make their livelihood and have done so for a long time—a phenomenological knowledge, based on lived experience, wayfinding and dwelling in the places that sustain you (Ingold 2000). Knowledge acquired through the senses is held in common and remembered through repeated performances, oral retellings, narrative reenactments, and rhythmic mnemonics. The social memory of these experiences is inscribed on the land and in the material culture, not necessarily alphabetically, but through sign and symbol. Social memory is inscribed through *inukhuit* (or "inukshuks," the stone monuments seen throughout Inuit territory), tepee rings, caribou blinds, caches, and other stone formations. They are found in clothing and songs. The memories and the knowledge are reenacted in stories, dances, and string games. The commons are kept alive in people's kitchens in their town homes, and at their hunting camps on the land; and the human relationship to the commons is renewed through ceremonies, such as when the people of Ulukhaktok greet and feed the sun, each year when it returns. Or, when the Blackfoot gather each summer for the sun dance. Common sense dictates the people always be grateful and never take for granted those things that make life possible in the first place: in the South, the rise of the sun each day, and the collective memory of the once great bison herds, and in the North, the return of the sun each spring, and the now precarious caribou herds, and the land that sustains them.

Over 30 years ago, during the last big oil crisis, Thomas Berger (1977/1988) consulted northern Canadians about the conditions under which a natural gas pipeline should be built through their land to ship natural gas to midwestern American markets. Berger's first stop on his northern tour was Aklavik, a small community in the Mackenzie River delta of the Northwest Territories, a place where I had spent a few years of my childhood. A former special constable with the Royal Canadian Mounted Police, the man who allegedly had killed the infamous Mad Trapper, spoke first. Lazurus Sittichinnli told Thomas Berger, "I know all this land" because I've earned my living on the land for "a long time." And then he said:

I can see that for the future,
for my grandchildren,
and the future for their children,
I can see
that everything is spoiling,
and I don't like
what I see. (E. Chambers 1989, 270).

This message was repeated 30 years later by one of the Elders in Ulukhaktok. "It seems like our earth is getting tired," Mary Akoakhion sighed. "You know how it is when people get old; well, our earth is getting old, too" she said. "And the weather is getting bad, very quickly" (Chambers 2010). Perhaps, as Voltaire once observed, common sense is not so common after all.

Just as the people of Ulukhaktok don't take for granted the return of the sun or the caribou, I mustn't take for granted this second chance I've been given to learn to live differently. When I was a young child living in Aklavik and Inuvik, in the Canadian North, even when I was a young woman living in Yellowknife, I did not understand "the great gift," as David Malouf (Rabinovitch & Wachtel 2009) has called "the presence of one another"—old-timers and newcomers. While I did venture out of doors periodically camping and canoeing—the outside world seemed dangerous and wild; "out-of-doors," as the slightly old-fashioned English expression goes, was *nature*. I felt at home with *culture*: at the kitchen table, with my grandmother's stories of our uncommonness and the fidelity of our blood to royalty in some faraway land. While the outside world was an unpredictable and dangerous place, the school with its alphabetic literacy and its ceremonies of modernity was predictable and safe; it, too, was culture. I haven't come across equivalents for the words *nature* or *culture* in Inuinnaqtun or Blackfoot. Both languages have words for *home,* as well as songs and stories aplenty to find your way home when you are lost.

One thing I seem to have in common with my mother and my grandmother is a deep estrangement from home, from the commons, from the common ground, and even the common good. Exile, self-imposed or otherwise, wounds deeply. My mother moved so many times before her 69 birthday that I lost count. She celebrated her birthday, the last as it turned out, a little too hard and ended up in the hospital, once again. She never left. And my grandmother, Alice Clarke, lived out her last years in the South, but always grieved for her northern home and her northern life. What Emily Dickinson said of her mother, I could say of my grandmother: "Home was so far from home." A victim of a stroke, Alice Clarke lived the last decade of her life in a seniors' lodge in Kamloops, British Columbia. She was rebellious to the end; mollified somewhat by her daily ounce of Tia Maria, prescribed, she said, by the attending physician, and by the Peter Jackson cigarettes she chain-smoked silently in front of a television, and by the stories she watched in a language that she no longer understood.

I do not want to take for granted my treaty rights and my treaty responsibilities; and I do not want this for my children, or my grandchildren either. I do not want to take for granted this opportunity I have been given to live differently than my ancestors. This last chance to stop moving, to start listening: ". . . to find my place on the planet," as Gary Snyder (1974) says, "and to dig in and take responsibility from there" (101). "To dig in" sounds oddly agrarian for my blood, and the planet too big a place, too big a responsibility. But to find "my place," right here—to be responsible for how I live here, how I work this common ground with others—that does sound like common sense, and worthwhile labor. Work that is worth doing as best I can.

And as treaty people, I believe, this is our common countenance. And, if curriculum scholars and practitioners, such as myself, consider the matter carefully, this IS *our* work. It is work that needs to be done, for a' that, and for the common good; it is work best done together.

ENDNOTES

1. At Blackfoot Crossing in southern Alberta, the site of the signing of Treaty 7, Frank Weasel Head told a class of undergraduate education students, both Blackfoot and Euro-Canadian, that "not just Indians have treaty rights; we are all treaty people." The treaties formalized a shared relationship from which both parties benefit and for which both bear responsibilities. Year later, Roger Epp published a collection of essays with the title, *We Are All Treaty People;* he credits the phrase to Muriel Lee, an Ojibwa-Cree who said: "on these prairies, we are all treaty people."

2. Oral histories from witnesses to the negotiations and signing of the treaties report that the indigenous people, in each instance, agreed to the terms because the promises made on behalf of the Crown were to "last as long as the grass grew, the river ran, and the sun shone—to an Indian that meant FOREVER" (Fumoleau 1973, 75). While witnesses report this poetic wording, it is not included in the actual text of the numbered treaties.

3. Chamberlin credits the phrase "ceremony of belief" to Frank Weasel Head from an interview about a horse quirt originally owned by Crop Eared Wolf. Frank Weasel Head explained that carvings on the quirt recorded dreams rather than actual events. The text of the carvings was, in Frank's words, " 'a ceremony of belief, not a chronicle of events, and the reading of it was a crucial part of its power, then and now.' It was a charm" (179). The same could be said of the treaties.

REFERENCES

Aboriginal Affairs and Northern Development Canada. 2010. "Treaty Guides." Last modified 15 September 2010. Accessed February 19, 2012. http://www.aadnc-aandc.gc.ca/eng/1100100028653/1100100028654.

Aboriginal Affairs and Northern Development Canada. 2011. "Giant Mine Remediation Project." Accessed February 19, 2012. http://www.aadnc-aandc.gc.ca/aiarch/mr/nr/s-d2007/2–2951-bk-eng.asp

American Association of Petroleum Geologists, Energy Minerals Division. "Oil Shale." Accessed February 19, 2012. http://emd.aapg.org/technical_areas/oil_shale.cfm

Berger, Thomas R. (1977) 1988. *Northern Frontier, Northern Homeland: The Report of the Mackenzie Valley Pipeline Inquiry.* Vancouver: Douglas & McIntyre.

Chamberlin, J. Edward. 2003. *If This Is Your Land, Where Are Your Stories? Finding Common Ground.* Toronto, Canada: Vintage.

Chambers, Cynthia M. 1989. "For Our Children's Children: An Educator's Interpretation of Dene Testimony to the Mackenzie Valley Pipeline Inquiry." PhD dissertation, University of Victoria, Victoria, Canada.

———. 2008. "Where Are We? Finding Common Ground in a Curriculum of Place." *Journal of the Canadian Association for Curriculum Studies* 6 (2):113–128. Accessed January 24, 2012 https://pi.library.yorku.ca/ojs/index.php/jcacs/issue/view/864/showToc.

————. 2010. "'I Was Grown up Before I Was Born': Wisdom in Kangiryarmiut Life Stories." *Transnational Curriculum Inquiry* 7 (2): 5–38. Accessed January 24, 2012. http://nitinat.library.ubc.ca/ojs/index.php/tci.

Chambers, Cynthia M., & Helen Balanoff. 2009. "Translating 'Participation' from North to South: A Case Against Intellectual Imperialism in Social Science Research." In *International perspectives on education, PAR and social change*, edited by Dip Kapoor & Steve Jordan, 73–88. New York: Palgrave MacMillan.

Chambers, Cynthia, Erika Hasebe-Ludt, & Dwayne Donald. 2002. "Creating a Curriculum of Métissage." *Educational Insights* 7 (2). Accessed January 24, 2012. http://ccfi.educ.ubc.ca/publication/insights/v07n02/metissage/metiscript.html.

Chambers Erasmus, Cynthia M. 1989. "Ways with Stories: Listening to the Stories Aboriginal People Tell." *Language Arts* 66 (3): 267–275.

Cixous, Hélène, & Mirielle Calle-Gruber. 1997. *Rootprints: Memory and Life Writing*. London, UK: Routledge.

Connerton, Paul. 1989. *How Societies Remember*. New York: Cambridge Univ. Press.

Elliott, Bruce S. 2004. *Irish Migrants in the Canadas: A New Approach*, 2nd ed. Montréal, Canada: McGill-Queen's Univ. Press.

Energy Mineral Division, American Association of Petroleum Geologists. 2009. "Oil Shale." Accessed on February 19, 2012. http://emd.aapg.org/technical_areas/oil_shale.cfm.

Epp, Roger. 2008. *We Are all Treaty People: Prairie Essays*. Edmonton, Canada: University of Alberta Press.

Fumoleau, Rene. 1973. *As Long as This Land Shall Last: A History of Treaty 8 and Treaty 11, 1870–1939*. [1973 edition published by McClelland & Stewart, Toronto; 2004 edition published by Univ. of Calgary Press]

Kurland, Philip B., & Ralph Lerner, eds. 2000. "John Locke, Second Treatise, Chapter 16, Section 03" *The Founders' Constitution*. Chicago: University of Chicago Press. Accessed February 19, 2012. http://press-pubs.uchicago.edu/founders/documents/v1ch16s3.html

Ingold, Tim. 2000. *The Perception of the Environment: Essays on Livelihood, Dwelling, and Skill*. London: Routledge.

Jockel, Joseph. 1987. *No Boundaries Upstairs: Canada, the United States and the Origins of North American Air Defence, 1945–1958*. Vancouver, Canada: University of British Columbia Press.

Hanrahan, Mairéad. 2006. "Where Thinking is Not What We Think." *New Literary History* 37: 179–195.

Herzfeld, Michael. 2006. "Spatial Cleansing: Monumental Vacuity and the Idea of the West." *Journal of Material Culture* 11 (1/2): 129–149.

McClearn, Matthew. 2009. "Mining: Sh*t Happens But You Move on: The Saga of a Contaminated Mine." *Canadian Business Online*, April 27. Accessed 24 January 2012. http://www.canadianbusiness.com/article/14756 – mining-sh-t-happens-but-you-move-on.

Rabinovitch, Sheila, producer, and Eleanor Wachtel, interviewer. 2009. "Dreaming Australia, Changing Visions of a Nation: David Malouf" [Radio broadcast]. *Writers & Company*, Toronto: Canadian Broadcasting Corporation. Broadcast

April 26, 2009. Accessed January 24, 2012. http://www.cbc.ca/writersandcompany/episode/2010/08/04/wednesday-4-august-2010-dreaming-australia-part-three-david-malouf/ http://www.cbc.ca/writersandcompany/archives/.

Robertson, J. Logie, ed. 1904; reprint 1963. *The Poetical Works of Robert Burns with Notes, Glossary, Index of First Lines and Chronological List.* Toronto: Oxford University Press.

Shiva, Vandana. 1997. "The Enclosure of the Commons." *(TWN) Third World Network.* Last modified January 20, 2012. Accessed January 24, 2012. http://www.twnside.org.sg/title/com-cn.htm.

Snyder, Gary. 1974. *Turtle Island.* New York: New Directions.

Watkins, Mel. 1977. *Dene Nation, Colony Within.* Toronto, Canada: University of Toronto Press.

Weasel Head, Frank. June 16, 2005. Lecture in the summer institute *Connecting with Kitaowahssinnoon*, Faculty of Education, University of Lethbridge, Lethbridge, Canada.

CHAPTER 2

FORTS, CURRICULUM, AND ETHICAL RELATIONALITY

DWAYNE DONALD

I BEGIN WITH REFERENCE TO THE CONFERENCE THEME that inspired this chapter: "An Uncommon Countenance: Provoking Past, Present, and Future Perspectives within Canadian Curriculum Studies." I find the concept of "an uncommon countenance" as suggested by William Pinar (2008) and subsequently picked up by the conference organizers, to be an extremely important, timely, and a provocative *problématique* for us as curriculum scholars to engage with together. However, I'm also simultaneously curious and cautious about how the suggestion of an "uncommon countenance" for Canadian curriculum is interpreted and understood. What is at stake in denoting uncommonness in our curricular considerations? My concern is that the condition of being "uncommon" might be misunderstood as affiliated with celebrations of diversity, difference, and cosmopolitanism that sometimes operate in an axiological void, and thus provide little meaningful guidance on how to proceed.[1]

One of the more meaningful ways to fill this void is to attend to the historical nature of our experiences and understandings—to attend to the ways in which the past occurs simultaneously in the present, and deeply influences how we imagine the future. This desire to bring more historical consciousness to curriculum deliberations is advocated by David Geoffrey Smith (2003) who wisely advises:

> To think about the future, it is best to work backwards, tracing trajectories to the present moment, carefully working out the lineages that brought current

conditions into being. Only then can thoughts of "what is to be done" be meaningful. (37)

This stance is also implied by the conference subtheme. The conceptual linking of past, present, and future as intimately interdependent provides an ethical standpoint from which to see more clearly how any theory of the present state of affairs involves a confluence of past and future. For the purposes of curriculum studies in the Canadian context, then, the reissuing of George Tomkins's (2008) book on Canadian curriculum history is indeed a significant event. The book provides a detailed and valuable genealogical account of Canadian curriculum history that deepens our understandings of curriculum studies in Canada, where we have been, where we are, and where we might be going.

Tomkins' study, however, leaves off around 1980, which is about the time that curriculum scholars at my home university were just beginning to have an impact nationally and internationally. As a beginning scholar working at the University of Alberta, I take seriously the idea that the works of Drs. Ted T. Aoki, Max van Manen, David Geoffrey Smith, Terry Carson, jan jagodzinski, and Jean Clandinin, among others, are inheritances that make a claim on me and provide direction on how to proceed. Genealogically speaking, they are my curriculum forebears. However, as an indigenous person, I am also acutely aware that the Cree and Blackfoot Elders who have taught me are also curriculum forebears that deeply influence the spirit and intent of my work. The challenge is to figure out how to bring these two seemingly disparate influences together in meaningful ways.

The particular challenge facing the field of curriculum studies in Canada is to come to terms with the history of Aboriginal-Canadian relations and try to reimagine the terms by which these influences can come together. Attentiveness to Aboriginal-Canadian relations is needed because the ways in which the relations are conceptualized has a distinctive bearing on the ways in which indigenous issues are taken up in educational contexts as curricular and pedagogical considerations. Now, in light of the fact that indigenous Elders are still largely unwelcome in university settings, and in light of the fact that indigenous knowledge systems are still largely marginalized, isolated, and rendered invisible in university settings, it seems that the relationship needs much repair work. Following the wise advice of David Geoffrey Smith, I wish to suggest that any meaningful deliberations on the future of Aboriginal-Canadian relations must work backward, beginning with a thoughtful accounting of the present state of affairs and revealing the very deep linkages to the past. This approach, and the emphasis on the interconnectivity of past, present, and future, seems to be commonsensical though. "Nothing new here," you might be saying to yourself. Following

Tomkins (1986), however, I think that the challenges posed to the curriculum field by indigenous peoples and their memories, experiences, and knowledge systems have "some kind of deep psychic significance" in the Canadian context that makes the significance of ongoing indigenous presence and participation difficult to acknowledge and comprehend (440). It has to do with the power of creation stories. Let me explain.

The particular type of "creation story" that I'm interested in has to do with nation and nationality. The beliefs that citizens hold regarding the genesis of their nation-state and the stories that they have been told about the birth of their country have a significant impact on the institutional, political, and cultural character of the country, and the preoccupations of the people. Perhaps the nation-state that best exemplifies this theory is the United States. The creation story of America begins with English settlers, searching for freedom and independence, who cling to the eastern shores of a new land, and persevere despite the constant threat and fear of *Indian* attack. If we follow the theory that such beginnings have thus influenced the development of the American nation, Americans can then be described as a people preoccupied with perceived threats to their freedom and way of life, and frequently motivated to act on their fear of the intentions of outsiders and enemies, be they Indians, British colonists, African slaves, slave owners, Spanish imperialists, communists, or (in the current context) Muslim terrorists and terrorist states. The mythological historical narrative of their nation-state has taught American citizens to fear perceived outsiders and regard them as threats to their freedom, independence, and way of life. What of Canada and Canadians then?

For many generations, Canadians have been taught that their country began as a fur-trading fort. In seeming tribute to this genesis, forts have been resurrected and maintained as national symbols, and are today ubiquitous structures on the geographical landscape of Canada. You cannot travel very far in Canada without encountering either a community that began as a fur-trading post or fort, a town or city that still uses the official title of "Fort" in its current name, or a historic site of a fort recreated as a museum. These celebrations of the history of the nation have fostered the development of a national logic—delineated by the fort walls—of insiders (settlers) and outsiders (Indians). The creation story of Canada continues to haunt our contemporary Canadian society by defining the terms according to which Aboriginal peoples and Canadians speak to each other about history, memory, place, and the land.

What, then, does this creation story teach about Aboriginal-Canadian relations? Here I want to remind that curriculum is "a highly symbolic concept" and "an extraordinarily complicated conversation" (Pinar et al. 1995). I do so to emphasize the point that the ways in which Aboriginal-Canadian relations are conceptualized, and thus expressed in curriculum considerations, is deeply embedded within our national narrative and mythically symbolized by the fort. In using the word "myth" in this case, I don't mean to suggest that someone has made something up. Instead, I believe that myths are actually truths about culture and conventional views of history that have both been deeply influenced by the stories of our country that we have been told in school.

The work of Roland Barthes is helpful to understand the power of myth. Barthes builds on the semiology of Saussure to articulate a semiological structure for myth as a way to "bring myth to order, to read it and therefore to provide the basis for a viable critique" (Allen 2003, 45). In this semiotic structure, the signifier is the "acoustic or graphic element" and the signified is the "mental concept conventionally associated with it" (Rylance 1994, 35). To demonstrate, consider this Barthesian first-order semiological system (Barthes 1972, 115) (see fig. 2.1).

In this example, the signifier of the fort connotes the typical visual or graphic portrayal of forts—of how they are imagined. This imagined fort depends on prior experience with forts; we know how they are supposed to look, in an archetypal way. In the context of western Canada, this signifier "fort" conjures in many minds the signified concept of the frontier. Forts and fortresses are built to assert sovereignty over an area or people, to physically separate insiders from outsiders, and to provide surveillance over a border area. Therefore, forts are typically built in these overlapping, contested, and emergent areas that we call frontiers. Finally, when signifier and signified come together as sign, the predominant image conjured is this imagined fort, situated at its *natural place* on the frontier. The fort and the frontier, then, have a deep semiotic and symbolic association.

Barthes's key contribution to our understandings of mythologies comes through his theoretical tracing of the ways in which first-order semiological systems get coopted by second-order semiological or myth-producing systems. "Myth acts on already existent signs, whether they be written statements or texts, photographs, films, music, buildings, or garments.... Mythology takes this sign and turns it into a signifier for a new signified,

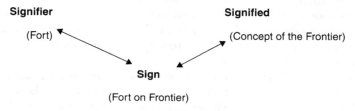

Figure 2.1   Barthesian First Order Semiological System

a new concept" (Allen 2003, 42–43). Myth, then, transforms first-order meanings into second-order meanings.

Recall that the previous diagram depicting a first-order semiological system produced a sign termed "Fort on Frontier." In the process of transforming this sign into the domain of mythology, then, an adaptation of Barthes's second-order semiological system looks like this (see fig. 2.2).

Barthes (1972) argues that myth raises the sign produced from the first-order semiological system (shown in the previous diagram) to a second-order level, turning that sign into a new signifier for a new signified and thus a new "mythologized" sign. Consider, then, that the first-order sign "Fort on Frontier" conjures images of a typical fort established on a perceived frontier. In light of the developmental myth of the West, however, the sign "Fort on Frontier" acquires deeper, mythological significance. This appropriated first-order sign, now as second-order signifier, becomes symbolic of the process through which wild and underutilized lands were civilized through European exploration, takeover, and settlement. The signified "Civilization in Wilderness" locates the conceptual place that the fort occupies in the mythological landscape of the colonial imaginary. The myth of civilization, serving as an organizing and rallying point for modernity, is posted on the terrain in the form of the fort. The "Fort on Frontier" signifies the material manifestation of this process. In this example, building a fort on contested lands is a sovereign act motivated by the myth of modernity—a myth founded on the belief that the Eurocentric version of progress and development brings benefits to all (Dussel 1995, 64). The key point here is that the fort, seen through the lens of myth in Canada, symbolizes, and is a sign, of the development of the West. The fort, then, is a mythic sign that initiates, substantiates and, through its density, hides the teleological story of the development of the nation.

This teleology has morphed into a national ideology that has shaped the institutions and conventions of Canadian society and operates according to an

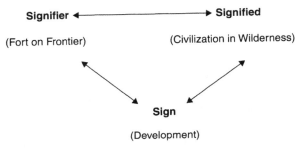

Figure 2.2   Barthes's Second-Order Semiological System

assumption of Aboriginal peoples as being outside accepted versions of nation and nationality. More to the point, the high historical status given to the fort in Canadian history has been telescoped to the present context as a sociospatial organizer of peoples and cultures that delimits *and* explains difference as irreconcilable. This, then, is the pedagogy of the fort (Donald 2009a).

Fort pedagogy works according to an insistence that everyone must be brought inside and become like the insiders, or they will be eliminated. The fort teaches us that outsiders must be either incorporated, or excluded, in order for development to occur in the desired ways. The strange difference of indigenousness is thus rendered incomprehensible to Canadian citizenship because it cannot be reconciled with the teleological dream of nation and nationality that has been propagated in schools for many generations (Donald 2009b). Schools and curricula are predicated on these logics and both have served to enforce epistemological and social conformity to Euro-Western standards established and presumably held in common by *insiders*. Outsiders and their knowledges have been actively excluded from meaningful participation in Canadian public institutions like schools and universities. The daily operations of schools and classrooms are heavily influenced by colonial frontier logics and often replicate the pedagogy of the fort in troubling ways.

So, how can these relations be decolonized, transformed, and thus renewed? How do we overcome the power of the creation story? I argue that decolonization, on a broad scale and especially in educational contexts, can only occur when Aboriginal peoples and Canadians face each other across these deeply learned divides, revisit and deconstruct their shared past, and engage critically with the realization that their present and future is similarly tied together. After all, as Kainai Elder Andy Blackwater advises, our tepees are all held down by the same pegs now (Chambers & Blood 2009).

An important consideration of this work, though, concerns the spirit and intent of this engagement. On what and whose terms can we begin decolonization? I think Willie Ermine's notion of ethical space is especially helpful in reimagining Aboriginal-Canadian relations. Ermine (2007) understands ethics as the basic human "capacity to know what harms or enhances the well-being of sentient creatures" (195). Ethics is concerned with our basic humanity and our cherished notions of good, responsibility, duty, and obligations. Ethics constitutes the framework of cultural boundaries that we recognize and respect as part of our daily lives.

For Ermine (2007), ethical space is the area between two entities, the points of contact that entangle and enmesh. Imagine that the two entities are Aboriginal and Canadian. Ethical space is a space of possibility—it speaks in the language of possibility—but it can only be created when it is affirmed that we are dealing with two different entities, worldviews, and knowledge systems. Once we affirm the existence of that other entity, then ethical space emerges as a possibility. The idea of ethical space entertains the possibility of a meeting place. The space offers a venue to step out of our allegiances, to detach from the circumscriptive limits of colonial frontier logics, and enact a theory of human relationality that does not require assimilation or deny indigenous subjectivity.

Inspired by this idea of ethical space, as well as the repeated reminder from Elders that we must attend to our relations—that it's all about relationships—I have conceptualized a curricular and pedagogical imperative called ethical relationality. Ethical relationality is an ecological understanding of human relationality that does not deny difference, but rather seeks to more deeply understand how our different histories and experiences position us in relation to each other. This form of relationality is ethical because it does not overlook or render invisible the particular historical, cultural, and social contexts from which a standpoint arises. Rather, it puts these considerations at the forefront of engagements across frontiers of difference.

Ethical relationality describes a curricular and pedagogical vision for a historicized and decolonial reframing of Aboriginal-Canadian relations that places indigenous philosophies and wisdom traditions at the forefront as guiding ethical principles. Emphasis on indigenous philosophies is necessary because, until quite recently, Canadians have generally practiced an *un*ethical form of relationality with Aboriginal peoples directed toward benevolent incorporation within Canadian nationality and citizenship. Canadians have tried to bring *their* Indians in from the wilderness. This form of relationality is unethical, and rooted in colonial frontier logics and fort pedagogy, because it fails to support the organic continuance of indigenous ways. It seeks to eliminate them. Ethical relationality, then, is an ecological curricular and pedagogical imperative that calls for more ethical understandings of Aboriginal-Canadian relations. Sustained attentiveness to Aboriginal-Canadian relations and willingness to hold differing philosophies and worldviews in tension creates the possibility for more meaningful talk on shared educational interests and initiatives. I believe that this organic tension provides potential sources of creativity that can be simultaneously life-giving and life sustaining for us all.

ENDNOTE

1. Here I am referring to the various "post" theories—postmodernism, postcolonialism, poststructuralism—that often promote hybridity as a new utopic form of subjectivity worthy of celebration. At times, these theoretical celebrations can amount to a troubling fetishization of culture and identity in the "third space" (Bhabha, 1990) at the expense of sustained deliberations on social power and difference. See Donald (2011, 6–9) for more on this.

REFERENCES

Allen, Graham. 2003. *Roland Barthes*. London: New York: Routledge.

Barthes, Roland. 1972. *Mythologies*. Translated by Annette Lavers. New York: Hill and Wang.

Bhabha, Homi. 1990. "The Third Space." In *Identity: Community, Culture, Difference*, edited by Jonathan Rutherford, 207–221. London: Lawrence and Wishert.

Chambers, Cynthia, & Narcisse Blood. 2009. "Love Thy Neighbour: Repatriating Precarious Blackfoot Sites." *International Journal of Canadian Studies* 39–40: 253–279.

Donald, Dwayne. 2011. "Indigenous Métissage: A Decolonizing Research Sensibility." *International Journal of Qualitative Studies in Education*, 1–23. Accessed November 28, 2011. doi:10.1080/09518398.2011.554449.

———. 2009a. "The Pedagogy of the Fort: Curriculum, Colonial Frontier Logics, and Indigenous Métissage." PhD Dissertation, University of Alberta.

———. 2009b. "The Curricular Problem of Indigenousness: Colonial Frontier Logics, Teacher Resistances, and the Acknowledgment of Ethical Space." In *Beyond Presentism: Re-Imagining the Historical, Personal, and Social Places of Curriculum*, edited by James Nahachewsky & Ingrid Johnston, 23–41. Rotterdam, The Netherlands: Sense Publishers.

Dussel, Enrique. 1995. *The Invention of the Americas: Eclipse of "the Other" and the Myth of Modernity*, translated by Michael Barber. New York: Continuum.

Ermine, Willie. 2007. "The Ethical Space of Engagement." *Indigenous Law Journal* 6 (1): 193–203.

Pinar, William. 2008. "Introduction." In *A Common Countenance: Stability and Change in the Canadian Curriculum*, by George Tompkins, xi–xxiv. Vancouver: Pacific Educational Press.

Pinar, William, William Reynolds, Patrick Slattery, & Peter Taubman. 1995. *Understanding Curriculum: An Introduction to the Study of Historical and Contemporary Curriculum Discourses*. New York: Peter Lang Publishing, Inc.

Rylance, Rick. 1994. *Roland Barthes*. London: Harvester Wheatsheaf.

Smith, David Geoffrey. 2003. "Curriculum and Teaching Face Globalization." In *International Handbook of Curriculum Research*, edited by In William Pinar, 35–51. Mahwah, NJ: Lawrence Erlbaum.

Tomkins, George. 1986. *A Common Countenance: Stability and Change in the Canadian Curriculum*. Scarborough, ON: Prentice-Hall.

———. 2008. *A Common Countenance: Stability and Change in the Canadian Curriculum*. Vancouver: Pacific Educational Press.

CHAPTER 3

AOKSISOWAATO'OP: PLACE AND STORY AS ORGANIC CURRICULUM

NARCISSE BLOOD, CYNTHIA CHAMBERS, DWAYNE DONALD, ERIKA HASEBE-LUDT, AND RAMONA BIG HEAD

AN OUTLINE

OPENING

Round 1
 Narcisse Blood: *Iinísskimm* Calls to the Woman
 Ramona Big Head: "Strike Them Hard!" The Baker Massacre Play (I)
 Cynthia Chambers: *Matónni*—Just Yesterday
 Dwayne Donald: Communication Is Gonna Get Out of Place
 Erika Hasebe-Ludt: The DTES: Downtown Eastside Vancouver

Round 2
 Narcisse Blood: Ayoungman's Prophecy
 Ramona Big Head: "Strike Them Hard!" The Baker Massacre Play (II)
 Cynthia Chambers: Magpies
 Dwayne Donald: What Does a Rock Mean?
 Erika Hasebe-Ludt: Japanese Language School, DTES

Round 3
 Narcisse Blood: Worrisome Dreams
 Ramona Big Head: "Strike Them Hard!" The Baker Massacre (III)

Cynthia Chambers: Building Dwelling
Dwayne Donald: The Museumization of *Papamihaw Asiniy*
Erika Hasebe-Ludt: Grandview/*Uuquinak'uuh* Elementary School, East
  Vancouver

CLOSING

OPENING

As a research collective, we have spent the last several years conceptualizing
a praxis of *métissage* that could be applied to curriculum studies in Canada.
The usefulness of texts of *métissage* to the field of curriculum studies is in
the ways that they can demonstrate connectivity while also simultaneously
re-cognizing difference. By drawing on multiple sources and contexts, creating texts of *métissage* can provoke a collective wondering regarding the connectedness of history, memory, and story.

  Chambers, Hasebe-Ludt and Donald (2002), working with autobiography as a critical point of departure, have theorized *métissage* as a curricular
practice that can be used to resist the priority and authority given to official
texts and textual practices. This curricular form of *métissage* shows how personal and family stories can be braided in with larger narratives of nation
and nationality, often with provocative effects. Thus, rather than viewing *métissage* as solitary research and textual praxis, this form of *métissage*
relies on collaboration and collective authorship as a strategy for exemplify-
ing, as research practice and text, the transcultural, interdisciplinary, and
shared nature of experience and memory. *Métissage*, in this example, calls
for authors to work "collectively to juxtapose their texts in such a way that
highlights difference (racial, cultural, historical, socio-political, linguistic)
without essentializing or erasing it, while simultaneously locating points of
affinity" (Chambers et al. 2008).

  In this chapter, we perform a curricular *métissage*[1] focused on the personal
and public significance of particular places and place-stories. This focus
is inspired by indigenous wisdom traditions that emphasize the personal
and intimate connectivity that people feel to the land and stories linked
to specific places. We are particularly inspired by the Blackfoot concept
aoksisowaato'p, which refers to the ethical importance of visiting a place as
an act of relational renewal that is life-giving and life-sustaining, both to the
place and to ourselves. Stories told of places where *aoksisowaato'p* has been
enacted have the organic power to give and sustain life in similar ways.

  Our *métissage* is organized around one central place-story that comes
from Blackfoot oral traditions. This organizing place-story will be told
in phases throughout the duration of the text. Remaining mindful of this

central place-story, and in preparation for the performance, each researcher has created his or her own text that articulates the particular relationship that he or she has with a specific place. From this process emerged a place-story, influenced by known place-stories also about that place. The researchers shared these stories with each other and then worked together to weave a shared script that includes the central place-story.

ROUND 1

NARCISSE BLOOD: *IINÍSSKIMM* CALLS TO THE WOMAN

A long time ago there was another drought, and in our stories, one way of remembering these events is about recognizing relationships, because the stories that we tell, they're not just stories. They are stories about knowing and acknowledging how we survive these severe droughts. Chambers (2006) reminds us that if you're living off the land and you don't know the stories, it can be fatal. If we apply this concept to the present day, it can still be fatal. Contained in the stories are the protocols of honoring and acknowledging the relationship to oneself first, to one's family, to the community, and to the nonhuman relations; these are the stories.

The stories also contain what you might call scientific knowledge today, as well as psychology. Thus, it is important to remember these stories because they address the importance of protocol, or how we relate to the world around us. My colleague Dwayne Mistaken Chief has articulated in English what protocols mean in Blackfoot: they are the boundaries to yourself first, and the boundaries to others, and to the natural world. If you know the stories you'll know those boundaries. If you don't know these stories, you will violate and desecrate the boundaries.

Many years ago, there was another time of starvation, of severe drought. The women were gathering wood along the Bow River. One of them was having trouble keeping the kindling bound. She told her companions to go on ahead. While she was tying the wood more securely, she heard someone singing. She looked around: Where was it coming from? It was coming from a tree. She approached the tree and saw that it was coming from a nest. She climbed up and looked into that nest, and sitting on a buffalo tuft was an *iinísskimm,* and the *iinísskimm* sang again. And in the song were the words: "Take me. I am holy. I will call the buffalo for you. When you sing these songs I am gifting to you, the buffalo will come, and you will be able to hunt and the people will be well fed. Remember the famine, the drought."

Because she was able to call the buffalo with the *iinísskimm*, the *iinísskimm* was placed in a very special place in our altar for smudging. The *iinísskimm* also guides us to where the buffalo are through our dreams. Our

Elders tell us that we receive our instructions through these dreams when Morning Star is at its brightest, just before we wake up. The *iinísskimm* still has relevance today.

RAMONA BIG HEAD: "STRIKE THEM HARD!"
THE BAKER MASSACRE PLAY (I)

In the early morning hours of January 23rd, 1870, in minus 30 degrees weather, Major Eugene M. Baker and his troops, under the direction of General Philip H. Sheridan, of the US Cavalry attacked a peaceful Blackfeet camp, along the Marias River killing approximately 217 people, mostly elderly women and children (Phillips,1996 82), many of whom were also suffering from the deadly disease, smallpox. The order was given by General Sheridan, "Tell Baker to strike them hard!" Baker was originally looking for Mountain Chief's camp. However, he found Chief Heavy Runner's camp first. Prior to this expedition, Baker was given a direct order that Heavy Runner was a peaceful chief, and that he and his people were not to be molested. However, after five days of marching in subzero temperatures, Major Baker and his troops came across Heavy Runner's camp, and although he was clearly informed that this was the wrong camp, he struck anyway.

The fall of 2001 marked the second year of our Elder Mentor Program at Kainai High School on the Blood Reserve in southern Alberta. One of the first events planned was a field trip to the site of the 1870 Baker Massacre. My colleague and social studies teacher, *Appioomahka* (Dwayne Donald), and our Elder advisor, *Kinakksaapo'p* (Narcisse Blood) were quite adamant that we take our students and Elders to this site. As for me, I had never before heard about the Baker Massacre.

On our way, *Kinakksaapo'p* began to tell me the story. He explained that the Blackfoot referred to the site as *Otsito'totsahpiwa* (the place where they were burned). The location of the Baker Massacre is along the Bear River, otherwise known as the Marias River, approximately ten miles southeast of present-day Shelby, Montana.

Natowapiisaaki (Carol Murray), the Tribal History Project Director at Blackfeet Community College in Browning, Montana, tells a story of how the old people on the Blackfeet Indian Reservation referred to the Baker Massacre site as "the bad place," or a place where something bad happened. *Kinakksaapo'p* added that, in the past, *Otsito'totsahpiwa* or the Baker Massacre site was avoided by the Blackfeet. No one would go near the site, for it marked one of the darkest moments in Blackfeet history.

As we walked through the massacre site 131 years later, I could feel the somber atmosphere of the place. It was a beautiful fall afternoon, yet I felt a sad presence and heaviness at this site. We sat and listened to stories from direct descendants of the survivors of this massacre. As the stories unfolded before me, all I could feel was anger. The anger was followed by feelings of frustration and helplessness. To attempt to articulate my feelings was futile. I simply did not have the voice for it.

Kinakksaapo'p informed me that one of our ancestors, *Natohkyiaakii* (Holy Bear Woman), had been one of the children who survived what Darrell Kipp, a great-grandson of Chief Heavy Runner. This specific story is often referred to as a "*horrific blow*" to the Blackfeet (Alberta Learning 2012). In the aftermath, *Natohkyiaakii* and the other children, who were orphaned that morning, trekked in freezing cold temperatures to nearby camps, where some walked the 90 miles, in a trail left behind by the army, to Fort Benton.

Their stories will never be found in any textbook. *Natowapiisaaki* (Carol Murray) shared the following: at the onset of the attack, which took place early in the morning of January 23rd, 1870, during one of the coldest winters on record, many of the young children scattered and ran to the nearby riverbanks. They did not have time to grab any warm clothing with them. The children frantically dug into the frozen riverbank with their bare hands in order to dig a hole to crawl into and shelter themselves from the flying bullets. Later, soldiers would find many young children hiding in the tall grass, freezing and shivering.

In one of the tepees, a mother, with a baby in her arms, screamed at her two other young daughters to run! As the girls were about to run out of the tepee, the younger sister was hit in the forehead by one of the deadly bullets. As the surviving daughter turned to her mother, she witnessed another bullet penetrating the baby, which also pierced her mother. So, this young girl was forced to run out of the tepee alone.

Another little girl ran to a nearby tepee and hid under a backrest. Frozen with fear, she peered through the slits of the backrest, and witnessed a soldier rip open the tepee and begin shooting indiscriminately at anyone that moved.

As *Natowapiisaaki* recounted these stories, I felt a cold chill running through my veins. The images in my mind were of the children, including *Natohkyiaakii* (Holy Bear Woman), running for their lives. Was my great-great-grandmother one of those children frantically digging, with bare hands, into the frozen riverbank? Or was she one of the little girls, frozen with terror, shivering in the tall grass while this unbelievably traumatic incident was unfolding before her?

I sat there, in my anger, asking no one in particular, why didn't I know about this? This massacre should never have been forgotten. My grandmother, *Ksikawo'tan* (Annie Bare Shin Bone), was 90 years old when she passed away. She was a granddaughter of *Natohkyiaakii*. And yet, she had never shared this story with me. As we drove away from the Baker Massacre site that fall of 2001, all I could think of was that this story has to be told. And the best way I know how to tell a story is to put it on stage.

CYNTHIA CHAMBERS: *MATÓNNI*—JUST YESTERDAY

> *As we walk our own ground, on foot or in mind, we need to be able to recite stories about hills and trees and animals, stories that root us in this place and keep it alive.*
>
> Scott Russell Sanders, "Telling the Holy"

The *iinísskimm* story is like a single twig in a magpie's nest, a nest of songs, ceremonies, and stories. A large dome-like nest that holds the people's memory and knowledge of Blackfoot territory, and of how to live well in that place. Songs I have never learned, ceremonies I rarely attend, and stories I have only recently begun to hear, and even more recently, to remember.

Two decades ago, I landed in Blackfoot territory. A bit like the magpie, a tough and an adaptable old bird that ranges all over western Canada, an erratic wanderer who sometimes heads north instead of south in autumn and winter (Salt and Salt 1976). A bit like me, who wandered throughout the west and north, until I landed in Blackfoot territory, two decades ago. In Blackfoot, they say I arrived *matónni*—just yesterday.

And since yesterday, I've heard some of the stories. Like the time, long ago—I've also learned that it really doesn't matter *how* long ago—a long time ago, the bison went underground. And when the bison disappeared, the people went hungry. At this time, *Náápi,* the creator and trickster, was walking around, making things and teaching human beings how to live in that place; creating chaos and causing grief where he went. But when the buffalo disappeared underground *Náápi* did a good thing; he saved the people from starvation; he found a way to bring the buffalo back.

More recently, I heard the stories about how the buffalo went away again. Maybe *Náápi* was still causing trouble, even if he wasn't around anymore, at least in a human form, to help fix the problems he had created. So this time, when the buffalo disappeared, an *iinísskimm,* a buffalo stone, showed the people how to call the buffalo back (Wissler & Duvall 1908/1995).

And I've heard the stories about the last big famine on the prairies. Since the time of *Náápi,* the magpies flourished with the herds and the hunts. When the herds were gone, and the great hunts over, the magpies picked clean the last of the bones. I heard how those shiny white bones littered the prairies, the first crop picked up and carted to the nearest railway siding, paid five cents a ton. Bison bones shipped east, only to return, as fertilizer and ammunition. Then, along with all those who depended upon the bison—the vultures, the grizzlies, and the wolves—the magpies starved, and those that survived moved on. An early Alberta naturalist, Mr. Frank Farley

(Salt and Salt 1976) only recorded two magpies in the Red Deer-Lacombe area in all the years between 1892 and when my grandmother was born in 1911. Even more recently, I heard the story about the motherless calves bawling for milk and the close press of the herd, desperate orphans who followed human riders back to their camp (Punke 2007). What were those calves to do without their mothers, where were they to go?

By the time my great-grandmother and her family left England to farm in southern Manitoba, even the bones had come and gone. The few remaining bison herds sought refuge in Blackfoot territory, *kitáowahsinnoon*. By 1911, when my grandmother was born in Winnipeg, the last herds too were gone. By then, the only plains bison to be found in Canada were in the national parks. Descendants of those bawling orphaned calves, imported from Montana.[2] In Blackfoot time, this all happened *matooni*, just yesterday.

Now—*annohk*—bison herds no longer graze the grasslands, no longer ford the Old Man River at Blackfoot Crossing. They can no longer offer themselves up to human beings so they and their children may live. But the spirit of the bison, or *iinii*, still dwells in Blackfoot territory. They are alive in the songs, the ceremonies, and the stories. And they are loose in the world, just as *Náápi* is.

These stories don't "explain" much; they don't really signify, represent, or deconstruct. They are metonymic, perhaps, but not metaphoric. The "meaning" of the story can't be reduced down to a slick "theme." All that these stories hold cannot be spiraled into a scope and sequence or thinly sliced into objectives for easy digestion. Although these bare-bones stories resist becoming lesson plans, they hold lessons and suggest outcomes. Although they've never won an Oscar, they do remind us of an "inconvenient truth"[3]—all human beings survive on the good graces of other beings. The *iinísskimm* story, the spirits of *Náápi*, and the buffalo, remind humans, that while famine may be underground, its return is inevitable.

A current curricular slogan in Alberta (2006/2008) is: "Education is our buffalo." Catchy. But scary. The extirpation of the bison is a story about how quickly things can go terribly wrong. And how, once things have gone *that* wrong, how hard it is to make them right again. In this story, the buffalo could not be *brought* back, nor could they be *called* back. The result is a famine that still haunts the Great Plains and all life dwelling there. A cautionary tale indeed. The magpies outside my window seem ready to move on, in search of new bones to pick.

DWAYNE DONALD: "COMMUNICATION IS GONNA GET OUT OF PLACE"

In the Cree language, the Northwest Resistance, a time of open military conflict between Cree and Métis groups and Canadians in the early spring of 1885, is known as *e-mâyikamikahk* or "where it went wrong" (McLeod 1998, 58). These events are remembered in this way because it was a time of dramatic change in the relationships that the Cree and Métis had with the Canadian government, changing as it did from a predominantly peaceful and cooperative partnership to one of violent coercion. Although these confrontations originated among Cree and Métis peoples living in the region known today as north-central Saskatchewan, there was considerable fear among settlers on the Canadian Prairies that these events would inspire other Aboriginal groups to join in a general resistance to the assertion of Canadian control in their territory. This sense of panic led to the refortification of the palisaded walls of Fort Edmonton, the general armament of hastily formed militias, and the decision of large numbers of families to seek shelter and safety within the walls of the fort (Silversides 2005 68–69).

One prominent resident of Edmonton at the time, however, took his cues regarding any impending dangers from the habits of the Aboriginal peoples who were camped around the fort. Frank Oliver, founder and editor of Alberta's first newspaper *The Bulletin* and considered as one of the founding fathers of the city of Edmonton, wrote an article in 1929, in which he recounted his reaction to the news that a state of war existed in the neighboring Saskatchewan territory. Oliver (1955) notes that since his arrival in Edmonton in 1876, he had grown accustomed to Indian encampments around the fort and the nightly sound of beating drums:

> Between comings and goings there was always a group of Indian tents near the fort; and without exception for night after night, winter or summer and year after year, the drum sounded and the dance or gambling was kept up until early morning. It was a permanent and prominent feature of the life of Edmonton. (4)

When a telegram was received in Edmonton on March 27, 1885, which relayed the news that the Cree and Métis had acted to defend their lands, Oliver surmised that the community was not under threat as long as the Indian tents remained around the fort and the drums could still be heard. He recalls lying in his bed that same night and listening to the drums with a sense of relief (12).

However, the next morning the tents were all gone and the drums were no longer heard. Despite numerous indications that the conflict that was the Northwest Resistance would spread to the Edmonton area, the safety of the residents was not threatened in this way, and life soon returned to normal for them. Normal, that is, with the exception of one notable difference: the silencing of the drums had apparently marked the beginning of a new era. According to Oliver,

> The night the drum-throb ceased in Edmonton marked the end of the old
> way and the beginning of the new. It was the end of the road for the Red
> Man. His dominance had ceased; the land of his fathers was no longer his.
> The Indian drum has never since been heard in Edmonton. (15)

For Oliver, writing retrospectively in 1929, the silencing of Indian drums in
the aftermath of the Northwest Resistance signified a poignant fait accompli
to the Indian problem. After 1885, the Canadian people could focus
on the task of building a nation out of wilderness. For the Cree and Métis,
e-mâyikamikahk speaks of the time when their relationships with the newcomers got out of balance as the interests of the settlers gained precedence
over Native American's basic needs.

As a descendent of the *Papaschase* Cree, a band whose reserve was expropriated by Canadian government officials in 1888, I have inherited a personal familial understanding of the displacement and disenfranchisement
associated with *e-mâyikamikahk* (Donald 2004). Just three years after the
Northwest Resistance, the *Papaschase* Cree lands were expropriated because
government officials believed that the reserve would be in the way of the
growth of the bustling frontier town of Edmonton. After their lands were
expropriated, the members of *Papaschase* Cree were dispersed and their com-
munitarian connections slowly eroded. This institutionalized removal of
Indians from the place now called Edmonton, and their subsequent ironic
recreation as outsiders who do not belong in that place, is just one example of similar processes at other significant gathering places on the prairies
during this era (Donald 2009). The "spatial and ideological diaspora" of
Aboriginal peoples was absolutely necessary to realize the teleological dream
of the emerging Canadian nation and nationality (McLeod 1998).

One of the dire consequences of this diaspora experienced by Aboriginal
peoples is a disconnection from their traditional lands. Kainai scholar Leroy
Little Bear addresses this issue directly when he says that you know you
have an identity problem when the land doesn't recognize you (Blood &
Chambers 2006). According to Dr. Little Bear, when you don't know the
stories, when you don't know the songs, when you don't know the places,
then it's almost as if your mother has cut off ties with you. This is just one
example of the troubling legacies of colonialism that are remembered by
the Cree in the notion *e-mâyikamikahk*. When things went wrong for my
Papaschase Cree ancestors, and they were chased away from their traditional
lands, the resultant spatial disconnect from the land led to a gradual forgetting of the teachings that come from the land. This forgetting has been
bequeathed to me as a descendant of the *Papaschase* Cree. As a result, the

land of my ancestors doesn't recognize me, and I live with an identity problem. I don't speak or understand Cree very well. I don't know the songs, places, or stories as I should. When I visit the sacred sites on the prairies, like the buffalo stones, I can't speak to them using the language that the rocks know best. I was not taught to communicate with them in those ways.

Kainai Elder Bernard Tall Man once told me a prophetic story that speaks directly to e-mâyikamikahk and this particular kind of identity problem:

These Elders—when I was young I had an older brother that dances and he had this family that was adopting him. They were pretty well off. Anyways, the dance started and the circle at the middle, it's round like this. That's where the drummers are. They had an entrance on the east side. They come in and sit down. The Elders are seated on the south side of that. Further on, on the west side there's a stage where they have the chief and council. They all sit on that stage. To me, it seemed like they had respect for chief and council. There was one time during the dance, everybody took part. To me, that was fun for them. My brother, his name was Lawrence, but his other name was John, he'd say, when you finish dancing he'd say, "Matomaaniwaaksi . . . . " They're not telling the truth. That means they want to dance some more. And they start dancing again and they have a lot of fun. They don't get paid for doing that. They go there to have fun and carry on our tradition.

And I see the Elders just sitting there. They dance once in a while, these guys on the south side of that. All of a sudden there was silence. Just silence. One of the Elders got up. No, one of the Elders started teasing another Elder. Joking around with the other Elders. A lot of teasing on that. About a lot of things. This Elder, started with one Elder, started teasing this one Elder, and instead of this Elder retaliating to what went on from the other Elder—there was a lot of laughter after he was finished. This Elder started teasing another person, challenging another person too. After he was finished there was a lot of laughter. Then it just kept going like that until all of them.

And I kept seeing this Elder, the main one, looking like this at everybody participating. So, he's a leader. Somebody has to lead off and these are followers. And I noticed because I do a lot of observation. And he's a good role model. This is what you should be doing.

In the future—he got up and went on this side, real slow. He started to sing a song of praise for all his friends. Song of praise for all of them around the circle. The dance hall was just packed full. Went around, all of a sudden, at the east side, he seen this young boy. Oh, I'd say he's about five years old. And he had his legs like that, sitting on the floor just looking up at the Elder. He stopped. Told the audience, "I'm pleased that you gave us the opportunity to do what we want to do, the Elders. That shows that you have respect for us. But we did our song of praise for the Elders. This is our way of life. Anytime, anywhere, you sing a song of praise for the ones that you think. Don't be shy because right now you'll see some guys are shy. They have to get paid in order to get up and . . . I don't have to get paid. I just get up and sing a song of praise any place."

Said this guy, "This young boy, look at this young boy. He listened. He knows what I'm saying. He understands Blackfoot. He speaks Blackfoot. All of us speak Blackfoot and understand Blackfoot. There is a generation in the future that will be—they won't hear each other. Communication is gonna get out of place. They won't know what they're saying. Some Elder would get up and sing a song of praise and younger generation would still be talking away. They won't speak our language anymore. He'd be saying, 'Tsa waani oma niitsitapikoan?' What's that Indian talking about?"

We hear it now. That's why—the old man made a prediction that time and it's close to seventy years ago. I heard it. I witnessed it. And it's like that now.
(Donald 2003, 120)

ERIKA HASEBE-LUDT: THE DTES: DOWNTOWN EASTSIDE VANCOUVER

If we are to survive as a life form on the planet . . . collectively, we must come to the realization that . . . there can only be true prosperity if it is global prosperity, and we can only count our wealth in peace when we count it together. The good news is that . . . we are actually pushing beyond the human race in our consideration to imagine the welfare of all life on earth as a practical objective.
Bruce Mau and the Institute Without Boundaries, Massive Change

On a windswept spring afternoon, clouds racing across the North Shore Mountains, rain in the air, I responded to an invitation by Nova Scotia arts-based scholar Dorothy Lander to participate in a gathering of women artists, educators, and community activists in the Downtown Eastside of Vancouver.[4] We came together to talk about our work in public places and institutions, to illuminate three generations of women's contributions to the arts and to popular education, and to trace their footprints in the local sites that we work and live in. The place that we met at was the Japanese Language School on the corner of Jackson Avenue and Alexander Street, once a vibrant educational center for Vancouver's pre-World War II Japanese Canadian community clustered around nearby Powell Street. Today, this and other streets in the Downtown Eastside, the DTES, as it is called—sometimes affectionately, most often derisively—have a different appearance and a different story to tell.

We began by walking in solidarity through the neighborhood, reprising the route of the memorial walk for the 23 missing and murdered women of the DTES.[5] These women's stories and their fates are part of the stark reality of what is today the poorest and most destitute urban neighborhood in all of Canada, its streets and back alleys the center of this country's drug capital (Maté 2008); the women's disappearance and deaths are part of the legacy of a troubled national history of deprivation, expulsion, and racism.

Only a few blocks away, in the neighborhood bordering the DTES, in upscale, posh Yaletown, visual artist Pamela Masik is creating a series of 69 portraits of these women. Masik is a mostly known for her dreamy abstracts sought by wealthy collectors. Yet, she has worked for nearly four years now on this different project that "at times left her sobbing and puking in her studio, overcome by the tragedy that bleeds from her subject matter" (Baron 2009, n.p.).

> "What exists in my community also exists in me," Masik says. She calls her series "The Forgotten," and her work exudes the anger and sadness she feels knowing that dozens of women living in a world of abysmal poverty and incessant violence kept disappearing one after another for years, and hardly anyone cared...." I'm hoping to affect people emotionally so maybe they're inspired to do something....A lot of these women didn't have a voice, and their community didn't have a voice." Welcome to Pamela Masik's nightmare. It belongs to us all. (Baron 2009, n.p.)

The writer Evelyn Lau (2009), on a recent walk through the DTES, reflects on her past life as a 14-year-old runaway on these troubled streets. Walking along Hastings Street, she feels "the grey stream of misery" flowing between the buildings; she sees "the twisted faces stitching a jagged path down the sidewalk, the groups of dealers huddled in rank doorways;" she recalls living in a suite that "overlooked the alley where stoned youth staggered to squabble and shoot up" (n.p.). She writes about the pain of looking back, the mounting wave of panic that she cannot swallow, the fight for breath as she walks back to "trendy Yaletown and the land of Lululemon and purse-sized dogs" where she now lives, at the edge of the neighborhood that once was her only home in her homeless past.

At the end of the walk commemorating the women in this place, in CRAB Park on the edge of the Pacific Ocean, sits a memorial stone with the inscription:

> The heart has its own memory.
> In honour of the spirit of the people
> murdered in the Downtown Eastside.
> Many were women and many were Native
> Aboriginal women. Many of these cases remain unsolved. All my relations.[6]

ROUND 2

NARCISSE BLOOD: BURDENSOME DREAMS

This is about what was recorded in the *Piikani* winter account about the Frank Slide in the Crowsnest Pass on April 29, in 1903. This story is not included in the Interpretive Centre's[7] historical account of this fateful day.

The *Piikani* knew not to camp close to the mountain, as it was called the Moving Mountain. A *Piikani* man was working in the coal mines, and one morning he woke up extra-early and complained to his wife: "Geez, these dream beings can give real onerous instructions. We have to break camp right now and to a place further from here." After moving his camp, he went to work, and he came home to his recently moved camp tired, only to be awakened by a thunderous noise—the mountain sliding. Had he not moved, he and his wife would have been killed by the boulders and the rocks. The place where the dream beings had instructed him to camp was at a safe distance from the slide. And he said to his wife: "I will never question these dream beings again. They have saved our lives."

RAMONA BIG HEAD: "STRIKE THEM HARD!"
THE BAKER MASSACRE PLAY (II)

In the fall of 2004, three years after my first visit to the Baker Massacre site, I took a sabbatical from my teaching position at Kainai High School. I began the Master's in Education degree program at the University of Lethbridge. In the fall of 2005, I was back in the classroom teaching high school English and Drama. The following fall semester of 2006 started out just as hectic as any other year. However, my world came to a screeching halt on October 28, 2006 when I found my 22-year-old daughter, *Apaisapiaakii* (Galina), dead in my basement. She had hanged herself.

I have seven children, Carl, Galina, Shawnee, Aloni, Oshana, Jesse, and Saya. Their father also had three more children in his second marriage, Starly, Tisha and J-Man. So Galina is the second child of a total of ten siblings. At the time of her death, she had two children, three-year-old Teesh Ansch and two-year-old Joseph. She was also six months pregnant.

Galina was a brilliant young woman! She was gorgeous, bright, creative, compassionate, and loving. She was a gifted storyteller, writer, dancer, singer, and visual artist. However, she also suffered from severe depression and low self-worth. Her death impacted so many lives, but I choose to look at the 22 years of her life as God's gift to the rest of us.

Needless to say, another year would go by before I could even think about continuing with the MEd program. After a full year on the healing path, I slowly began to breathe in life, and I saw the sky once again. I knew that I wanted to complete what I had started. Therefore, I decided to submit a play on the Baker Massacre as the final project towards the fulfillment of my MEd degree.

When I finally made the decision to put the story of the 1870 Baker Massacre on stage, I felt confident that I could do it. Directing plays is not that difficult for me. In fact, between 1996 and 2008, I had directed approximately 22 drama productions involving well over 200 students at Kainai High School. The challenge, for me, was writing the play. I had never undertaken such a task. Most of the original productions that I had worked on were done in collaboration with my son, *Aamskapohkitopii* (Carl Brave Rock), and my students. In spite of the trepidation I felt, I knew that my soul was not going to rest until this play was written and staged. And on January 23rd, 2008, after I had asked the *Aamsskaapipikani* (the South Piegan or Blackfeet) Elders for their blessing, I officially became a playwright.

The most difficult part was writing the scene of the actual massacre. Writing this play began to trigger the memories and flashbacks of my own traumatic experience of my daughter's suicide. For example, one of the survivors of the Baker Massacre was *Kyo'tokan* (Bear Head). He was 12 years old at the time of the massacre. His account is heart wrenching. It was difficult for me to read his story. Yet, in order to move forward, I had to uncover the layers of atrocities that had taken place on that fateful morning:

> Chief Heavy Runner ran from his lodge toward the seizers [soldiers] on the bank. He was shouting to them and waving a paper writing that our agent had given him, a writing saying that he was a good and peaceful man, a friend of the whites. He had run but a few steps when he fell, his body pierced with bullets. Inside the lodges men were yelling; terribly frightened women and children, screaming—screaming from wounds, from pain as they died. I saw a few men and women, escaping from their lodges, shot down as they ran. Most terrible to hear of all was the crying of little babies at their mothers' breasts. The seizers all advanced upon the lodge....They shot at the tops of the lodges; cut the bindings of the poles so the whole lodge would collapse upon the fire and begin to burn—burn and smother those within. I saw my own lodge go down and burn. Within it my mother, my almost-mothers, my almost-sisters. Oh how pitiful were their scream[s] as they died, and I there, powerless to help them!
>
> Soon all was silent in the camp, and the seizers advanced, began tearing down the lodges that still stood, shooting those within them who were still alive, and then trying to burn all that they tore down, burn the dead under the heaps of poles, lodge-skins, and lodge furnishings; but they did not burn well.
>
> At last my seizer released my arm and went about with his men looking at the smoking piles, talking, pointing, laughing, all of them...I sat before the ruin of my lodge and felt sick. I wished that the seizers had killed me too. In the center of the fallen lodge, where the poles had fallen upon the fire, it had burned a little, then died out. I could not pull up the lodge-skin and look under it. I could not bear to see my mother, my almost-mothers, my almost-sisters lying there, shot or smothered to death. When I went for my horses [earlier that morning before the attack], I had not carried my many-shots gun. It was there in the ruin of the lodge. Well, there it would remain. (Schultz 1962, 301–302)

I came to realize that all traumatic experiences are somehow related, whether it is unresolved historical trauma, or more recent traumatic experiences. I made the following journal entry just after reading Bear Head's account:

> *I still find it extremely difficult to read the story of the actual massacre. The images in my head and the sounds I hear consume me. Amid the sounds of guns, I hear heavy breathing of those running for their lives. I hear the screams of women, children and babies. I see red blood everywhere. I hear the silence of those who were killed instantly. I see Galina hanging in my basement. I hear my own screams as I panicked in fear. I hear the banging on the washer and dryer as I tried to get help. I didn't feel the cold on my bare feet as I ran outside screaming for help. My God! This is so hard! The pain is unbearable. A mother should never have to see her dead child.*

The connection between the Baker Massacre and my daughter's death was strong. One event triggered the other. The pain I felt from both of these traumatic incidents was of the same magnitude. I began to understand why I *could* write this play. My own personal trauma had given me the gift I needed to write. I know what it feels like to be so terrified and helpless when death is right in front of you. I felt the same feeling of shock and trauma as *Kyo'tokan* and *Natohkyiaakii*. My body was numb and lifeless as I sat there in the aftermath of Galina's death. Although I can never compare my tragedy to the Baker Massacre, I know that it is possible to experience that same kind of shock and pain today.

CYNTHIA CHAMBERS: MAGPIES

> *The sounds we make, the patterns we draw, the plots we trace may be as native to the land as deer trails or bird songs. The more fully we belong to our place, the more likely that our place will survive without damage.*
> Scott Russell Sanders, "Telling the Holy"

My mother's people came to Canada from Great Britain; they arrived on the grasslands with a dream of owning land. If they had to farm to get that land, they would. Like other immigrants, they brought the place-stories from their old home to their new one. And, nested inside those stories were beliefs about good and evil, luck and fortune, wilderness and civilization, nature and culture. Beliefs about magpies, those opportunistic scavengers with voracious appetites, who were acolytes of witches, omens of misfortune, and instruments of evil—arrogant and annoying pests, raucous thieves and wily predators—of other nests, nests of *nice* birds (Cornell 2009; Winterman 2008). In cahoots with other "bird brains" (Savage 1995), the crows and ravens.

The magpie's reputation for being a sidekick to the devil is as old as Noah and the Ark. The story goes he was the only bird who refused to board the ark preferring to sit outside "jabbering over the drowning world" (Swainson 1885, 77). Or, perhaps, the bad reputation comes from his bad seed: Noah sent out the raven and the dove after the great flood, the magpie's black-and-white plumage evidence of their illicit union. That sounds like raven business, but what about that dove?

And then there was the curse from Jesus. Two birds perched upon the cross where Jesus was hanging, the story goes, a dull bluebird and a magnificent magpie. While the timid bluebird wiped Jesus's tears, the wicked magpie mocked his suffering with her beautiful plumage. And so Jesus blessed the bluebird for all time, and then he cursed the magpie: "...thy color shall be sad and somber, thy life a hard one; ever, too, shall thy nest be open to the storm" (Swainson 1885, 5).

Yes, and open to the storm their nests have been. In 1804, when Lewis and Clark first encountered black-billed magpies, in what is now South Dakota; they were unafraid of humans, taking food right out of their hands, and entering their tents (Ryser 1985). Apparently, it doesn't pay to be bold. Seventy years after Lewis and Clark first sighted them, the bison were gone and so were the magpies. Several decades later, when there were enough towns and farms for the birds to make a livelihood, the magpies returned to the prairies. They learned how to feed their naked and helpless young from the dumpster instead of the buffalo jump, from the ticks off cattle instead of bison. Instead of being grateful, ranchers and farmers alike hated the magpies. For over a half-century, they shot and trapped them, poisoned their food and dynamited their rookeries (Morache n.d.). Bounties were posted and Alberta children collected five cents per pair of magpie feet in the 1930s (Wetaskiwin & District Heritage Museum 2005): all to no avail. Determined opponents still call for their demise, others spray them with hoses and bait their food with cayenne pepper. The Government of Alberta (2005) posts diagrams for building a better magpie trap on their website. Magpies are the birds that "everyone loves to hate."

Well, not everyone. For the Blackfoot, magpies (or *mamiá'tsikimi*), along with the stars and the spirits are the "above beings" or *spomitapiksi* (Blackfoot Gallery Committee 2001). When Walter McClintock (1968/1999), a young Yale graduate brought his notebook and camera to Blackfoot country in 1896, he asked Brings-Down-the-Sun to tell him about the birds. The old man began his lesson with a story about the magpie.

> The birds you see making so much disturbance near the camp, chattering while flying from tree to tree, and looking eagerly for scraps, are called *Ma-mi-as-ich-ime* (long tails or magpies). I look upon them as my friends

because they always come to my coyote bait, when I am catching eagles. They say to each other, "Long tails fly on ahead and fasten your provision bag to another tree." If you take notice you will see them flying ahead of each other, continually in search of food. The women often sing these words as a slumber song to children. (481–482)

The magpies and their cousins, the ravens, are talented messengers and the people depend upon them. Once, long ago, when the buffalo refused to go over the jump, the people were starving.[8] A young woman offered herself to one of the bulls, if only the herd would jump over the cliff. When the young woman's father realized what had happened, he went in search of his daughter. In one version of the story, the father asked a magpie for help: "Ha! Long Tail *mamiá tsikimi*," he said, "you are a beautiful bird. Help me. Look everywhere as you travel about, and if you see my daughter, tell her I wait here for her." The magpie delivered his message to the young woman, and then returned with her reply: the father was to wait here for daughter. But before she could come, the buffalo bulls discovered the man, and they bellowed; they hooked him with their great horns and trampled him with their great hooves, until not a tiny piece of his body remained. The daughter wailed in mourning and the buffalo reproached her.

You see now how it is with us. We have seen our mothers and fathers go over the buffalo jump, our relations killed so your relations may eat. But we will pity you. If you can bring your father back to life, you both can go back to your people. (106)

The daughter begged the magpie. "Pity me. Help me. Find a little piece of my father's body and bring it to me." The magpie poked around in the trampled mud with his long beak and finally picked out something white, a small fragment of bone, and flew back to the woman with it. She covered the bone with a blanket and sang a special song; and then her father breathed and sat up. The magpie was so happy; he flew round and round making a great noise. The buffalo were so amazed that they agreed to teach the buffalo dance and the buffalo song to the man and his daughter. "Now, go home now," they said. "Do not forget what you have seen. Teach it to the people." And they did.

In another version of the story, the helper was the raven, an albino. Either way, magpie or raven, was a witness to this contract between bison and humans, to have compassion for one another because they depend on each other. And, when humans broke this great covenant once again, well, magpie and raven witnessed that, too. The stories show us how to act like relations, and then they show us what happens when we forget how to do so.

DWAYNE DONALD: WHAT DOES A ROCK MEAN?

What does a rock *mean*? To Aboriginal peoples of the prairies, rocks are significant, and deeply spiritual, markers on the land because of their visual prominence on the open prairie. In the past, they could be seen from miles away, and this enabled travelers to orient themselves as they traveled throughout their territory. Rocks were helpers in this regard, and continue to be respected and honored for providing guidance in this way.

Two tenets of traditional indigenous philosophy support the notion that rocks are spiritual entities. The first is that rocks are manifestations of ancient forms of life that provide people with connections to the past. Rocks remind us of the creation of the world and human kinship with all subsequent forms of life stemming from creation and the work of the Creator (Hill 2008; Little Bear 1998). Rocks are viewed as animate in that they have vitality to them, an internal hum of energy that, in a spiritual way, retells the stories of Creation. This energy reminds us of where the rocks have been, and what they have seen prior to occupying their present place. As Willie Ermine (1995) explains, the fundamental insight gained from viewing energy in this way is that all existence is connected, and that the whole of creation is enmeshed in each entity that comprises it (103).

To the Cree, considerations of life-forms like rocks, as organic entities, as energy, as heat, as movement are also insights into "*muntou*" (Ermine 1995, 104), the mystery of life that manifests itself in diverse forms. *Muntou* inhabits the rocks and the places where rocks dwell. To delve into the energy of these entities is to place oneself in a web of relationality and acknowledge the connectedness of all beings. In this view, rocks comprise the landscape and give energy to the world in the same way that plants, animals, and people do. As such, they are considered the ancient relatives of more recent forms of life. Indigenous languages allow for people to speak to and pay homage to rocks without being thought crazy because the foundational philosophies that support the cultures conceptualize rocks as animate, as relatives, as spirits. As such, rocks have their own stories to tell. Vine Deloria (1991) expressed these ideas this way:

> Power and place are dominant concepts—power being the living energy that inhabits and/or composes the universe, and place being the relationship of things to each other...put into a simple equation: Power and place produce personality. This equation simply means that the universe is alive, but it also contains within it the very important suggestion that the universe is personal, and therefore, must be approached in a personal manner...The personal nature of the universe demands that each and every entity in it seek and sustain personal relationships. (22–23)

Another second spiritual quality of rocks, deeply connected to the first, is that rocks are located at places that have a history—a story—and wisdom on how to live a good life comes from looking closely at the place and listening carefully, over and over again, to the story. Specific rocks become significant to the people when the story of their meaning and significance and how they got to their present place becomes an essential way of teaching about the land and living well on it (Christiansen 2000, 34–46; Bullchild 1985, 167–171). Read the words of Dudley Patterson, a Western Apache Elder:

> Wisdom sits in places. It's like water that never dries up . . . You must remember what happened at them long ago. You must think about it and keep thinking about it . . . You will be wise. People will respect you. (Basso 1996, 126)

The important point about rocks and place-stories is that the rocks, as animate entities, have an energy to them that is forever in flux—constantly changing, transforming, combining, and recombining. This cyclic energy is what gives the rock its spiritual quality.

When one sees the world in this way there are two general premises that result. One is that the constant flux process of energy means that everything is related through the cyclic nature of energy flows. The second is that we must look at the world holistically and search for regular observable patterns in nature as a way to make sense of the world and our place in it. As Leroy Little Bear (2000) explains, the earth is the place "where the continuous and/or repetitive process of creation occurs. It is on the earth that cycles, phases, patterns—in other words, the constant motion or flux—can be observed" (78). This search for patterns accounts for the emphasis on renewal in indigenous ceremonies and prayers. The desire is to honor cycles, patterns, and flows through ceremonial avowal of human affiliations with the land and significant places. Through prayer and ceremony, we participate in the natural patterns and renew intimate relationships with those entities that give us life.

There are rocks on the prairies that are still visited, and considered prominent sites of spiritual renewal and pilgrimage for Aboriginal peoples. These rocks, though, are what are left of a large interconnected network of buffalo stones that dotted the landscape a short time ago. Archaeologists have termed these networks of rocks the Ribstone Complex. According to Solomon Bluehen, an Elder from the Little Pine First Nation in Saskatchewan, these ribstones are the dwelling places of the guardian spirits of the buffalo (Wormington & Forbis 1965, 170). The lines on the stones represent ribs, while the holes are symbolic of bullet or arrow holes. Elder Bluehen tells us that originally there was only one ribstone that was brought to the top of a hill by "Little People," who told an old man of its spiritual powers. They said that it would be the last buffalo on the prairies. Since this time, other ribstones have been created from the original one. And since this time, the Cree and Blackfoot and other nations have considered the buffalo stones sites of pilgrimage where offerings are left and prayers said to the Creator. The prayers ask for continued blessings and that their people continue to be provided what they need to live well. The interconnected buffalo stones are reminders of the intimate nature of the relationships between people, the buffalo, and the Creator. They are considered life-giving and life-sustaining sites of sacred renewal.

There is one particular buffalo stone considered to be central to the Ribstone Complex that has been removed from its place on the prairie. It once sat on a prominent hill above a tributary of the Battle River named Iron Creek in the region we now call east central Alberta. This rock was a spiritual protector of the buffalo and a powerful reminder of all the generous gifts provided the people by *iihtsipáítapiiyo'pa*—the Source of Life to the Blackfoot people. The rock fell from the sky, a gift from the Above Beings. It is known to the Cree as *papamihaw asiniy*—flying rock—because of the way it got to the earth. The story is that the people witnessed the rock's fiery fall from the sky. They watched the flying rock tumble down and then disappear from their view when it hit the earth. This was viewed as a very significant spiritual event.

When the people went to the place where *papamihaw asiniy* had landed, they approached it cautiously and with reverence. The life force, energy, and the heat that the flying rock brought to the earth must have scorched the grass in a wide circle extending far outside of the impact impression it made on the land. What could this rock mean?

The fact that the rock landed at a place where the traditional territories of the Blackfoot and Cree overlap was not overlooked. The area was contested as both tribes vied for access to the rich resources there. That is why they often found themselves at war over it. But, perhaps *papamihaw asiniy* brought a message from the Creator that the Cree and Blackfoot should change the way they regarded this land and the resources it gave them. Perhaps the flying rock was sent to this contested territory by the Sky Beings to remind the people that no one can own the land or the buffalo. These were to be held in common and respectfully shared by all.

ERIKA HASEBE-LUDT: JAPANESE LANGUAGE SCHOOL, VANCOUVER DOWNTOWN EASTSIDE

Once Powell Street was the busy commercial center of Vancouver's pre-World War II Japantown, with flourishing sushi shops, grocery stores, fish markets, and restaurants—Aki's, Kamo's, Fujiya's, Yoshida's, and many more. Oppenheimer Park was home to the baseball field where the legendary Asahi team played. The Buddhist temple on Jackson Avenue across from the park was where many families and community members worshipped, where weddings and funerals, and Sunday School were held.

When Dorothy invited me to the nearby Japanese Language School on Alexander Street to hold our meeting in one of its classrooms, I asked my husband Ken what he remembered about the school. He had gone there for seven years during the late 50s and early 60s, twice a week in the afternoon after regular school, with his younger sister Elaine. "I was there for a long time," he told me. "When I was five, I spoke perfect Japanese. I went to school and lost it just like that." Japanese school was a "pain in the neck," he said, having to read and write and do the question-and-answer exercises from the textbook. Then, at home, he had to tell his parents about the lessons all over again, in Japanese, to make sure that he wouldn't forget what he had already lost once earlier in his childhood. Ken's memories of the building on Alexander Street are of dusty hallways and classrooms without much furniture, most of them unused and too cavernous for the small groups of *Nissei* and the *Sansei* second- and third-generation Canadian Japanese students that were propelled there by their parents' efforts to keep alive the mother tongue in danger of being lost—because its use was forbidden in the English-only curriculum of public schools, because the shame of being labeled "Jap" and "enemy alien" silenced it among the community, because the *Issei's* homeland and language was the target of national hatred, because the desire to be accepted and belong to that English-speaking nation burned in every young and old *Nikkei's* heart.

In his latest book entitled *A Fair Country: Telling Truths About Canada*, John Ralston Saul (2008) has called upon this nation to begin a different kind of dialogue and relationship between Canadian immigrant and indigenous peoples, and to remember

> our real tragedies. The aboriginal community has suffered from endless acts of injustice, violence and dishonesty, including the trashing of treaties signed in good faith;...the persecution of the Métis was another; [and] there was the legalized anti-Asian racism, which culminated in the internment of the Japanese Canadians during the Second World War. "We are going down to the middle of the earth with pick-axe eyes," Joy Kogawa writes, "...we are the despised rendered voiceless." (31)

In Vancouver, as in many other places, Japanese Canadians were left homeless too, without a neighborhood of their own. The language school on Alexander Street was the only building returned to the community after the *Nikkei* were allowed to return to the West Coast in 1949. Powell Street and its surroundings became a different kind of neighborhood then. Robbed of "Little Tokyo's" vibrant business and community activity from before the war, the hotels became temporary residences for the homeless poor from more than just one racial background. The Vancouver Asahi Japanese-Canadian baseball team had been forced to disband in 1941 after the Japanese attack on Pearl Harbor. The Asahi continued to play baseball in the internment camps, but never played together again as a team after World War II. To this day, as everywhere across Canada, there is no longer any place that could be called Japantown.

But today the Japanese Language School remains open, perseveres in its efforts to provide community programs for their twenty-first century clients—Japanese by ethnic and linguistic heritage and otherwise. There is still the Powell Street Festival, and the Cherry Tree Festival, that once a year celebrates the cultural heritage of this diasporic community. Recently, the city of Vancouver proposed to uproot the last few Japanese Sakura, the remaining ones of the 21 cherry trees that were planted more than 30 years ago by *Issei* seniors in the grounds of the Oppenheimer Park, as a memorial to the *Nikkei* community that once made a home of this place.[9] Along with the trees, there was a rock with a plaque engraved with haiku poetry that had been placed in the park to commemorate the history of Japanese Canadians in Vancouver (*Vancouver Courier* 2008). The rock is still there, but the plaque has disappeared. No one knows what happened. And now the city wants to redevelop the park, take out the trees that, it claims, are "declining" and replace them with "young, sturdier species" someplace else. My husband, who incidentally works for the Parks Board, says that, on the contrary, the Sakura are still sturdy and would stay that way for many years. Their fate, after a lengthy debate between the Parks Board and advocates for the preservation of the Legacy Sakura, remains undecided, tenuous at best. But the cherry trees in Oppenheimer Park were blossoming once again this spring.

ROUND 3

NARCISSE BLOOD: MR. AYOUNGMAN'S PROPHECY

In the course of doing our work on learning from place, Dr. Vivian Ayoungman remembered the following story, and now she understood the significance and relevance of this prophecy. One day her father, Arthur Ayoungman, told Vivian:

This is a story your grandfather told me many years ago when I was still very young. We were by the Bow River, and your grandfather told me: "Come here, my son. Let me show you something." And he pointed to the river and said: "Look, my boy. Look how clean and pristine this water is. We can drink directly from this water. We can swim in this water. But, my son, in the near future, you will not be able to drink from water anymore. You won't be able to swim anymore in this river, because of what is upstream. Upstream is the town of Calgary, and it is going to grow bigger, and the people upstream are going to damage this water by throwing and dumping their waste into this river."

And this has come about.

RAMONA BIG HEAD: "STRIKE THEM HARD!"
THE BAKER MASSACRE PLAY (III)

On Wednesday, January 23rd, 2008, it was exactly 138 years since the massacre and seven years since my first introduction and visit to the site. I was part of a delegation who were paying homage to our ancestors at the Blackfeet Community College's commemoration ceremony of the 1870 Bear River massacre. It was a cold morning, as I stood on the bluffs overlooking the Bear River where *Isokoyoomahka* (Chief Heavy Runner) and his people had camped.

I met *Natowapiisaaki* (Carol Murray) at this site. *Natowapiisaaki*'s passion about Blackfeet history, and the Baker Massacre in particular, is extremely powerful and infectious. She has made it a personal mission for her community to never forget this tragedy. Because of her dedication and research on this topic, many people of this generation are experiencing a reawakening of this story.

As we stood on the bluffs, she pointed to an area on the frozen Bear River where *Isokoyoomahka* (Chief Heavy Runner) walked onto the ice carrying a piece of paper, which stated that he was a peaceful chief. "That's where he was shot," she said. His body was found frozen on the ice in the aftermath. She also named Black Eagle as the other body that had been identified lying dead next to him.

When we turned around, we saw more and more people began showing up. I counted eight school buses. Of the approximately 200 people, who arrived that morning, there was a mixture of young children, adults, and Elders present. The young ones, of course, took off down the hill. I stood there and smiled as I watched little boys wrestling in the snow. They seemed oblivious to the cold. My mind flashed back getting a glimpse of what this traumatic day would have been like 138 years earlier. Mostly it was the children who had survived the massacre, and they were probably not much different in age from these little ones. Little boys were probably wrestling in the snow the day before the massacre, totally oblivious of what fate had in store for them the next morning.

I found a quiet place on the bluffs and made my tobacco offering. My prayer, spoken in my own Blackfoot language, became very emotional. At that moment, I began to feel the magnitude of the events. I prayed to the grandfathers and grandmothers, and called on *Isokoyoomahka* (Chief Heavy Runner) and *Natohkyiaakii* (Holy Bear Woman) to guide me as I begin to write the play. I humbly asked them to help us to be just as strong and resilient as they had been.

As a result of my experiences and successes in working with young people in theatre, I knew that this play could only be staged by children. My rationale was that since most of the survivors of the massacre were children, it only makes sense that they tell the story. I had a feeling that magical things would happen, and the magic that did happen surpassed everything that I had ever before experienced with my plays at Kainai High School.

When I began writing this play, I initially thought that I would stage it only in Blackfoot country. However, in April 2008, with the encouragement of my supervisor, *Aaksistoyiitapiaaki* (Dr. Cynthia Chambers), I submitted a proposal to *Performing the World* 2008, a conference in New York City. The following month, I received a notification of acceptance to this conference. I immediately submitted another proposal to my administration at the Kainai Board of Education. They were all extremely supportive. *All I had to do was raise the money.*

In June 2008, I held open auditions for the entire school district. I wanted to include the younger students. A total of 23 students auditioned. Some sang in spite of their front teeth being missing, some did monologues, some danced, and some read poetry. The following week I went to my planning committee and declared that, since we didn't have the money anyway, we were taking all 23 children to New York City!

Rehearsals began in July 2008. I was still working on the play. After rehearsals, I would rush home and work on the next scene for the following day. Plus, I was lobbying everyone I knew for money. In September 2008, we had a major breakthrough with our funding and we were able to take a total of 73 people to New York City, where we had the debut of our play.

"Strike Them Hard!" The Baker Massacre Play opened at *Performing the World* in New York City on October 4, 2008. There were delegates from all over the world. It was an honor to share this story with them. When we returned home, we had two sold-out performances at the Historic Empress Theatre in Fort Macleod, Alberta. The response was amazing! On January 23rd, 2009, things had come full circle. I fulfilled my promise to bring the play to the Blackfeet Reservation in Browning, Montana. We performed at the Bear River Massacre Commemoration hosted by the Blackfeet Community College.

For 139 years, the Baker Massacre has been relatively obscure. Today, there is a full-length play that chronicles all of the significant events, including the Blackfeet perspective, leading up to the massacre. With all our shows combined, we performed this play to approximately one thousand people. Therefore, there is a good chance that the traumatic events that took place on January 23rd, 1870 at Chief Heavy Runner's camp will not be forgotten ever again, especially among the Blackfoot. The cast and crew were a huge part of my journey with this play. Lasting memories and friendships were created throughout this whole process. I will never forget these people. I am deeply indebted to each of them. They were a key part of my healing journey.

The following is a letter I wrote to my daughter at the conclusion of my journey with the Baker Massacre story:

To my dear Galina;

I love you more and more everyday. I know if you were here, you would not have missed my opening night for anything! You would have been in the audience taking it all in. Afterwards, you would have come backstage and hugged me and congratulated me. You would have been my sounding board throughout this process. You would have been so proud of me.

Yet, as I write this, I know that you were there on opening night! You were in the audience. You did hug me and congratulate me. You were my sounding board and you are proud of me.

My girl, you gave me the strength to do this. I didn't think I could carry on without you, but you gave me the courage to keep going.

I dedicated this play to you, my girl, because you were the gifted writer. You were the storyteller. You were the creative one. You were the one who was not afraid to tell the painful stories.

This project has been one of the most memorable accomplishments in my life and I can't wait until the time comes when I can sit with you and tell you all about it.

You are in a place with the ancestors, and I hope they aren't too mad at me for the way I chose to tell their story. If they are . . . can you take care of it?

Until we meet again,

Mom.

CYNTHIA CHAMBERS: BUILDING DWELLING

We cannot create myth from scratch but we can recover or fashion stories that will help us to see where we are, how others have lived here, how we ourselves should live.

Scott Russell Sanders, "Telling the Holy"

Today, magpies are my neighbors, if not my friends. We "live and labor" next to one another (Herriot 2000). They wake me each dawn with their screeching and yammering, I only grumble in return. They dart in and out of the large spruce trees, perch on fences and bare branches, and strut around the yard like they own the place. They build large, untidy nests in the deciduous trees in nearby fields (Savage 1995). Mates for life, the couples work together. Often the males bring the sticks, while the female rearranges them in the nest. Twig by twig, over 40 or so days, they arrange over 500 sticks (Birkhead 1991) to form large domed fortresses up to 4 feet tall and 40 inches around (Salt & Salt 1976; Cornell 2009). They cement the sticks together with mud, and line the nest with fine rootlets and stems, hair and grass, ready it for the clutch of new eggs (Savage 1995).

My mother loved to garden. Moving dirt, planting trees, nurturing end-of-season shrubs bought for half-price or less. Growing up in Vancouver, my mother moved numerous times before she followed her mother to the Yukon. There she met my father. For the few years my mother, father, and I were a family, we moved frequently as well. From Vancouver to Saskatoon. And then to Edmonton, where we moved from apartment to apartment until my parents finally built a bungalow in a new suburb at the outskirts of the city. When we moved into 14317–98 Avenue: there were no streets, no sidewalks. No suburban order, just dirt and mud. My mother went to the country and dug up young saplings to transplant in her first real yard, of her first real house and home.

After 14317–98 Avenue in Edmonton, my mother and I traveled alone, moved often. So often, I attended 21 schools in four provinces, two territories, and one American state. And after that I flew the nest, my mother and her third husband moved another 60 times before she died. Wherever she moved and whenever she could, my mother gardened and landscaped. A relentless migrant and a perpetual stranger to new circumstances, she never seemed to tire of sculpting a home with fire-sale shrubs and pots of pansies.

In his evocative essay, "Building, Dwelling, Thinking" Martin Heidegger restores an older, less used meaning of the German *bauen,* as "dwelling," still present in the word "neighbor," meaning "one who dwells nearby" (Ingold 2000, 185). For Heidegger this older meaning of dwelling precedes the "high-and-mighty modernism" preoccupied with building as cultivation and construction. Preoccupied with a compulsion to bring rational order to uncivilized, and thus dirty, troubling spaces.

Empire was constructed in each village, town, and city to which my mother and I moved. Seemingly empty, unproductive landscapes were cultivated and put to use. The commons was divided into the public and the private. Civility and order was brought to public spaces with buildings and monuments that replicated the ideals of the European nation-state: city halls and parliament buildings. Gardens, such as the Galt Gardens in the center of Lethbridge, parks, and boulevards were cultivated. With the buffalo went the tipi. British sensibilities about "being civilized" (Herzfeld 2006) and aesthetics about domestic space molded the private domains of the newcomers, their houses, and their front and backyards.

The newcomers believed they needed to build, to dwell. But for Heidegger this was ass-backwards. "To build is in itself to already dwell" . . . "*Only if we are capable of dwelling,*" he said, "*only then can we build*" (Heidegger 1971, 160, emphasis in original). And this is true for all the other beings that dwell in these places. The magpies are dwelling beside me as they build their nests.

My mother continued to buy and sell houses, and to cultivate new gardens, sometimes digging up old ones and taking her plants with her to the next place. But she was continually restless, caught up in the current of mobility and migration. *Only if we are capable of dwelling, only then can we build,* said Heidegger. Perhaps planting trees, potting peonies, and deadheading marigolds was my mother's way of rearranging each house into a home, hoping that it would become a "place of maximal security" (Ingold 2000, 160). But instead, each new place became another point of flight; she was, it seems, incapable of being at home, at least for long.

Canada is a country occupied by such migrants. Perhaps not all as pathologically rootless as my mother. In Blackfoot, they call us "the newcomers," the ones who have just arrived. With our spades and shovels and seeds, with our high-and-mighty modernist ideas about cleanliness, order, and being civilized, and how those values must be represented in the landscape at any cost. And of course in the curriculum as well.

I arrived in Blackfoot territory 20 years ago, *matónni*, just long enough to know that to dwell here, I have a lot to learn and that there are beings willing to teach me. There are stories to help me learn how to dwell in this place, dwell, rather than occupy a condo, or build a career.

DWAYNE DONALD: THE MUSEUMIZATION OF *PAPAMIHAW ASINIY*

Then one day, a newcomer visited the flying rock and, not comprehending its power and spiritual energy, he had it carried away in a horse cart. This was John McDougall, a Methodist missionary working in the area. McDougall viewed the spiritual reverence for *papamihaw asiniy* as a major obstacle to his Christianizing and civilizing efforts. From McDougall's perspective, in spite of the evidence of offerings around it, the stone was just a meteorite. Evidence of his civilizing motives can be found in one of his books recounting his missionary work with the Cree, Blackfoot, and Stoney wherein McDougall (1971) describes a thirst dance ceremony that he attended in the valley of Iron Creek within sight of *papamihaw asiniy*. He concludes the section with this grand statement: "To-day we have a wild nomadic heathen life, but doubtless in the near to-morrow this will give way to permanent settlement, and the church and school will bring in the clearer light of a larger and fuller revelation" (89). It seems McDougall misunderstood the significance of the rock and considered its removal a necessary part of his civilizing mission.

Papamihaw asiniy was clearly out of place at McDougall's Victoria Mission where it sat, when described by a traveler who saw it there in 1866:

> In the farmyard of the mission-house there lay a curious block of metal of immense weight; it was rugged, deeply indented, and polished on the outer edges of the indentations by the wear and friction of many years. Its history was a curious one. Longer than any man could say, it had lain on the summit of a hill far out in the southern prairies. It had been a medicine stone of surpassing virtue among the Indians over a vast territory...And it was no wonder that this metallic stone should be a Manito-stone and an object of intense veneration for the Indian; it had come down from heaven; it did not belong to the earth, but had descended out of the sky; it was, in fact, an aerolite. (Butler 1968, 304)

Once the people of the area realized the flying rock had been removed, they considered the act a very bad sign, foretelling of terrible things to come. Elders prophesied that war, disease, and famine would result (Cuthand 2007, 16; Dempsey 1984, 37–38). In the four years following McDougall's civilizing act, these prophecies came true. The buffalo became much harder to find. Warfare and killing increased, as the hungry people competed for the scarce buffalo still to be found in the area. Smallpox killed approximately half of all Aboriginal peoples living on the prairies in 1869–1870 (Alberta Historical Review, 1963). The people were soon languishing on reserves.

Once McDougall realized his possession of the flying rock did not bring him more converts to Christianity, he shipped *papamihaw asiniy* from his Victoria Mission to Ontario. It was placed on a pedestal between the two front doors of the chapel on the campus of Victoria College in Cobourg. Students could touch it as they entered the building for prayers. Eventually, it was donated to the Royal Museum of Ontario. The flying rock then sat in that place for almost a century.

While at the museum, the rock attracted the attention of curious scientists from around the world. In 1886, a scientist working at Victoria College subjected *papamihaw asiniy* to its first scientific investigation. Scientists who wanted to know more about the rock chipped off samples of various sizes. They were then sent to the Field Museum Natural History in Chicago, Smithsonian Institute in Washington DC, Natural History

Museum in Vienna, American Museum of Natural History in New York, British Museum Natural History in London, and the Geological Survey of Canada in Ottawa. In a strange twist of its story, offerings were being made *from* the flying rock instead of *to* it. Those offerings were sent away to strange places, further distanced from the prairies where the flying rock had a place and a story that the people remembered. But that is what happens in a museum. The story of the artifact and the significance of the place that it comes from must be ignored. The artifact must be depersonalized and renamed, its original power and place must be removed and replaced so that it can be objectified, analyzed, and shelved.

John Willinsky (1998) has written in detail on the role of the museum in the colonial project, and makes this statement regarding the processes involved:

> the educational qualities of Western imperialism began with the amateur naturalist gathering specimens and artifacts while recording the lay of the land.... The themes of discovery, conquest, possession, and dominion are about ways of knowing the world, of surveying, mapping, and classifying it in an endless theorizing of identity and difference.... Over the last five centuries, the spectacles of empire were harnessed through what might be termed an exhibitionary pedagogy. The West came to see the world as a lesson in its own achievement. (85)

By removing *papamihaw asiniy* from its place, McDougall began a process that became much more than simply civilizing and Christianizing the Indians in the area by removing a sacred rock. The removal of the rock allowed the place to be reimagined. It allowed the prairies to be redefined in ways more conducive to Euro-Canadian notions of land use. To rename *papamihaw asiniy* as Manitou Stone and place it in a museum is a sovereign act. Canadian sovereignty over the area, at the expense of indigenous peoples, was achieved through the assertion that the significance of the land and places where rocks and stories dwell was superseded by the dream of open empty land so attractive to settlers. The creation story of the Canadian West depends on the transformation of the land to better serve the needs of market capitalism, the habits, and priorities of *Homo Oeconomicus*,[10] the Economic Man. Anything indigenous leftover from settler development was regarded as unfortunate detritus best located in a museum storeroom, or summarized in the margins of scientific notes. In those days, *papamihaw asiniy* had no place within the future of Canada.

The flying rock was returned to the prairies in 1972. It was renamed the Manitou Stone. It now sits openly on display at the Royal Alberta Museum. Some people think that *papamihaw asiniy* should be liberated from the museum and put back in its place, thus given back to the people that know its story. Repatriating *papamihaw asiniy* would bring much spiritual healing to the communities most affected by its removal. Such healing would mark a new era for Aboriginal peoples in Canada.

ERIKA HASEBE-LUDT: GRANDVIEW/*UUQUINAK'UUH* ELEMENTARY SCHOOL

> *Start a relationship with the land where you live. Ask that land what it needs from you. Because the truth is the land is the basis for everything... One of the important questions is to ask: What does the land need from you? (Jensen 2006, n.p.)*
>
> Derrick Jensen, *Tearing Down the Master's House*

When you walk further east from the Downtown Eastside, a dozen blocks or so, you come to the other neighborhood bordering the DTES, Grandview Woodlands. On Woodland Drive you find Grandview Elementary School, with its Coast Salish name *Uuquinak'uuh* prominently displayed on one of the outside walls. I have been visiting there too, as part of our life writing and literacy project in Canadian cosmopolitan sites. In these sites, and in schools such as Grandview, teachers and students are documenting their lives and their relationships with their surroundings, and with the larger world. This urban city block on which *Uuquinak'uuh* School sits is located just off "The Drive," Commercial Drive, that is, the vibrant hub of former "Little Italy," now one of Vancouver's many gentrified mixed neighborhoods, with an eclectic mosaic of savvy youth, middle-class upwardly mobile young families, middle-aged hippies, edgy artists and others of all ages practicing art-full and alternative lifestyles, and older working-class men and women with zesty European accents in their English. The Drive, however, is also divided from east to west by socioeconomic status and race. The side where Grandview school sits, with its First Nations co-op housing, is on the "wrong side" of The Drive, the less prosperous one. The school's statistics reflect the poverty many of the children and parents live with. Just recently, Marguerite, the teacher who is doing a life writing and photography project with her grade one and two students, told me that *Uuquinak'uuh*, with its large indigenous student population, is losing three teachers due to budget cuts,

> teachers we cannot afford to lose, with 67 identified special needs out of a total of 168 students, and 12 more pending. The school board is treating all of the schools equally, but we know that equal is not fair! (Marguerite Leahy personal communication, May 2009)

In light of the school board's "Aboriginal enhancement policy," this seems even less acceptable. But the good news is that the parents organized a protest march, called it "Mothers for Education," and had a big turnout, with people marching in solidarity along both sides of The Drive. Marguerite emailed me:

> The parents and grandparents were all fired-up to speak out against cuts that affect their children. We had about 70 people carrying signs and chanting with drums. The trustees said that they were blindsided and did not know the effect of all the number crunching and changes in the Aboriginal weighting formula. The superintendent said that he would review the proposed changes in light of the ramifications for schools like Grandview. We'll see. At least they came out on Mother's Day. A big step for our parents.... The only bad part was when we got to the park, there was so much dope in the air— right at the children's playground! Commercial Drive parents smoking while their children are on the slides and swings.... (Marguerite Leahy personal communication, May 2009)

Lester Pearson, the Canadian Nobel Peace Prize politician, claimed that the well-being of a civilization depends on its ability to respond creatively to human and environmental challenges (Mau 2004). An immense challenge for us within and across our creative and critical disciplines is to figure out what this means for our children in their schools and homes today. Spending time in the Downtown Eastside and at *Uuquinak'uuh* brought home to me how difficult this is in these neighborhoods that live at the edge of hope. To creatively imagine and realistically create "massive change" for a better world (Mau 2004), in the small, vulnerable places children dwell and seek refuge in, takes a courage and wisdom on the part of adults. Helping children live and learn well in places where neglect thrives and no one in the official care services seems to care, at least not enough, is an urgent task for all of us. One of the ways to take care and to care is to document life these places truthfully, like Marguerite and her students do, to tell these stories to each other and to the people in the institutions responsible for the care of our young. Thomas King (2008) reminds us that the truth about stories is that that's all we are, and, as Laguna storyteller Leslie Silko's words, warns us:

> Don't be fooled.
> They are all we have, you see,
> all we have to fight off
> illness and death. You don't have anything
> if you don't have the stories. (Silko 1977 as cited in King 2008, 14)

It is our obligation, King tells us, to take care of the stories and to take care of the land where the stories are unraveling, as a matter of physical and spiritual survival, as part of "the webs of responsibilities that bind all things" (23) that hold us in relationality.

78

NARCISSE BLOOD ET AL.

ENDNOTES

1. This *métissage* was originally performed by Narcisse Blood, Cynthia
Chambers, Dwayne Donald, and Erika Hasebe-Ludt at the 4th Biannual
Provoking Curriculum Conference: "An Uncommon Countenance:
Provoking Past, Present, and Future Perspectives Within Canadian
Curriculum Studies" in Ottawa, Ontario, Canada in May 2009.
Subsequently, another version was performed by Ramona Big Head,
Cynthia Chambers, Dwayne Donald and Erika Hasebe-Ludt under the
title *"Aoksisowaato'p ki aokakio'ssin*: Imagining Organic Curriculum for
Relational Renewal" at the "6th International Globalization, Diversity,
and Education Conference" in Spokane, WA, USA (February 2010).
Ramona Big Head's parts were adapted from her Master's project " 'Strike
Them Hard!' The Baker Massacre Play" (Lethbridge: University of
Lethbridge 2008). The symposia consisted of oral storytelling and shared
reading of the scripts that lasted approximately one hour. The storytelling
and readings were augmented with visual images and audio recordings to
provide a multi-sensory and intertextual experience for the audience.
2. See Parks Canada website for a history of the re-introduction of bison into
Canada through the newly formed national parks of Elk Island National
Park and Buffalo National Park http://www.pc.gc.ca/pn-np/ab/elkisland
/natcul/natcul1bi_E.asp
3. See Davis Guggenheim, *An Inconvenient Truth*. (Hollywood: Paramount,
2006).
4. In March 2009, Dorothy Lander and her co-investigators "traveled coast to
coast, from Antigonish, NS to Tofino, BC by rail (plus bus, cab, and ferry),
making 15 'whistlestops' to meet with rural and urban women's art and
advocacy communities." For more information see http://womenmaking
waves.wordpress.com/the-whistlestop-project.
5 See http://www.missingpeople.net/home.html for more information on this
event and the continuing activism focused on the missing and murdered
women of the Vancouver Downtown Eastside.
6. The inscription on this memorial stone is found at http://www.missingpeo
ple.net/home.html
7. For more information about the official government interpretation of the
site of the Frank Slide see the Interpretive Centre's website http://www
.frankslide.com/
8. The version of the story related here is adapted from the one reported by
George Brid Grinnell in *Blackfoot Lodge Tales: The Story of A Prairie People*
(Lincoln, NB: University of Nebraska/Bison Books, 2003).
9. For more information and updates on the Legacy Sakura, see http://www
.canada.com/vancouvercourier/news/story.html?id=53f6b9e1-dd4c-4c67
-b091-9887bb17349d&k=29274
10. *Homo Oeconomicus* is most often translated as "Economic Man." However,
the term *homo* actually refers to the human species as a whole and not just
"man." See John Persky. 1995. "The Ethology of *Homo Economicus," Journal
of Economic Perspectives* 9 (2): 221–231.

REFERENCES

Alberta Historical Review. 1963. *Smallpox Epidemic of 1869–70* 11 (2): 13–19.

Alberta Learning. (2012). *First Nations, Metis and Inuit perspectives in curriculum.* Retrieved on September 23, 2011:   http://ignitionindustries.com/clients /albertaeducation/ltb/fnmi/

Alberta Teachers Association. 2006, rev. 2007/2008. Education is Our Buffalo: A Teachers' Resource for First Nations, Métis and Inuit Education in Alberta. Edmonton, AB: Alberta Teachers' Association.

Baron, Ethan. 2009, 4 May. A Message in Angry Strokes. *The Province.* Retrieved September 21, 2009, from http://www.theprovince.com/news/todays-paper /message+angry+strokes/1561063/story.html

Basso, Keith. 1996. Wisdom Sits in Places: Landscapes and Languages Among the Western Apache. Albuquerque, NM: New Mexico Press.

Big Head, Ramona. 2008. *"Strike them hard!" The Baker Massacre play.* Unpublished Master's project, University of Lethbridge, Lethbridge, Alberta.

Birkhead, Tim. 1991. The Magpies: The Ecology and Behaviour of Black-billed and Yellow-Billed Magpies. London, UK: T & A D Poyser.

Blackfoot Gallery Committee. 2001. *Nitsitapiisinni: The Story of the Blackfoot People.* Toronto: Key Porter Books.

Blood, Narcisse, & Cynthia Chambers, producers/writers/directors. 2006. *"Kaaáhsinnooniksi: If the Land Could Speak..."* [Digital-video documentary]. (Produced in cooperation with Alberta Community Development Branch and the University of Lethbridge.)

Bullchild, Percy. 1985. The Sun Came Down: The History of the World as My Blackfeet Elders Told It. New York: Harper & Row.

Butler, William. 1968. The Great Lone Land: A Narrative of Travel and Adventure in the North-West of America. Edmonton: Hurtig.

Chambers, Cynthia. 2006. ""The Land is the Best Teacher I Ever Had": Places as Pedagogy for Precarious Times." *JCT: Journal of Curriculum Theorizing* 22 (3): 27–37.

Chambers, Cynthia, Erika Hasebe-Ludt, & Dwayne Donald. 2002. Creating a Curriculum of Métissage. *Educational Insights* 7 (2) [Online]. Retrieved April 15, 2004, from http://ccfi.educ.ubc.ca/publication/insights/v07n02/toc.html

Chambers, Cynthia, Erika Hasebe-Ludt, Dwayne Donald, Wanda Hurren, Carl Leggo, & Antoinette Oberg. 2008. Métissage. In *Handbook of the Arts in Qualitative Research: Perspectives, Methodologies, Examples, and Issues*, edited by J. Gary Knowles & Ardra L. Cole,141–153. Thousand Oaks, CA: Sage.

Christensen, Deanna. 2000. Ahtahkakoop: The Epic Account of a Plains Cree Head Chief, His People, and Their Struggle for Survival, 1816–1896. Shell Lake, SK: Ahtahkakoop Publishing.

Cornell Lab of Ornithology. 2009. *All About Birds: Black-billed Magpie.* Ithaca, NY: Cornell University. Retrieved July 16, 2009, from http://www.allaboutbirds.org /guide/Black-billed_Magpie/lifehistory

Cuthand, Doug. 2007. *Askiwina: A Cree World.* Regina , SK: Coteau Books.

Deloria, V. (1991). *Indian Education in America.* Boulder, CO: American Indian Science and Engineering Society.

Dempsey, Hugh. 1984. *Big Bear: The End of Freedom*. Vancouver, BC: Douglas & McIntyre.

Donald, Dwayne. 2003. "Elder, Student, Teacher: A Kainai Curriculum Métissage." Unpublished Master of Education Thesis, University of Lethbridge. Lethbridge, Alberta.

———. 2004. "Edmonton Pentimento: Re-reading History in the Case of the Papaschase Cree." *Journal of the Canadian Association for Curriculum Studies* 2 (1): 21–54.

———. 2009. "The Pedagogy of the Fort: Curriculum, Aboriginal-Canadian Relations, and Indigenous Métissage." Unpublished doctoral dissertation, University of Alberta, Edmonton, Alberta.

Ermine, Willie. 1995. Aboriginal Epistemology. In *The Circle Unfolds: First Nations Education in Canada*, edited by Marie Battiste & Jean Barman, 101–112. Vancouver, BC: UBC Press.

Government of Alberta. 2005, 01 July. *An Improved Magpie Trap*. Edmonton, AB: Alberta.ca Agriculture and Rural Development. Retrieved November 11, 2008, from http://www1.agric.gov.ab.ca/$department/deptdocs.nsf/all/agdex3496

Grinnell, George Bird. 2003. *Blackfoot Lodge Tales: The Story of a Prairie People*. Lincoln, NB: University of Nebraska Press/Bison Press.

Guggenheim, Davis, dir. 2006. *An Inconvenient Truth* [DVD]. Hollywood: Paramount.

Heidegger, Martin. 1971. *Poetry, Language and Thought*. Translated by Albert Hofstadter. New York, NY: Harper and Row.

Herriot, Trevor. 2000. *River in Dry Land: A Prairie Passage*. Toronto: Stoddart.

Herzfeld, Michael. 2006. "Spatial Cleansing: Monumental Vacuity and the Idea of the West." *Journal of Material Culture* 11 (1/2): 129–149.

Hill, Don. 2008. "Listening to Stones." *Alberta Views* September: 40–45.

Ingold, Tim. 2000. The Perception of the Environment: Essays in Livelihood, Dwelling and Skill. New York, NY: Routledge.

Jensen, Derrick. 2006. *An Interview with Derrick Jensen: Tearing Down the Master's house*. Retrieved December 1, 2007, from http://www.worldproutassembly.org/archives/2006/08/an_interview_wi_6.html

King, Thomas. 2008. "The Art of Indigenous Knowledge: A Million Porcupines Crying in the Dark." In *Handbook of the Arts in Qualitative Research: Perspectives, Methodologies, Examples, and Issues*, edited by J. Gary Knowles & Ardra L. Cole, 3–25. Los Angeles, CA: Sage Publications.

Lau, Evelyn. 2009, February 19. Evelyn Lau: A Homeless Past Stirs Again. *The Georgia Straight*. Available from http://www.straight.com/article-201936/homeless-past-stirs-pain.

Leahy, Marguerite, electronic mail correspondence, May 12, 2009.

Little Bear, Leroy. 1998. "Aboriginal Relationships to the Land and Resources." In *Sacred Lands: Aboriginal Word views, Claims, and Conflicts.*, edited by Jill Oakes, Rick Riewe, Kathi Kinew & Elaine Maloney, 15–20. Canadian Circumpolar Institute Press: Edmonton.

———. 2000. "Jagged Worldview Colliding." In *Reclaiming Indigenous voice and vision*, edited by Marie Battiste, 77–85. Vancouver, BC: UBC Press.

Massacre of Piegan in 1870. 1932, April 3. *The Billings Gazette.*

Maté, Gabor. 2008. In the Realm of Hungry Ghosts: Close Encounters with Addiction. Toronto, ON: Alfred A. Knopf Canada.

Mau, Bruce, & the Institute Without Boundaries. 2004. *Massive Change: A Manifesto for the Future Global Design Culture.* London/New York: Phaidon Press.

McClintock, Walter. 1968/1999. *The Old North Trail: Life, Legends, & Religion of the Blackfeet Indians.* Lincoln, NB: University of Nebraska/Bison Books.

McDougall, John. 1971. Pathfinding on Plain and Prairie: Stirring Scenes From Life in the Canadian North-West. Toronto, Ontario: Coles.

McLeod, Neil. 1998. "Coming Home Through Stories." *International Journal of Canadian Studies* 18 (Fall): 51–66.

Montana Fish, Wildlife & Parks. n.d. *Living With Magpies.* Helena, MT: Montana Government. Retrieved July 10, 2008, from http://www.ictws.org/history .phphttp://fwp.mt.gov/wildthings/livingwwildlife/magpies/default.html

Morache, Martel. n.d. *Fifty Years of Game Management (1938–1988) in Idaho.* Idaho Chapter of the Wildlife Society. Retrieved July 10, 2008, from http://www.ictws .org/history.php

Oliver, Frank. 1955. "The Indian Drum: An Incident in the Rebellion of 1885." *Alberta Historical Review* 3 (1): 3–15.

Persky, John. 1995. "The Ethology of Homo Economicus." Journal of Economic Perspectives 9 (2): 221–231.

Punke, Michael. 2007. Last Stand: George Bird Grinnell, the Battle to Save the Buffalo, and the Birth of the New West. New York: HarperCollins/ Smithsonian Books.

Phillips, William. S. 1996. *Total Warfare on the Marias.* Unpublished Master's thesis, Wake Forest University, Winston Salem, North Carolina.

Ryser, F. A. 1985. *Birds of the Great Basin.* Reno, NV: University of Nevada Press.

Salt, R. W., & J. R Salt. 1976. The Birds of Alberta: With Their Ranges in Saskatchewan & Manitoba. Edmonton, AB: Hurtig.

Saul, John R. 2008. *A Fair Country: Telling Truths about Canada.* Toronto, ON: Viking Canada.

Savage, Candace. 1995. *Bird Brains: The Intelligence of Crows, Ravens, Magpies and Jays.* Vancouver, BC: Greystone Books/Douglas & McIntyre.

Schultz, James W. 1962. *Blackfeet and Buffalo: Memories of Life Among the Indians.* Norman, OK: University of Oklahoma Press.

Silversides, B. 2005. *Fort de Prairies: The Story of Fort Edmonton.* Surrey, BC: Heritage House

Swainson, Rev. C. 1885. *Provincial Names and Folklore of British Birds.* London, UK: Trübner and Co.

Vancouver Courier. May 2, 2008. "Memorial Cherry Trees in Peril Due to Oppenheimer Park Redevelopment." *The Vancouver Courier.* Available from http://www.canada.com/vancouvercourier/news/story.html?id=53f6b9e1-dd4c -4c67-b091–9887bb17349d&k=29274

Wetaskiwin & District Heritage Museum. 2005, 12 December. "Mabel Josephine (Hougestol) Lee" In *The women of Aspenland, 1890s to 1960s.* Wetaskiwin, AB: Wetaskiwin Online.com. Retrieved May 16, 2009, from http://www.wetaskiwin online.com/museum/lee_mabel/index.html

Willinsky, John. 1998. *Learning to Divide the World: Education at Empire's End*. Minneapolis, MN: University of Minnesota Press.

Winterman, Denise. 2008, 28 March. "Why Are Magpies So Often Hated?" Available from *BBC New Magazine*. Retrieved May 10, 2009, from http://news .bbc.co.uk/2/hi/uk_news/magazine/7316384.stm

Wissler, Clark, & D. C. Duvall. 1908/2007. *The Mythology of the Blackfoot Indians*. Compiled and translated by D. C. Duvall. Lincoln, NB: University of Nebraska Press.

Wormington, Hannah M., & Richard Forbis, 1965. *An Introduction to the Archaeology of Alberta, Canada*. Denver, CO: Denver Museum of Natural History.

CHAPTER 4

Reconsidering Canadian Environmental Curriculum Studies: Framing an Approach to Ecojustice

Andrejs Kulnieks, Nicholas Ng-A-Fook, Darren Stanley, and Kelly Young

Responding to the Currently Emerging Ecojustice Movement

In the spring of 2009, we presented several papers on a panel at the 4th Biennial Provoking Curriculum Studies Conference. Our presentations evolved into a postconference discussion whereby each of our areas of concern about curriculum prompted us to reconsider how we might reconceptualize Canadian environmental educational curriculum. In this chapter, we build upon these initial conversations and respond to an emerging ecojustice movement. Nicholas Ng-A-Fook traces the ways in which his international intellectual studies, within the public schooling system here in Canada and the United States, have helped him to reconsider how, as a curriculum theorist, he might provoke the interdisciplinarity of fields like environmental education, indigenous, postcolonial studies, and curriculum studies to reconceptualize his (colonial) understandings of concepts like environmental sustainability, greenwashing, and ecojustice. Darren Stanley draws on transdisciplinarity and complexity theories to address the kinds of conditions that underlie the emergence of healthy living and learning organizations. Andrejs Kulnieks works from an ecojustice framework to reconsider how a deep analysis of language can foster a greater awareness of life histories in relation to place. Finally, Kelly Young considers the ways in which bringing forth an ecojustice education framework can illuminate metaphors that perpetuate antiecological habits of mind in the development of identity formation.

Much of our theorizing is informed by an ecojustice perspective that, according to Bowers and Martusewicz (2004), involves a cultural analysis of the social and ecological crisis in the course of investing the ways in which root metaphors such as anthropocentrism, patriarchy, ethnocentrism, individualism, progress, mechanism, economism, and so on, reproduce taken-for-granted hierarchies within what we call Canadian curriculum studies. We recognize and note the importance of diverse temporal and spatial relationships and how our language mediates a world full of complex interdisciplinary topographies and sociocultural landscapes of understanding are caught up in a larger crisis of perceptual disconnection.

AN AUTOBIOGRAPHICAL STUDY OF ENVIRONMENTAL EDUCATION CURRICULUM POLICY

We share this planet, our home, with millions of species. Justice and sustainability both demand that we do not use more resources than we need.

Shiva 2005, 50

During the summer of 2000, I returned to university to further my professional intellectual development as a science and history high school educator. At that time, our union was challenging the Ontario government's (led by Premier Mike Harris) restructuring of curriculum policies (standardized outcomes and testing), amalgamation of school boards and educational administration, as well as increasing a high school teacher's overall workload. Mike Harris also made major cuts to the environmental education programs that existed within Ontario schools as part of the new curriculum that supported the economic rhetoric of his "common sense revolution." At that time, the immediate or future impacts of such restructuring of the system and its respective curricular policies in relation to concepts like "environmental sustainability" were not part of my epistemological stance, either inside or outside the school curriculum. Nonetheless, it was during this era of major curriculum reforms that I returned to graduate school at York University.

During that summer, I was first introduced to the international field of curriculum studies and its respective historical discursive trends in a course titled "Introduction to Curriculum Studies." Like happenstance, the course instructor just happened to be William F. Pinar who was invited to share his insights with us as a visiting professor. In fact, I was also fortunate enough to study with scholars like Lous Heshusius (1996), Leesa Fawcett (Alsop & Fawcett 2010), Constance Russell (2005, 2006), Deborah Britzman (1998) who asked us then, as students, to reconsider among other things the kinds of short- and long-term relationships we seek to sustain (or repress) between self and the other, while inhabiting different urban and rural environments. Celia Haig-Brown (2008) who later agreed to be my thesis advisor always pushed us to question as to how we might decolonize our daily inhabitations of what Bowers (2009) calls the cultural commons.

Indeed, my lived curriculum within these courses was an intellectual turning point for me. William F. Pinar introduced us for the first time to *currere* (an autobiographical methodology for curriculum theorizing), as a legitimate form of educational research within the disciplinary structures of schooling. During our coursings of that summer term he encouraged us to study, to linger, within the "verticality" and "horizontality" of the interdisciplinary and international theoretical topographies (see Pinar 2007), while we deconstructed our different lived experiences in relation to concepts like environmental education, sustainability, and ecojustice.

Such intellectual study afforded us opportunities to reconsider our epistemological stances, while contemplating the complicated conversations already taking place both outside and within what Chambers (1999, 2003) has eloquently and quite succinctly called the topos of Canadian curriculum studies. Our challenge, at that time as burgeoning curriculum theorists, as administrators, teachers, and graduate students was in many ways to reread and rewrite our lived experiences in relation to the various topographies of curriculum theory—to develop a language of our own. Ones that began at home, as Chambers (1999) reminded us then, but also journeyed elsewhere.

For my thesis, I utilized *currere* as a strategy for bridging an inter/disciplinary and complicated conversation between women and gender, postcolonial, indigenous, and curriculum studies. Then at Louisiana State University, I studied the ways in which my teachings of colonialism's cultural, historical, and national narratives suppressed and continue to silence the stories of the colonized, including our relationships to the environment itself (Ng-A-Fook 2007). Although public institutions of schooling house an ensemble of knowledges and practices that reproduce and inscribe colonialism's culture, they also provide spaces to teach alter/native historical narratives, where we might continue to challenge the sustainability of our present colonial relationships through our inhabitations of different rural and urban environments. The potential social significance for revisiting our intellectual histories within curriculum studies via autobiographical research is that it becomes a way for reconceptualizing both the content and the purpose of our presence in relation to concepts like environmental sustainability, greenwashing, and ecojustice.

During my first year as an assistant professor at the University of Ottawa, the Ontario Ministry of Education established the Curriculum Council and published its first report: *Shaping our Schools, Shaping our Futures*. The report provides important and relevant strategies for administrators, teachers, students, and community-based environmental partners to teach the next generation of Canadian citizens how we might continue to recapitulate our industrialized educational system (its manufactured curricular arteries) toward creating a more sustainable environmental future. However, the current reconceptualization of the Ontario curriculum as becoming more inclusively green—a greener way of shaping our schools, shaping our futures—also fails in many ways to address such intergenerational calling forth across the territories that we now inhabit. Instead, this report pays homage to our future actions by evoking the thrilling names and concepts scattered over the history of educational scientism and technology, while forgetting the very experiences that take place under our feet (Jardine 1992; Gough 2006). This is what Young (2009) calls the historical and present mechanistic and commodified approaches that colonize our daily curricular actions. Although somewhat greener, the document in many ways continues to narrate the classical narratives of technological progress with which we "enlighten" ourselves today. Its current narrative plot of technological progress fails in many ways to offer solutions to the ongoing Canadian problem of over consumption: a problem that is ever more present due to our expanding global population, and its respective stockpiling of economic enclosures.

In 1968, Hardin defined a technological solution as an educational narrative that advocates for change "only in the techniques of the natural sciences, demanding little or nothing in the way of change in human values or ideas of morality" (101). Furthermore, as Young (2009) warns us, the Curriculum Council Report also fails to provide narrative accounts that question how our curriculum policy documents remain steeped in the technical root metaphors of overall and specific expectations, which reinscribe anthropocentric and individualistic pedagogical approaches for environmental education within our future curricular designs. At the same time, this report pushes teachers, communities, and students to take action, just now, so that we may sustain our narrative and material existence as a species at least in the near future.

When I was a young boy, during the silence of dark mornings, after my father had been on call all night, I would often whisper at the side of his bed

"Dad, will we leave to go hunting soon?" "Just now," was often his prescribed cultural reply. "Just now," is a prevalent Guyanese expression in our family, which means anywhere from five minutes from now to an hour, to four, or in some cases three days, or maybe more. Yet, implicated in this temporal cultural reference to time, is that there is always just enough time available, for ecojustice to come, just now. Today, how might we provoke an asking of narrative moments, of thinking, of doing, that takes time now to think about the things we do, could do just now, and/or put off doing just now?

In response to such questioning, "environmental education rests," the report narrates, "on a foundation of knowledge from both science and social studies/geography" (5). Furthermore, it advocates for the integration of such interdisciplinary knowledge across the school curriculum. Such interdisciplinary integration is an important beginning toward greening the curriculum within our schools. Instead, Gough (1999) asks us to reconsider our conceptions of literacy to take into account a more nuanced understanding of environmental education as a intertextual practice situated within the interdisciplinary terrains of the arts and humanities, which in turn move beyond the current conceptual narrative enclosures of the places we now inhabit. To the next generation, our provincial government reassures the public that they

> will receive the best possible education in the world, measured by high levels of achievement and engagement for all students. Successful learning outcomes will give all students the skills, knowledge and opportunities to attain their potential, to pursue lifelong learning, and to contribute to a prosperous, cohesive society. (1)

This governmental "regime of truth" is applied toward disciplining environmental education within our schools, under the standardized political and multinational guise of assessment and accountability (Foucault 1980). Meanwhile, a student's "subjective" presence within their daily activities (within their narrative accounts) is deliberately ignored. Is this another promise to take the narrative lead out of our curricular gas? In an Orwellian sense, we continue to (re)count how well the cows and pigs are growing within our educational enclosures in order to generate future biopower for the corporate industrial machine. Such narratives of "successful" learning outcomes and economic prosperity continue to advocate for, what Gough (1999) calls, unsustainable narratives of consumer fiction. Meanwhile our Canadian resource-based economies continue to rely on each global citizen's cohesive ability to prosperously produce, export and consume more oil, trees, and fisheries.

The current storied vision of Ontario education sees schooling through the lenses of a governmental system taking on primarily, what Greene (1995) calls, a technical point of view; what the Ministry of Education research branch calls evidence-based learning. This narrative plot advocates for political reform as "benevolent policy making, with the underlying conviction that changes in school can bring about progressive social change" (11). Like many others, our family often tries to devise technical ways, a daily environmental education curriculum if you will, and responsible local and global citizenship practices, in which we might decrease the evils of contributing to overpopulation, overhunting and harvesting of living things, both taking and giving to the commons without relinquishing any prosperous privileges we now enjoy from our stockpiling of economic enclosures. In turn, we struggle with taking an ecological account of our daily household economy.

As teacher educators, how might we then reconsider (autobiographically) the ways in which our curriculum as planned, implemented, and lived provokes environmentally responsible citizens of every kind, that in turn understand how shaping the stories taken up in our schools is interrelated to how we conceptualize the future shaping of the ecological territories that many of us now call home? For now, the Curriculum Council Report continues, at least for me, to attune our earthy mindfulness toward narrative accounts of environmental sustainability as a form of greenwashing, of an ecojustice to come just now.

We can trace the term "greenwashing" back to 1986, where Westerveld (1986) critiqued the hotel industry practice of placing green cards in each room, promoting reuse of guest towels, in order to save the environment. However, Westerveld observed "that in most cases, little or no effect toward waste recycling was being implemented by these institutions due in part to the lack of cost-cutting by such practices" (as cited in Ng-A-Fook 2010, 51). For example, now with the Curriculum Council Report in circulation, how much are schools doing in terms of effecting waste reduction? The report acknowledges that due to "the absence of specialized teacher training and expertise, there is likely a gap between the environmental education 'intended' in Ontario's curriculum and that which is taught and received in the classroom" (Ontario Ministry of Education 2007, 2). And yet, how does placing a green card within each of our curriculum designs work to reduce industrial consumer consumption taking place both inside and outside of schools? This questions aside, Westerveld suggests that the objective of this type of corporate "green campaign" is about increasing profits and not necessarily about diminishing our ecological impact. Consequently, he labeled such green campaigns and other outwardly corporate environmentally conscious acts with an underlying purpose of profit increases as greenwashing.

In a sense, we can reread the Curriculum Council Report, and its respective resource documents, as a yet another technocratic and corporate narrative of greenwashing, which seeks to place overall and specific green expectations in every classroom. Do these green expectations help us profit toward shaping "successful" environmentally responsible citizens within a cohesive Ontario society? Is there such a cohesive thing? And, what might the interdisciplinary narrative visions of such "successful" expectations look like? As teacher educators, teachers, and graduate students, how might we then draw upon autobiographical research strategies to reconsider our intellectual histories and epistemological stances, while taking up environmental education reforms in Ontario like *Shaping our Schools, Shaping our Future* that move beyond our "common sense" assumptions as one approach for framing ecojustice through the school curriculum?

RECONSIDERING TRANSDISCIPLINARITY AND COMPLEXITY THEORY

Everyone in a complex system has a slightly different interpretation. The more interpretations we gather, the easier it becomes to gain a sense of the whole.
Margaret J. Wheatley

Human beings are good at recognizing as well as creating patterns in time and space. Alas, the kinds of patterns that generally have crept into many of our actions and thinking reflect the rather linear nature of a Euclidean world of straight lines, flat shapes, and regular figures. The natural world, however, is nothing at all like this. We have done a great job in flattening out the world and removing much of its jagged, bumpy, organic self. Thankfully, there are so many other structures that seem to have escaped our collective attention as a kind of pattern unto itself—trees, riverbeds, clouds, mountain tops, sand dunes, flocking patterns of birds, schools of fish, and so on. And yet, what kinds of patterns were these? It seems clear to me now that such attention comprises a transdisciplinary quality and feature of what we call learning. Moreover, learning seems to be less of a quality that pertains to human beings, not something that takes place in structures called school and classrooms, but something that reflected many scales of organization all at once, from the neurological to the biological, to the social, and ecological. For these reasons, I started to think about learning in light of complex dynamical systems of all kinds (Stanley 2005).

Transdisciplinary thinking then is an emerging philosophy that underpins many contemporary and still-emerging understandings of a number of complex phenomena like health (Albrecht, Freeman & Higginbotham 1998), education (Davis & Sumara 2006), and ecology (Orr 1992, 1994). Here, I ask us to reconsider a view of ecojustice framed by transdisciplinary thinking, linking it with complexity thinking as a concern for the self-organizing, emergent properties of nested systems. Nature and society need not be conceived of as separate phenomena or domains of study although, historically speaking, much of contemporary society has done well to understand the world as such. It would seem, however, that the world has "come undone" where a loss of coherence and meaning has created disconnections across, and between, many different scales of organization, ranging from the cell assemblies, organic systems, biological beings, social and cultural forms, local ecologies, and the planet itself (Ratson 1993). This fragmenting of the world has come into being as a result of particular pervasive, dominant metaphorical constructions that reflect certain culturally and historically rooted patterns of thought and action. In recent times, more integrated, holistic views of worldly phenomena have emerged including a transdisciplinary discourse known as complexity science to offer some potentially promising insights for an ecologically sensitive and just pedagogy.

How does a view of transdisciplinarity and complexity theory help us to reconsider and reconceptualize Canadian environmental education curriculum? To be sure, there is ample evidence that documents the extent and degree of many of the world's most significant problems can be taken up by teachers and students through such theoretical frameworks (Capra 1996). Moreover, the major problems and concerns of our time—AIDS, other diseases, hunger, poverty, violence, terrorism—simply cannot be studied and understood in isolation as they are systemic, interconnected, and interdependent in nature. These problems, which reflect a "crisis of perception" (Capra 1983), reflect an inadequate and, perhaps, inappropriate view of the world. Specifically, the world continues to be seen, described, and interacted with as if it were a machine-like organization. To be sure, it has become more pressing with each published report like *Shaping our Schools, Shaping our Futures*, and shared conversations about people's lived experiences of living in poverty, violence, and destruction of local ecologies that, as a collective, we need to take action and do things a little differently than we have in the past.

There are, one might surmise, different solutions and approaches to many of the world's problems, however, a radical shift in our collective thinking is still required. This already emerging, and still seemingly, radical shift is the view of the world as an integrated whole as opposed to being a collection of parts and disciplinary foci—at least from a purely intellectual perspective. It is a deep ecological and holistic view that reflects the need for healing, health, and holiness, and an awareness that human beings are already and always have been embedded within the world that is fundamentally interconnected and interdependent. Surely, such a stance must draw upon a diverse collection of views and disciplinary concerns. Indeed, one might say that an interdisciplinarity is required. For many researchers, scholars, and practitioners, the turn to interdisciplinary work brings up many concerns and the need to answer complex questions, address broad issues, explore disciplinary and professional relationships, solve problems that are beyond the capacity of any one discipline, and achieve unity of knowledge, no matter the scale.

How might we then take up ideas that matter within the contexts of transdisciplinarity and complexity theories? Diversity, for example, is not merely important in social matters—gender, sexuality, place of origin, ethnicity, and so on—it is a principle of some importance for all scales of organization: it is a principle that works across all scales of organization. Connectivity is another important notion, not only for the coherence of a given scale of organization (i.e., phenomena) but also for the coherence of seemingly separate and different "layers" or "levels" of life. Life, viewed as interactions that beget nothing more than further interactions, gives rise to many different scales of organization all at once—physiological, biological, social, cultural, political, and ecological. The inherent connections and relationships between and among these different scales cannot be ignored, as an ecojustice perspective reminds us the role and importance that culture plays in the ways in which people look at the world. And, from a purely environmental perspective, one, which places human beings "outside" of the rest of the world, is likewise problematic. The embeddedness of each scale of phenomena must be a part of any conceptual framework. Again, such a view may be impossible. But, surely, viewing the world through a set of shared principles, principles drawn from or shared by complexity science, facilitate a side step around the need to focus on so many different disciplinary perspectives. A transdisciplinary perspective like ecojustice or complexity science, two resonating perspectives, seems to offer just what is needed to heal the world that is cut up, disassembled, and destroyed by our actions and ways of thinking. An ecojustice perspective, a perspective rooted, partly, in how certain cultural and root metaphors shape what human beings do, is required to make some amends.

What would happen, then, if we reconsidered learning as a phenomenon that unfolded across multiple scales of organizations at once? In other words, if ecology is concerned with matters of relationship, what might the ecological function of schools be, if we were to envision our lives and the world as thoroughly embedded living structures caught up in this restless conversation that we might call life? And, how might transdisciplinarity and complexity theory provide us alternative possibilities for reconsidering such curricular questions?

RECONSIDERING CANADIAN ENVIRONMENTAL CURRICULUM THROUGH PLACE-BASED LEARNING

Oral culture also means much more than telling stories. It means learning how to hear them, how to nourish them, and how to let them live.

Bringhurst 2006, 175

Working in the field of education for over 15 years, both as teacher and with teacher candidates, I am continually reminded of the importance of developing a deeper awareness of the relationship between language and identity formation. Understanding the implications of Rosenblatt's (1978) work regarding how the reader is an integral aspect of the text can be viewed as a starting point to my research regarding interpretive practices. My research on aesthetic focal practices includes the work of collage as well as that of the creation of poetic work such as songwriting is something that cannot be separated from my musical performances. Having worked with various poems over a course of time, both visually and musically, has allowed me to also broaden my understanding of processes of translation that take place when we move from one for of artistic creation to another.

Now my position as program coordinator at the Nipissing University Muskoka campus provides me with a unique opportunity to think about how intact ecosystems can help learners develop a deeper understanding of place through rethinking their relationships with the places they inhabit. In my research, I question: How does identity formation and place-based learning play an important role in understanding human relationships with natural and reconstructed environments? Having worked with students in K-12 classrooms has helped me reconsider the importance of fostering a keen interest in all areas of multiple-literacies as outlined in the Ontario curriculum. One way to do so is through asking learners to work with stories that outline the ecologies that we, as humans depend on for our survival. These stories can be found throughout all world cultures, but are often overshadowed by stories adopted by popular culture to prioritize of pursuing financial interests.

The literature on environmental education is chronologically dwarfed by the antiquity of the wisdom of its mostly biocultural practitioners. It is the contention of scholars like Longboat (2007) and Sheridan (1994) that the Oral Tradition is an environmental issue. The development of environmental literacy as an academic concern flourishes in the comparatively minute realm of environmental education. Biocultural loss includes a disconnection between people and the place where indigenous knowledges and languages have grown and thrived since time immemorial.

In *Vanishing Voices*, Nettle and Romaine (2000) write: "A small change in the social environment, such as the loss of control of resources to outsiders, can have drastic consequences which pass right through the domains of culture and language" (79). In addition to the autobiographical nature of this work, such research also draws upon educational criticism, environmental thought, traditions illustrated by biocultural examples of learning in landscapes representing knowledge in the form of a story interpreted through a hermeneutic lens. The interdisciplinary nature of this work posits a biocultural ethic for environmental education and challenges the naturalizing of settler cultures in the North American continent.

Clearly, the relentless generation of garbage, nuclear waste, and other forms of pollution impact the health of ecosystems. It is difficult to move away from unhealthy relationships with the earth without a deep questioning of our current systems for producing and learning language. Engaging with focal practices as outlined by Borgmann (1992), and subsequently Sumara (1995), is a way of becoming immersed in an environmental literacies curriculum. Focal practices are described as processes of engaging with an activity from a preliminary phase to a concluding achievement. Examples of focal practice activities can range from gardening and cooking with ancestral foods to the development of critical literacy skills and beyond. Borgmann (1992) explains that focal practices include taking part in activities from their beginnings to a state of completion as a way to remedy the postmodern condition of unnatural realities that machines of modern technology inspire. Although Borgmann uses this term to move beyond urban ways of engaging with the world, Sumara (1996b) applies this concept of focal practice to reading and writing practices. Moreover, Bringhurst (2002) suggests that every place has its own literature. Learning to listen to languages inherent in their natural settings makes it possible to move beyond linear ways of thinking that monolingual cognitive influences perpetuate. In addition, learning different ways of translating and representing places can contribute profoundly to the relationship that learners can develop with the places they live. To develop an awareness of local plants and animals is a step toward becoming less dependent on the ecologically irresponsible practice of shipping plants and animals thousands of miles for nonlocal consumption.

How then does identity formation and place-based learning help us to reconsider Canadian environmental education curriculum? Indigenous focal practices require participants to engage with a series of tasks from a beginning point to a state of completion. Examples of ecologically relevant focal practices range from being part of eco-poetic processes commonly associated with Oral and Literary Tradition, to growing, harvesting, collecting, and preparing foods that one has contributed to or engaged with in some way, shape, or form. This type of consumption is a way that we, as educators, can help learners understand that human life is part of the ecosystems that we live in and that give us the sacred gift of life.

The word "sacred" is deep with Christian imagery. Throughout the colonization of North America, there has been a gradual shift of beliefs that define what makes a place sacred due to processes of secularization. The etymology of the word sacred is something set apart for a specific purpose (The Oxford English Dictionary 1971, 2616). Turner's (1980) and Gatta's (2004) investigations about how settler culture has conceptualized and developed the notion of sacred helps clarify how systems of belief can negatively shape cultural attitudes about human relationships with local as well as unfamiliar territories. Mythopoetic engagements with place produced, recorded and living in the Oral Tradition can help recover the idea that all places are, to some degree, sacred. The particular location of some places contributes to the ancestral conviction of their sacredness. Basso (1996), Bringhurst (2006), Cajete (1994), and Devereux (1996), among others, suggest that these places are sacred to people because of engagement and the opportunity to develop experiences within them. Wilson (1993) suggests that these memories resonate with us beyond our own lives and that living bodies carry with them the memory of ancestral experiences. Moreover, Cajete postulates that the spiritual component is an essential element of developing an understanding of place and that taking part in ancestral activities is an important way of developing an appropriate and good relationship with Mother Earth. It is our engagement, whether by becoming part of the air that we breathe, or by providing us with the water that makes up a majority of our body mass, as well as other interactions we have with what Abram (1996) defines as the "more-than-human-world," that helps us to understand the sacredness of place.

Helping educators and students consider how their own focal practices have helped them shape and continue to influence their own identities is one way to awaken an awareness of their potential in the curricula of public systems of education. One way that we can work to better understand the intricacies of language is by creating opportunities for learners' right to foster an excitement about developing aesthetically pleasing forms of expression that include poetry and other ways of telling stories about learning. I ask students to reconsider ways in which they have developed deeper understandings about the places that they live in.

Intergenerational knowledge is often shared through their place-based life-stories. In addition, many of the stories describe how to work with focal practices that involve growing and preparing food that are in-tune with healthy ways of being. Becoming aware of the importance of these ecologically centered practices can help learners generate a desire to learn more about themselves and their relationship with the places that they live in. By asking learners to have deep discussions about what they know about in terms of growing and preparing the food that they eat is a good place to start. Eco-poetic reflective practices that can generate an excitement about these practices can be a potential curricular window for reconsidering our approaches to address the importance of ancestral knowledge and place-based learning within our future classrooms.

RECONCEPTUALIZING CANADIAN ENVIRONMENTAL CURRICULUM THROUGH A DEEP ANALYSIS

All education is environmental education.

Orr 1992, 81

When I returned to the academy as a K-12 educator in the mid-nineties, my graduate work centered around "language, culture and teaching," through the interdisciplinary framework of the graduate program in education at York University. It was during this time that I was introduced to David Orr's (1992) work on ecological literacy, and his assertion that indeed, "all education is environmental education." To this day, Orr continues to influence my research. My areas of interest emerged from my readings, courses, and conference experiences, as they intersect among language and literacy, curriculum theory, environmental ecojustice education, and most importantly, from years of learning from indigenous Elders.

The first two areas of research that influenced my work were literacy and curriculum theorizing. I spent a considerable amount of time reading in the area of philosophical hermeneutics (Gadamer 1976), and studied with Dennis Sumara (1995, 1996a, 1996b), and Warren Crichlow (Crichlow & McCarthy 1993) in the areas of literacy and curriculum. I continued to read the work of Maxine Greene (1995) on the work of the imagination in education, Madeleine Grumet (1988) on the importance of rumination, Louise Rosenblatt (1978) on reader-response theory, and William Pinar (Pinar 1994) in terms of understanding of curriculum as *currere*—a course to be run, and on the importance of autobiography in educational research. In addition, for several years I was fortunate to learn from my experiences with "curriculum reconceptualists", a group of curriculum theorists who meet at the annual Journal of Curriculum Theorizing (JCT) conference in Bergamo, Ohio. All of these experiences provided me with a wide base of theories to reconsider curriculum theorizing in terms of rethinking my lived experiences as child who grew up in the Ontario public school system.

I was also fortunate to have had the experience of studying under Joe Sheridan (1994) in the area of indigenous storytelling and environmental learning. It was during this time that I reconsidered the relationship between language and landscape as we read Keith Basso's (1996) book, wisdom sits in places: Landscape and language among the Western Apache, Cajete's (1994) doctoral work on an ecology of indigenous education, Edith Cobb's (1959) work on the ecology of imagination in childhood, and Wendell Berry's (1995) work on conservation. Simultaneously, I was introduced to the growing field of ecojustice education that involves a cultural analysis of the environmental crisis (Bowers 2002), and I spent many years learning from indigenous Elders at Trent University. From these influences, my doctoral work traced the indigenous roots of environmental education through an analysis of my experiences with the guiding and scouting movement. Using archival, and environmental, and autobiographical methods, I brought together research in the areas of curriculum theorizing, ecojustice education, and indigenous knowledges.

During that period of intellectual study, I ruminated on my engagement with nature as a child. Through my writing, I recalled spending hours in my local woods frolicking about and climbing trees. I began to realize what an impact my experiences with natural spaces had on my life. In turn, I began to use an ecojustice education framework in my teacher education courses. Since then, I am often asked "what exactly is ecojustice education?" In response, ecojustice is a framework for bringing forth a cultural analysis of the environmental-social crisis. On a personal level, ecojustice is also a connection to a group of scholars who teach in faculties of education with this framework. In brief, ecojustice education is, at least for me, an interdisciplinary field of research that brings together indigenous knowledge and indigenous environmental studies (Apffel-Marglin and PRATEC 1998; Bowers & Apffel-Marglin 2004; Cajete 2000; Cruikshank 1981, 1990; Laduke 1999; McGregor 2004; Sheridan & Longboat 2006; with ecofeminism (Plumwood 1994, 2002; Shiva 1993; Warren 2000, 1997), and the fields of deep ecology, sociology of knowledge and sociolinguistics (Abram 1996; Berger & Luckmann 1967; Bowers 2001, 2005, 2007; Brown 1977; Cobb 1959; Lakoff & Johnson 1980; Leopold 1948; Snyder 1990 as some examples). By proposing that an ecojustice framework be used in reconsidering environmental curriculum through a deep analysis of language and metaphor, I am addressing the taken-for-granted assumption that ecology and environmental issues are strictly part of a science curriculum. Rather, from an ecojustice perspective, the ecological crisis is a cultural crisis and therefore ecojustice pedagogy is well positioned across all curricula from K-postsecondary.

How can a deep analysis of language and metaphor play afford us opportunities to reconsider our human relationships with natural and reconstructed environments? For Bowers (2001) and Merchant (1980), root metaphors are explanatory frameworks derived by means of the mythopoetic narratives and prevailing experience that influenced thinking and human conduct across a wide range of cultural experience. Since these root metaphors are entrenched in, and are taught as part of the dominant discourse through a privileging of cultural narratives that perpetuate antiecological habits of mind (Young 2008), it is the work of ecojustice educators to identify these metaphors and cultural narratives, and to expose the ways in which classroom curricula influences identity formation, ways of thinking, and perceptions.

Although there are many areas of concern for ecojustice educators, this focus of my reconsideration primarily involves "analyzing the deep cultural assumptions or root metaphors that underlie both social inequalities and ecological degradation and are carried forward inter-generationally" as outlined on the ecojustice education website—www.ecojusticeeducation.org (Bowers & Martusewicz 2004). Revealing root metaphors at work in dominant cultural narratives can lead toward a development of ecological literacy that can ultimately foster an understanding of the importance of human relationships with the natural world.

By recognizing the power of language and the need to bring attention to the ways in which language is a barrier between humans and the natural world, root metaphors reveal the ways in which language can hide and illuminate taken-for-granted associations. For example, by engaging in a close analysis of the words, "dirt" and "soil"; the word *dirt* is often associated as something bad, and *soil* with something good. However, these are the same. When analyzing the meanings of and associations of words such as "drain" and "stream," the word *stream* is often associated with something valued, natural and ecological, while *drain* is associated with something unvalued, human-made, and mechanistic (Martusewicz, Edmundson, & Lupinacci 2012). One might consider the ways in which a drain and a stream flow into the same systems, and whether it would be more likely to pour something like "Drano" into a stream or a drain. Another example involves questioning: How is the body like a clock or computer? How is it different? How is the body like a plant? It is through these powerful examples that we begin to recognize the prevailing associations that words have via root metaphors.

The close analysis of root metaphors can lead toward a deeper connection between culture and the environmental and social crisis that include a consideration of the forms of enclosure are part of everyday life. For example, by questioning how water, genetically modified grain, airways, woodlands and meadows, and so on, have been enclosed and privatized may lead to an analysis of the effects of global warming, the degradation of ecosystems, the development of greenhouse gases, a rapid loss of species, hunger and poverty, and so on. All of these analyses involve a deep analysis of language and metaphor and a consideration of the ways in which humans have and continue to develop antiecological habits of mind. A close analysis of root metaphors then, plays an important role in understanding human relationships with natural and reconstructed environments.

How does a deep analysis of language and metaphor help to reconsider environmental education curriculum? Reconsidering environmental education curriculum through an ecojustice approach to language learning involves an identification of the ways in which the Ontario Ministry of Education Report, *Shaping our Schools, Shaping our Future* (2007) continues to be dominated by a failed science model that draws upon a commodified approach to environmental education (Young 2009). By tracing the origins of environmental education to a separation between science and indigenous environmental education models, and by identifying the ways in which environmental education continues to be subjugated by a science model that does not take into account the cultural roots of the environmental crisis (Young 2009), it is imperative for us to reconsider the importance of bringing together science, ecojustice education, and indigenous environmental studies into a reconceptualist model of environmental education (Longboat, Kulnieks, & Young 2009). Indigenizing environmental education involves both a science and indigenous model for environmental learning (Kulnieks, Longboat, & Young, 2010, 2011). In all cases, reconsidering environmental education involves a connection between the ways in which language, and specifically root metaphors play a significant role in the development of anti-ecological habits of mind.

In addition, by addressing the failure of Ontario Ministry of Education's revised 2006 documents, titled, *The Ontario Kindergarten Program* and *The Ontario Curriculum Grades 1–8* to include methods for students to identify the ways in which culture plays an important role in the social and environmental crisis (Young 2009), an ecojustice approach can move beyond simply raising environmental issues. Such a curriculum can help to facilitate a greater understanding of the ways in which sustainable relationships with the earth are an important part of the educational process. Ultimately, reconsidering Canadian environmental curricula by fostering cultural literacy and ecological habits of mind involves a study of relationships through a deep analysis of language and metaphor.

As educators, how can we help students name root metaphors? How has the field of Women's Studies been successful in naming language in terms of the root metaphor patriarchy in order to illuminate gender inequalities? (Consider policeman vs. police officer as one example) How are root metaphors such as "progress" and "individualism" (that are taken-for-granted as positive) related to consumerism? How might you use some of the materials at www.ecojusticeeducation.org in your teaching practices?

REFERENCES

Abram, D. 1996. *The Spell of the Sensuous: Perception in a More-than-human World.* New York: Pantheon Books.

Albrecht, G., S. Freeman, & N. Higginbotham. 1998. "Complexity and Human Health: The Case for a Transdisciplinary Paradigm." *Culture, Medicine and Psychiatry* 22 (1): 55–92.

Alsop, S., & L. Fawcett. 2010. "And After This Nothing Happened: Traditional Ecological Knowledge and Science Education." *Cultural Studies in Science Education* 5: 1027–1045.

Apffel-Marglin, F., & PRATEC. 1998. *The Spirit of Regeneration: Andean Culture Confronting Western Notions of Development.* London: Zed Books Ltd.

Basso, K. 1996. *Wisdom Sits in Places: Landscape and Language Among the Western Apache.* Alburqurque, NM: University of New Mexico Press.

Berger, P., & T. Luckmann. 1967. *The Social Construction of Reality: A Treatise in the Sociology of Knowledge.* Garden City, NY: Anchor.

Berry, W. 1995. "The Conservation of Nature and the Preservation of Humanity." In *Another Turn of the Crank,* edited by W. Berry, 64–85. Washington, DC: Counterpoint.

Borgmann, A. 1992. *Crossing the Postmodern Divide.* Chicago: University of Chicago Press.

Bowers, C. A. 2001. *Educating for Eco-justice and Community.* Athens, GA: The University of Georgia Press.

———. 2002. "Toward an Eco-justice Pedagogy." *Environmental Education Research* 8 (1): 21–34.

———. 2005. *The False Promises of Constructivist Theories of Learning: A Global and Ecological Critique.* New York: Peter Lang Publishing, Inc.

———. 2006. *Revitalizing the Commons: Cultural and Educational Sites of Resistance and Affirmation.* Lanham, MD: Lexington Books.

———. 2007. *Handbook for Faculty on How to Introduce Cultural Commons and Ecojustice Issues into Their Courses.* Retrieved July 6, 2008, from http://cabowers.net

———. 2009. "Educating for a Revitalization of the Cultural Commons." *Canadian Journal of Environmental Education* 14: 196–200.

Bowers, C. A., & F. Apffel-Marglin .2004. *Re-thinking Freire: Globalization and the Environmental Crisis.* Mahwah, NJ: Lawrence Erlbaum Associates.

Bowers, C. A., & R Martusewicz. 2004. *The Ecojustice Dictionary.* Retrieved January 25, 2008, from http://www.ecojusticeeducation.org

Bringhurst, R. 2002. "The Tree of Meaning and the Work of Ecological Linguistics." *Canadian Journal of Environmental Education* 7 (2): 9–22.

———. 2006. *The Tree of Meaning: Thirteen Talks.* Kentville, Nova Scotia: Gaspereau Press.

Britzman, D. 1998. *Lost Subjects, Contested Objects.* New York, New York: State University of New York Press.

Brown, R. 1977. *A Poetic for Sociology: Toward a Logic of Discovery for the Human Sciences.* Cambridge, MA: Cambridge University Press.

Cajete, G. 1994. *Look to the Mountain: An Ecology of Indigenous Education.* Skyland, NC: Kivaki Press.

Cajete, G. 2000. *Ecology of Native American Community.* Athens: University of Georgia Press.

Capra, F. 1983. *The Turning Point: Science, Society, and the Rising Culture.* Toronto: Bantam Books.

————. 1996. *The Web of Life: A New Scientific Understanding of Living Systems.* New York: Anchor Books.

Chambers, C. 1999. "A Topography for Canadian Curriculum Theory." *Canadian Journal of Education* 24 (2): 137–150.

Chambers, C. 2003. "As Canadian as Possible Under the Circumstances: A View of Contemporary Curriculum Discourses in Canada." In *The Internationalization Handbook of Curriculum Research,* edited by William F. Pinar, 221–252. Mahwah, NJ: Lawrence Erlbaum Associated.

Cobb, E. 1959. "The Ecology of Imagination in Childhood. Daedalus." *Journal of the American Academy of Arts and Sciences* 88 (Summer): 537–548.

Crichlow, W., & C. McCarthy, eds. 1993. *Race, Identity and Representation in Education.* New York: Routledge.

Cruikshank, J. 1981. "Legend and Landscape: Convergence of Oral and Scientific Traditions in the Yukon Territory." *Arctic Anthropology* xviii (2): 67–93.

————. 1990. *Life Lived Like a Story: Life Stories of Three Yukon Native Elders.* Vancouver, BC: University of British Columbia Press.

Davis, B., & Dennis J. Sumara. 2006. *Complexity and Education: Inquiries into Learning, Teaching, and Research.* Mahwah, NJ: Lawrence Erlbaum Associates.

Devereux, P. 1996. *Re-envisioning the Earth: A Guide to Opening the Healing Channels Between Mind and Nature.* New York: Simon & Schuster.

Foucault, M. 1980. *Power/Knowledge.* New York, NY: Pantheon Books.

Gadamer, H. G. 1976. *Philosophical Hermeneutics.* Translated by D. E. Linge. Los Angeles: University of California Press.

Gatta, J. 2004. *Making Nature Sacred: Literature, Religion, and Environment in America from the Puritans to the Present.* New York: Oxford University Press.

Gough, N. 1999. "Rethinking the Subject: (De)constructing Human Agency in Environmental Education Research." *Environmental Education Research* 5 (1): 35–48.

————. 2006. Shaking the Tree, Making a Rhizome: Towards a Nomadic Geophilosophy of Science Education. *Educational Philosophy and Theory* 38 (5): 625–645.

Greene, M. 1995. *Releasing the Imagination: Essays on Education, the Arts, and Social Change.* San Francisco, CA: Jossey-Bass Publishers.

Grumet, M. 1988. *Bitter Milk: Women and Teaching.* Amherst, MA: University of Massachusetts Press.

Haig-Brown, C. 2008. "Taking Indigenous Thought Seriously: A Rant on Globalization With Some Cautionary Notes." *Journal of the Canadian Association of Curriculum Studies* 6 (2): 8–24.

Hardin, G. 1968. "The Tragedy of the Commons." In *Classics in Environmental Studies,* edited by Nico Nelissen, Jan Van Der Straaten, & Leon Klinkers, 101–114. Utrecht, NL: International Books.

Heshusius, L. 1996. "On Tending Broken Dreams." In *From Positivism to Interpretivism and Beyond,* edited by Lous Heshusius & Keith Ballard, 128–135. New York: Teachers College Press.

Jardine, D. 1992. "A Bell Ringing in the Empty Sky." In *Contemporary Curriculum Discourse: Twenty years of JCT*, edited by William F. Pinar, 266–277. New York, NY: Peter Lang Publishing, Inc.

Kulnieks, A., D. Longboat, & Kelly Young. 2010. "Re-indigenizing Curriculum: An Ecohermenutic Approach to Learning." *AlterNative: An International Journal of Indigenous Scholarship 6* (1): 16–24.

————2011. "Indigenizing Curriculum: The Transformation of Environmental Education." In *Contemporary Studies in Canadian Curriculum: Principles, Portraits and Practices*, edited by Darren Stanley & Kelly Young, 351–374. Calgary, AB: Detselig.

Laduke, W. 1999. *All Our Relations: Native Struggles for Land and Life – Selection*. Cambridge, MA: South End Press.

Lakoff, G., & M. Johnson. 1980. *Metaphors We Live By*. Chicago, IL: University of Chicago Press.

Leopold, A. 1948. *A Sand County Almanac, and Sketches Here and There*. Oxford: Oxford University Press.

Longboat, D. R. 1998. "The Indigenous Environmental Education Program: A Model for Learning and Sharing of Naturalized Knowledge Systems." Unpublished manuscript, Toronto, ON.

————. 2007. "Kawenoke the haudenosaunee archipelago: The Nature and Necessity of Biocultural Restoration and Revitalization." Unpublished doctoral dissertation, York University, Toronto, ON.

Longboat, D., Andrejs Kulnieks, & Kelly Young. 2009. "Beyond Dualism: Toward a Transdiciplinary Indigenous Environmental Studies Model of Environmental Education Curricula." *The EcoJustice Review: Educating for the Commons* 1(1): 1–18.

Martusewicz, R., J. Lupinacci, & J. Edmundson. 2012. *Teaching for Diversity, Democracy and Sustainability: An Ecojustice Approach*. New York: Routledge.

McGregor, D. 2004. "Coming Full Circle: Indigenous Knowledge, Environment and Our Future." *American Indian Quarterly* 28 (3–4): 385–410.

Merchant, C. 1980. *The Death of Nature: Women, Ecology, and the Scientific Revolution*. San Francisco: Harper & Row.

Nettle, Daniel, & Suzanne Romaine. 2000. *Vanishing Voices: The Extinction of the World's Languages*. Oxford: Oxford University Press

Ng-A-Fook, N. 2007. *An Indigenous Curriculum of Place*. New York: Peter Lang Publishing, Inc.

Ng-A-Fook, N. 2010. "An/other Bell Ringing in the Sky: Greenwashing, Curriculum, and Ecojustice." *Journal for the Canadian Association of Curriculum Studies* 8 (1): 41–67.

Orr, D. W. 1992. *Ecological Literacy: Education and the Transition to a Postmodern World*. Albany, NY: State University of New York Press.

————. 1994. *Earth in Mind: On Education, Environment, and the Human Prospect*. CA: Island Press

————. 2002. *The Nature of Design: Ecology, Culture, and Human Intention*. New York: Oxford University Press.

Ontario Ministry of Education. 2006a. *The Ontario Curriculum Grades 1–8*. Toronto: Queen's Printer for Ontario.

———. 2006b. *The Ontario Kindergarten Program*. Toronto: Queen's Printer for Ontario.

———. 2007. *Shaping Our Schools, Shaping Our Future*. Toronto, ON: Queen's Printer for Ontario.

Pinar, W. F. 1975/2000. "Search for a Method." In *Curriculum Studies: The Reconceptualization*, edited by W. Pinar, 415–424. Troy, New York: Educator's International Press.

———. 1994. *Autobiography, Politics and Sexuality: Essays in Curriculum Theory 1972–1992*. New York: Peter Lang Publishing, Inc.

———. 2007. *Intellectual Advancement Through Disciplinarity: Verticality and Horizontality in Curriculum Studies*. Rotterdam: Sense Publishing

Pinar, W. F., W. Reynolds, P. Slattery, & P. Taubman, P. 1995. *Understanding Curriculum*. New York: Peter Lang Publishing, Inc.

Plumwood, V. 1994. *Feminism and the Mastery of Nature*. London: Routledge.

———. 2002. *Ecological Culture: The Ecological Crisis of Reason*. New York: Routledge.

Ratson, G. A. 1993. *The Meaning of Health: The Experience of a Lifetime*. Trafford: Victoria, Canada.

Rosenblatt, L. 1978. *The Reader, the Text, the Poem*. Carbondale, IL: Southern Illinois University Press.

Russell, C. L. 2005. "'Whoever Does Not Write is Written': The Role of 'Nature' in Post-post Approaches to Environmental Education Research". *Environmental Education Research*, 11 (5): 433–443.

———. 2006. "Working Across and with Methodological Difference in Environmental Education Research." *Environmental Education Research* 12 (3/4): 403–412.

Sheridan, J. 1994. *Alienation and Integration: Environmental Education in Turtle Island*. Unpublished doctoral dissertation, University of Alberta, Edmonton, AB.

Sheridan, J., & D. Longboat. 2006. "The Haudenosaunee Imagination and the Ecology of the Sacred." *Space and Culture* 9 (4): 365–381.

Shiva, V. 1993. *Monocultures of the Mind: Perspectives on Biodiversity and Biotechnology*. Penang, Malaysia: Third World Network.

———. 2005. *Earth Democracy: Justice, Sustainability, and Peace*. Cambridge, MA: South End Press.

Snyder, G. 1990. *The Practice of the Wild*. New York: North Point Press.

Stanley, D. 2005. "Paradigmatic Complexity: Emerging Ideas and Historical Views of the Complexity Sciences." In *Chaos, Complexity, Curriculum and Culture: A Conversation* edited by William Doll, M. Jayne Fleener and John. St. Julien, 133–152. New York: Peter Lang Publishing, Inc.

Sumara, D. 1995. "Response to Reading as a Focal Practice." *English Quarterly* 28 (1): 18–26.

———. 1996a. *Private Readings in Public: Schooling the Literary Imagination*. NY: Peter Lang Publishing, Inc.

————. 1996b. "Using Commonplace Books in Curriculum Studies." *Journal of Curriculum Theorizing* 12 (1), 45–48.

———— *The Oxford English Dictionary.* 1971. London: Oxford University Press.

Turner, F. 1980. *Beyond Geography: The Western Spirit Against the Wilderness.* New York: Viking Press.

Warren, K. J. 1997. Ed. *Ecofeminism: Women, Culture and Nature.* Bloomington, IN: Indiana University Press.

————. 2000. *Ecofeminist Philosophy: A Western Perspective on What It Is and Why It Matters.* New York: Rowman and Littlefield.

Wheatley, M. 2002. *It's An Interconnected World.* Accessed June 12, 2012 from http://margaretwheatley.com/articles/interconnected.html.

Wilson, S. 1993. "An Indigenous American's Interpretation of the Relationship Between Indigenous Peoples and People of European Descent" Paper presented at *The World Indigenous Peoples Conference Education.* Wollongong, NSW, Australia.

Young, K. 2005. "Developing Ecological Literacy as a Habit of Mind in Teacher Education" *The EcoJustice Review: Educating for the Commons* 1 (1): 1–7.

————. 2008. "Ecological Habits of Mind and the Literary Imagination." *Educational Insights* 12 (1): 1–9.

————. 2009. "Reconceptualizing Elementary Language Arts Curriculum: An Ecojustice Approach." In *Early Childhood Currricula: Reconceptualist Perspectives,* edited by L. Iannacci & P. Whitty, 299–325. Calgary, AB: Detselig Enterprises.

PART 2

CURRICULUM, CULTURE, AND LANGUAGE

CHAPTER 5

Educational Rights: Language Rights and Rights to a Plural Education

Denise Egéa-Kuehne

PHILLIPSON (1992) REMINDS US THAT "THE PRIMARY GOAL of all declarations of human rights...is to protect the individual against arbitrary or unjust treatment" (93). Although concerns about human rights in general go back several centuries, the rights of minorities and linguistic rights in particular, have been given some serious attention only more recently. In the United States, the dominance of English has been taken for granted, at least until 1981 when Senator S. I. Hayakawa brought this issue before Congress, introducing—without any success—a constitutional amendment to make English official (Crawford 1992). I open with a very brief overview of the progress on linguistic human rights since the end of World War I, and how they address education.[1]

In Europe, especially since the end of the World War I and the treaties that reshaped Europe, efforts toward specifically trying to codify linguistic human rights took a more systematic approach. The *International Covenant on Civil and Political Rights* (1966) specifically states:

> In those States in which ethnic, religious, or linguistic minorities exist, persons belonging to such minorities shall not be denied the right...to enjoy their own culture...or to use their own language. (Article 27)

Several organizations and resolutions directly address education, promoting either: (1) the teaching of "regional" minority languages from preschool through university (e.g., *Kuijpers Resolution* 1987); (2) access to education in one's own native language (*Universal Declaration on Indigenous Rights* 1988, see Weissner 2007); (3) the teaching of both the native language and the official language (*International Seminar on Human Rights and Cultural Rights* [Brazil] 1987); or (4) the learning at school of two foreign languages (Fédération Internationale des Langues Vivantes 1988, 1989). However, international conventions have their own limitations and remain vague, in particular regarding legal status that is seldom clearly specified.

UNESCO recommended that the UN "adopt and implement a universal declaration of linguistic rights," even though it may be difficult to agree on the definition of what a linguistic human right is, or on the scope of the declaration. Surely, setting a "normative, inalienable standard" for linguistic human rights would be a major step for minorities toward helping legitimate their native languages, and do so through education.

Jacques Derrida identified two "interdicts" that threaten minority languages.

TWO INTERDICTS

First and foremost the master ... took the figure of the schoolmaster.

Derrida 1998, 73

The role languages play in any society is worthy of the most serious attention on the part of *all* educators. Strong and clear communication is a necessity in all areas, but more especially, in schools where all children must have access to learning, and later to the democratic process where they must be able to "communicate, to give or receive information vital to their participation as citizens" (Thomas 1996, 137). In cases where educational opportunities are diminished or denied through linguistic control or coercion, some children may find themselves excluded from the learning process, and later, as members of the community, they may lose all ability to participate in the governing of their region and country, and in the decisions that affect their lives.

The two "interdicts" placed on languages identified by Derrida are both, first and foremost, a "... school thing, something which happens 'at school,' but barely a measure or a decision, rather a pedagogical structure. The interdict [is] coming from an 'educational system'" (Derrida 1998, 65–66, emphasis in original). He insisted on using the substantive *l'interdit* to stress its "*exceptional and fundamental*" character.

The first interdict, the interdicted language, places an interdiction on the native language to which access is restricted, if not denied: at school especially, children are not allowed to speak it, and may be severely punished.

When such a situation occurs, Derrida wrote, the object of the interdiction is "not a thing, not a gesture, not an action." What is interdicted is "access to the saying [*le dire*], that's all, to a certain saying" (Derrida 1998, 58). But the "that's all" does not point to a minor event. It is there to underscore a "fundamental interdict," an "absolute interdict": "the interdiction of the diction, of the saying." Derrida gave as an example (an example with the universality of the exemplary testimony) his own situation at the Algiers high school that he had attended. Though it had never been couched in the terms of a law— "no natural frontier, nor juridical limit"—students were allowed to choose, they had "the formal right to learn, or not to learn Arab or Berber . . . or Hebrew. It was not illegal, nor a crime. At least in the lycée" (59). Derrida stressed that nonetheless, the interdiction was there, but of a different kind, it functioned along different paths, "more cunning, peaceable, silent, liberal" (ibid.), but there nevertheless, and an aberration: in its home country, Arabic could be learned only as a foreign language; and Derrida did not recall that anyone ever took Hebrew at school.

In several countries, the language that is forbidden to speak freely may be offered in school as a subject of study, *but* as a foreign language. This aberration is common in the United States, where immigrants' languages (e.g., Spanish, Chinese, French, and German) are then learned from outside, "as the language of the other." As noted by Derrida, the percentage of students in high school taking a course in their native language as a foreign language is near zero. One reason is that other means of control are at work, and in any case, few minority or immigrant children with a native language other than the imposed dominant language reach high school.

The second interdict, the language that interdicts the use of all languages but the one setting the interdict is denied, is also "carried out in the schools" (Derrida 1998, 71), in the schoolyards and in the classrooms. The imposed, dominant, oppressor's language—the language of the (school) master—is supposed to be substituted for the native language, the home language, and to become the main language. However, "its sources, its norms, its rules, its law, [its history], are situated elsewhere" (72), anywhere but at home. For example, for Derrida, in Algiers, this language was and still is located in France, in what is called the *Métropole*. For the children that he and his peers were, it was "a distant country . . . not foreign [*étrangère*], . . . but strange [*étrange*], fantastic, phantasmagoric . . . a dream country, and thus at a non-objectivable distance" (73). Through the schoolmaster, this imposed language offered the model of a well-spoken, well-written language; it represented the language of the master, and symbolized the master himself (the colonized as well as the schoolmaster). From this distant country, strange and foreign, "came the paradigms of distinction, of correction, of elegance, and of the literary or oratory language" (ibid.).

For Derrida and his peers, the "metropolis" was beyond the Mediterranean Sea. In other instances and other situations of linguistic and cultural hegemony, this geographical distance may be no more than the distance between the "province" and the capital (Paris, London, Moscow, Madrid, and so on), the countryside and the metropolitan area, or between the inner city hood and the suburbs.[2] In every case, it is between the reality, the place and the context in which the dominated group lives every day, and the place of hegemonic power. In every case, between the standards of a literary, "correct" language imposed by the school, and the (interdicted) native language spoken at home; whether there is a sea, an ocean, or not, there is a space of "symbolic infinite dimension, a gorge for all the schoolchildren..., an abyss" (Derrida 1998, 75). Curricula take the form of some "doctrine of indoctrination" (76) whereas the content taught, as well as the teaching approaches are literally foreign to the students. The discipline where it is the most obvious, in any situation, in any country, is history; next is literature. They offer the students "the experience of a world without any sensible continuity with the one in which they actually live, almost without anything in common with [their] natural or social landscapes" (76).[3] This kind of teaching takes very little account of the practical needs of the minority children and almost none of their cultural needs. For example, Amadou Kourouma, a writer from the Ivory Coast who wrote in French but whose native language was Malinke, talked about "feeling in African," experiencing reality, emotions, life, and representing them in Malinke in all their dimensions, yet of the impossibility of being able to express those feelings in "classic French." Derrida described a similar experience, a description that again takes the form of a universal testimony:

> So you can perceive the origin of my suffering, since this language goes right through them through and through, the site of my passions, of my desires, of my prayers, the vocation of my hopes...always.... I have wondered whether one can love, enjoy, pray, die of pain, or die period, all in another language, or without saying anything to anyone, without even speaking. (14)

While Derrida stresses the gap that always exists between a literary culture and a nonliterary culture, additionally, "besides this essential heterogeneity, besides this universal hierarchy" (1998, 77), he also emphasizes the profound rift between the dominant literature ("its history, its works, its models, its death rites, its modes of transmission and celebration, its 'beautiful neighborhoods,' the names of its authors and publishers" (ibid.), and the indigenous culture unique to the dominated minority, be it Creole, African, Cajun, First Nation, Métis, Inuit and so on. Derrida stated this "cost of passage": "We entered into the French literature only by losing our accent" (ibid.). The decisive agent in this process is the school, and particularly, the teacher, which play the main part in promoting the dominant language and culture, and in facilitating the assimilation of the linguistically and socially diverse children to the dominant norms.

The consequences of these interdicts have a devastating impact on the cultures and languages of minorities, as described by Pfeiffer (1975) in his research among the Navajo:

> Navajo children are taught in a foreign language [English]: they are taught concepts which are foreign, they are taught values which are foreign, they are taught lifestyles which are foreign, and they are taught by human models which are foreign. The intention behind this kind of schooling is to mold the Navajo child (through speech, action, thought) to be like members of the predominant Anglo-Saxon mainstream culture. The apparent assumption seemingly being that people of other ethnic groups cannot be human unless they speak English, and behave according to the values of a capitalistic society based on competition and achievement. The children grow up in these schools with a sense of: (1) confusion regarding the values, attitudes and behavior taught at home; (2) loss of self identity and pride concerning their selfhood—their Navajo-ness; (3) failure in classroom learning activities; (4) loss of their own Navajo language development and loss of in-depth knowledge of their own Navajo culture. (133)

Some measures have been proposed in an attempt to minimize the damaging impact of the imposed language through education and the school system.

DROITS LINQUISTIQUES

For example, in 1993, *The Draft Declaration on the Rights of Indigenous Peoples* was completed by the Working Group on Indigenous Populations of the UN Sub-Commission on Prevention of Discrimination and Protection of Minorities. Since some articles concerning the rights to self-determination and land rights are controversial, the Draft Declaration has not yet been adopted.[4] This proposition contains, among others, two articles particularly interesting for education, which, although they are listed under different article numbers and are phrased somewhat differently, ask for the same rights:

Right to develop and promote one's own languages, "to revitalize, use, develop and transmit to future generations their histories, languages, oral traditions, philosophies, writing systems and literatures," (UN 1993, Part III, Art. 14) and to use them for administrative, cultural, judicial, educational, and other purposes. This necessarily includes preserving native or home languages, and be educated in one's own language. In a 1992 conference, Edouard Glissant[5] declared: "Each and every language must be protected against erasure as well as against fossilization." For him, it makes all languages unified in one exigency, even though it is not yet acknowledged by all: "Attitudes must change, we must break away from this inescapable movement of annihilation of idioms, by recognizing for all languages, powerful or not, the space and means to survive in a global concert."

Right to all forms of education, including the rights of children to have access to education in their own languages, and to establish, structure, conduct, and control their own educational systems and institutions (UN 1993, Part IV, Art. 15). Is there a "correct" way to teach languages, the way we talk about a "correct" (i.e., standard) way to practice it? Glissant (1992) asked. A "best" language pedagogy? Glissant believes that such claims affect "the [very] concept of language," as well as "the relation of one language with the others," and the theoretical framework of the various disciplines associated with languages, be it "to analyze them, . . . to translate them, . . . [or] to teach them." What must be questioned, "is the very principle (if not the reality) of the intangible uniqueness of a language" (n.p.).

Hence, multiplicity has permeated all vehicular languages, and it is now "internal to them," even as they seem to resist any changes. To varying degrees of complexity, there are now several English languages (British, American, Australian, South African, and so on), several Spanish (Columbian, Puerto Rican, Catalan, and so on), and several French (standard ["Parisian"], Quebecois, Creole, Cajun, and so on). This multiplicity means, "the implicit renouncing to the conceited aloofness of monolingualism, and the temptation to participate to the global entanglement." It is not without direct consequences. Glissant saw three in particular:

(1) The consolidation of old oral, vernacular, or composite languages, their fixation, and their transcription [it is the case of Creole, Cajun, and Malinke] . . . . There would be nothing to gain, and it would even be dangerous to defend these languages from a monolinguistic standpoint: it would be locking them in an ideology and a practice already obsolete.

(2) Today, all techniques of language learning or translation must take into account this internal multiplicity of languages, a multiplicity which goes much further than the former cleavages caused by the patois and dialects proper to each one of them.

(3) The "opacity" of each language, vehicular or vernacular, dominant or dominated, is increased beyond measure by this new multiplicity. (Glissant 1992, n.p.)

This internal multiplicity of languages makes it difficult to justify the quest for a fictitious, if not impossible, monolingualism. Consequently, it is neither desirable nor realistic to pretend to want to teach a Language with a capital L. It is just as fictitious or dangerous to want to pretend to a "yet unknown mode," an innovative and unique way to transcribe a language that is so far only oral (Cajun, Malinke) with the only goal to make it known as such among the world languages. For, Glissant asserted, "it is not enough to affirm the right to linguistic difference, or, the opposite, to interlexicality, to be sure to achieve them" (1992, n.p.). Such a strategy makes this oral language—rich with its images, varied in its structures, vital in its flexibility, so appropriate to express feelings or reality "in their totality"—run the risk of being petrified, fossilized, stripped of what makes its verve. Glissant insisted: "One must preserve opacity, create a hunger for the propitious obscurities of transference, and relentlessly deny the false commodities of the vehicular sabirs" (1992, n.p.). Claiming a right to linguistic difference is not sufficient to actually accomplish such differences within our educational systems.[6]

Concluding Remarks

Whereas the United States, holding on to a monolingual view of the world and a subtractive view of bilingualism, advocates a monolinguistic educational policy, many countries throughout the world have experienced and recognized the value of plurality and a plural education. They have realized that variety does not threaten a language, it enriches it, and it is entirely possible to teach and to learn one's own language, history, literature, and culture, plus those of other countries. Several nations manage this quite well. Their motivation is great, for they are aware that understanding both their own culture and others' is essential, if they are to preserve their identity in a plural world.

Remembering that all minorities do not seek assimilation, since in fact, some are eager to maintain their distinctiveness, and to transmit their culture and language to the next generations, the issue of linguistic and cultural rights was presented as a major concern. I discussed how absolute monolingualism is impossible when multiplicity is inherent in any language, even where education must face a double interdict: the interdicted language, and the language of interdiction. In response, several organizations and resolutions attempted to ensure international recognition of the neglected languages and linguistic rights, some directly addressing education: the right to develop and promote one's native language, and the right to all forms of education, including education in one's native language.

Before closing, it must be emphasized that research in education must forego the limited and limiting concept of language as simply a "tool" and separate from human experience, especially in linguistics and language learning and teaching, of course, but also in all disciplines. Language is constitutive of reality, experience, and identity (Cicourel 1983; Egéa-Kuehne 1996, 1997; Foucault 1979; Phillipson 1992). Through language, a sense of the culture, the institutional traditions, the ways of thinking, perceiving reality, and communicating are transmitted. Teaching only the technical and pragmatic aspects of a language and its mechanics while ignoring its social, cultural, and ethical dimensions is extremely insufficient. Language teaching that ignores the cultural and sociological dimensions of language learning works more toward assimilating learners than empowering them. Research has begun to address problems of equity in education and society, and has broadened its theoretical perspective. More studies are expected to look at languages beyond the national scene, on a global level. Some serious work is also needed on the ideological dimension of language and power, in education and society in general.

ENDNOTES

1. For details on the history of linguistic rights, see for example Capotorti 1979; Crawford 1992; Phillipson 1992; Sieghart 1983; Skutnabb-Kangas & Phillipson 1986, 1989; Woehrling 1990.

2. In the US, busing children to another school zone in order to implement the desegregation program is a tangible as well as symbolical attempt to bridge this gap. After several years, it has mostly failed for some of the reasons mentioned here.

3. It was the case in all colonial territories, where they learned the history of the colonizers' country. However, it also occurred in non-colonized *per se* countries. Grant (1995) mentions how "the Scots must be almost the only people in the world, except for colonial and dependent territories, whose children learn more about someone else's history than their own"; however, he also notes that "in countries such as Ireland and Catalonia, this has already been done." (10)

4. Source: UN Doc. E/CN.4/Sub.2/1994/56. http://www.unesco.org/most /lnlaw9.htm. *Draft Declaration on the Rights of Indigenous Peoples*: "The Draft Declaration on the Rights of Indigenous Peoples was completed by the Working Group on Indigenous Populations of the UN Sub-Commission on Prevention of Discrimination and Protection of Minorities in 1993. Since some articles concerning the rights to self-determination and land rights are controversial, the Draft Declaration has not yet been adopted." Examples of some article excerpts: "*Article 14*: Indigenous peoples have the right to revitalize, use, develop and transmit to future generations their histories, languages, oral traditions, philosophies, writing systems and literatures,

and to designate and retain their own names for communities, places and persons..." *"Article 15*: Indigenous children have the right to all levels and forms of education of the state. All indigenous peoples also have this right and the right to establish and control their educational systems and institutions providing education in their own languages, in a manner appropriate to their cultural methods of teaching and learning. Indigenous children living outside their communities have the right to be provided access to education in their own culture and language. States shall take effective measures to provide appropriate resources for these purposes."
Source: UN Doc. E/CN.4/Sub.2/1995/26. http://www.halcyon.com /pub/FWDP/International/95–12808.txt. Some examples: "29. National laws should ensure that the use of traditional languages in education, arts and the mass media is respected and, to the extent possible, promoted and strengthened..." "30. Governments should provide indigenous communities with financial and institutional support for the control of local education, through community-managed programs, and with use of traditional pedagogy and languages."

5. Edouard Glissant' paper, "Paysage de la francophonie," was presented at a colloquium organized with David Wills at Louisiana State University, April 23–25, 1992, titled *Echoes from Elsewhere/Renvois d'ailleurs*. During this colloquium, for the first time, Derrida presented the text of *Le monolinguisme de l'autre*. At the time, Edouard Glissant was Director of the Center for French and Francophone Studies at Louisiana State University, Baton Rouge. He is originally from Martinique. Quotes from Glissant's and Derrida's papers translated by Denise Egéa-Kuehne. No page numbers.

6. Some relatively more recent measures have been taken by UNESCO, in the form of declarations, recommendations, or conventions, such as *UNESCO Universal Declaration on Cultural Diversity* (November 2, 2001, http://portal.unesco.org/en/ev.php-URL_ID=13179&URL_DO=DO _TOPIC&URL_SECTION=201.html), or for example *Recommendation concerning the Promotion and Use of Multilingualism and Universal Access to Cyberspace* (October 15, 2003, http://portal.unesco.org/en/ev.php-URL _ID=17717&URL_DO=DO_TOPIC&URL_SECTION=201.html), and *Convention on the Protection and Promotion of the Diversity of Cultural Expressions 2005* (Paris, October 20, 2005), noting the following words: "*Recalling* that linguistic diversity is a fundamental element of cultural diversity, and reaffirming the fundamental role that education plays in the protection and promotion of cultural expressions."

REFERENCES

Cicourel, Aaron. 1985. "Text and Discourse." *Annual Review of Anthropology* 14: 159–185.
Crawford, James. 1992. *Language Loyalties*. Chicago: Chicago University Press.

116   DENISE EGÉA-KUEHNE

Derrida, Jacques. 1998. *Monolingualism of the Other; or, The Prosthesis of Origin.* Translated by Patrick Mensah, Stanford, CA: Stanford University Press.

Egéa-Kuehne, Denise. 1996. "Bachelard and Science Education: The Danger of Unitary Epistemology." *Journal of Curriculum Discourse and Dialogue* 3 (2): 23–34.

———. 1997. "Neutrality in Education and Derrida's Call for 'Double Duty.'" In *Philosophy of Education 1996*, edited by Frank Margonis, 154–163. Urbana, IL: Philosophy of Education Society.

Foucault, Michel. 1979. *Discipline and Punish: The Birth of the Prison.* Translated by Alan Sheridan, New York: Vintage.

Glissant, Edouard. 1992. "Paysages de la Francophonie." Paper presented at the colloquium *Echoes from Elsewhere/Renvois d'ailleurs*, Baton Rouge: Louisiana State University, April 23–25. No page numbers. Quotes translated by Denise Egéa-Kuehne.

International Seminar on Human Rights and Cultural Rights. 1987. Recife, Brazil, October 7–9, organized by the International Association for Cross-Cultural Communication.

Kourouma, Amadou. 1997. Communication at the Annual Conference of the American Council for the Teaching of Foreign Languages, Nashville, TN, November, 1997.

Kuijpers Resolution. 1987. Official Journal of the European Communities, No C 318, 30.11. 1987, pp. 160–164. Accessed December 27, 2011. http://www.minel res.lv/eu/epres/re871030.htm

Pfeiffer, Anita B. 1975. "Designing a Bilingual Curriculum." In *Proceedings of the First Inter-American Conference on Bilingual Education*, edited by Rudolph C. Troike & Nancy Modiano. Arlington: Center for Applied Linguistics.

Phillipson, Robert. 1992. *Linguistic Imperialism.* Oxford, England: Oxford University Press.

Skutnabb-Kangas, Tove, & Robert Phillipson. 1986. "Denial of Linguistic Rights: The New Mental Slavery." Paper presented at the 11th World Congress of Sociology, New Delhi, August 1986.

———. 1989. *Wanted! Linguistic Human Rights.* ROLIG-papir 44, Roskilde: Roskilde Universits-center.

Thomas, Lee. 1996. "Language as Power: A Linguistic Critique of U.S. English." *The Modern Language Journal* 80 (2): 129–140.

United Nations. 1966. "International Covenant on Civil and Political Rights." General Assembly resolution 2200A (XXI), New York, December 16, 1966. Accessed December 27 2011. http://www2.ohchr.org/english/law/ccpr.htm

———. 1966 [1993]. *Draft United Nations Declaration on the Rights of Indigenous Peoples.* General Assembly resolution 2200A (XXI), New York, December 16, 1966. Accessed December 27, 2011. http://cwis.org/fwdp/drft9329.html.

Wiessner, Siegfried. 2007. "United Nations Declaration on the Rights of Indigenous Peoples." General Assembly resolution 61/295, New York, September 13, 2007. Accessed December 27, 2011. http://untreaty.un.org/cod/avl/ha/ga_61–295 /ga_61–295.html

Woehrling, Jean-Marie. 1990. "Les institutions européennes et la promotion des droits linguistiques des minorités. Le projet de Charte européenne des langues régionales et minoritaires." Paper presented at the International Colloquium on Language Rights/Human Rights, Council of Europe, Strasbourg, November 15–17, 1990.

CHAPTER 6

THEORIZING ASIAN CANADA, REFRAMING DIFFERENCES

ROLAND SINTOS COLOMA

ASIAN CANADIANS ARE THE LARGEST VISIBLE MINORITY community in Canada, yet they remain at the peripheries of scholarly, policy, and educational discussions.[1] According to Statistics Canada, there are over 3.5 million Canadians of Asian descent in 2006, constituting about 11 percent of the national population. Based on projections by Statistics Canada, about one in five Canadians will be a member of a racialized minority group by the next decade. South Asians and Chinese will remain the largest ethnic minority groups, making up almost half of the total racialized minority population by 2017. The increase of Asian Canadians over the past 30 years and in the projected future are due to high immigration rates, with their impact acutely seen and felt in major metropolitan areas, such as Toronto, Vancouver, and Montréal (Bélanger & Caron Malenfant 2005; Li 2003). In spite of their strong numerical presence, however, Asian Canadians remain relegated to the margins of research and teaching in the fields of education in general, and of curriculum studies, in particular.

An inquiry into the study of Asian Canadians throws into sharp relief the status and health of "minority studies" in multicultural Canada (Bannerji 2000; Mackey 2002; Walcott 1997). Research and teaching on Asian Canadians should by no means be considered minor in the Canadian academe, if the term minor denotes an inferior or inconsequential position. Nor should it signify being less developed, since such a comparison relies on an academic standardized norm and teleology of achievement. The status of research and teaching of Asian Canadians as part of minority studies in

Canada, in actuality, reveals more about the rationalities, operations, and effects of mainstream intellectual and institutional discourses and structures. It also illuminates the possibilities and limits of various ontologies, epistemologies, and methodologies that are utilized and available for empirical and pedagogical work. In short, understanding the ways in which Asian Canadians are framed in scholarly and curricular discourses can shed light, not only on their internal histories and developments, but also on mainstream their disciplinary logics and practices. Such an inquiry, consequently, has relevance for other interdisciplinary fields, such as women's studies, and other area studies programs, such as Caribbean studies and Middle Eastern studies, whose intellectual currency, symbolic standing, and material allocation in scholarly and institutional venues continue to remain disputed and uncertain.

Admittedly, the study of Asian Canadians as a formal *institutional* enterprise does not exist in any Canadian university or college (Yu & Beauregard 2007). In other words, there are no Asian Canadian Studies programs that exist in any Canadian higher education institution.[2] Research institutes, centers, and undergraduate and graduate courses that *focus on Asia* are numerous and well supported in Canada. For instance, in the Greater Toronto area, the University of Toronto has the Asian Institute at the Munk School of Global Affairs, and York University has the Centre for Asian Research.[3] Much less attention and resources, however, have been provided for the development of research and teaching related to Asians in Canada, therefore leading to their invisibility as a racialized minority community (Coloma et al. 2012; Ty 2004). Faculty members with scholarly and teaching interests in Asian Canadians either include relevant readings in their general courses or, in rare cases, offer specialized courses on Asian Canadian studies.[4] Since Canada's academic and pedagogical gaze has been primarily directed externally to the west across the Pacific, my work as a scholar and the discussions in this chapter aim to shift the gaze to focus internally, and enact a key objective in the study of Asian Canadians: to examine the historical, sociocultural, and political conditions and forces that shape our knowledge about people of Asian heritage in Canada and in the diaspora.[5]

Toward this end, this chapter will outline, in broad preliminary strokes, an intertwined set of frameworks that aims to address the ways in which the research and teaching of race, minority subjects, and Asian Canadians in particular, are framed and construed in the Canadian academe. As a preview, the first framework examines *pan-ethnic* and *ethnic-specific* perspectives. The second takes an *intersectional* approach that accounts for the multiplicity of indices and positions within a racialized category. The third mobilizes a *transnational* lens that highlights the history, legacy, and workings of migration, imperialism, and globalization. The fourth framework underscores a *comparative* view to investigate how racialized communities have impacted and influenced one another. I put forward these frameworks as a heuristic tool in order to also think through the analytical terrain of my research on the history of Asian Canadian social movements and, borrowing from the 2009 Curriculum Studies conference title (Ng-A-Fook 2009), to provoke an onto-epistemological rethinking in regards to our theorizing and teaching of race, diaspora, and nation in Canadian curriculum studies.

FRAMEWORKS OF DIFFERENCE

The lack of formal institutional structure for the study and teaching of Asian Canadians has by no means limited its emergence and development as a *scholarly* endeavor. In his article, "The Lateness of Asian Canadian Studies," literary and cultural critic Christopher Lee (2007) argues that the long overdue emergence of Asian Canadian studies as an intellectual project is primarily due to two factors: (1) the scarcity of institutional programs in Canadian higher education to develop such theoretical and empirical lines of inquiry for faculty and students; and (2) the critique of identity politics that defers any referential closure between identitarian categories and the subjects or communities to which they putatively signify. If we take Lee's assessment as our point of departure, which attends to both historical materialist and post-structuralist concerns, how then do we pursue theorizing Asian Canada with a contested academic idiom and limited programmatic support, when the very intellectual foundation upon which we construct such a project is unstable and contingent, yet the struggle for formal institutional establishment and legitimacy requires referential clarity and fixity? In other words, how do we pursue a scholarly and pedagogical endeavor regarding the largest racialized minority population in Canada, a project that is already fraught with multiple, competing, and contradictory interests, investments, and effects?

I pursue the work of researching and teaching Asian Canadians mindful of the complexities, instabilities, and debates around the categories of "Asian," "Canadian," and "Asian Canadian." Rather than bracketing or simplifying these tensions, I see them as a rich opportunity to analyze their histories, operations, and legacies. By investigating the study of Asian Canadians as a scholarly and pedagogical field in the Canadian academe, I put under scrutiny what constitutes these terms, and highlight the possibilities of four frameworks—pan-ethnic, intersectional, transnational, and comparative—for intellectual, institutional, and curricular analyses. These frameworks are especially germane for Canadian curriculum studies as we grapple with the field's perennial questions: "*what* should be taught?" and "*how* should things be taught?" (Egan 2003, 12, italics in original). For

Kieran Egan, "Curriculum inquiry is educational inquiry; both properly address the *what* and *how* questions together and deal with all the ramifications of trying to answer, 'What should [students] learn, in what sequence, and by what methods?'" (15). Although the four frameworks below can be pursued in any sequence and in combination with each other, they enable scholars and practitioners to address both the content (what) and method (how) of curriculum inquiry by teaching and learning differently about race in general, and Asian Canadians, in particular.

PAN-ETHNIC FRAMEWORK

Asian Canadian as a pan-ethnic category is a powerful sociopolitical construct (Coloma 2006; Espiritu 1992). I posit its formation within the simultaneous and negotiated process of interpellation and identification that name and bring together a racialized coagulation of diverse ethno-national cultural groups (Althusser 1971; Fuss 1995). In other words, the term Asian Canadian is both imposed upon and claimed by a grouping of people based on political reasons and not on biological, genetic, or anthropological criteria. It is an interpellation generated and utilized by the Canadian government in the form of census and other biopolitical technologies of surveillance and management to sort, regulate, and allocate resources to various populations by race and ethnicity. It is also an identification that many Asians in Canada have self-ascribed as a collective identity for cultural solidarity and political mobilization (Li 2007). For instance, in Toronto where I live, are the fu-GEN Asian Canadian Theatre Company and the Asian Community AIDS Services.[6]

A central concept in theorizing Asian Canada is what sociologists Michael Omi and Howard Winant call racialization, which "signif[ies] the extension of racial meaning to a previously racially unclassified relationship, social practice or group" (Winant 1994, 59). They emphasize that race needs to be understood as "an unstable and 'decentered' complex of social meanings constantly being transformed by political struggle" (Omi & Winant 1994, 55). The concept of racialization with the signifier of race as fluid and negotiated is a productive entry point when researching and teaching about Asian Canadians, since it grapples with issues of diversity in pan-ethnic groupings.

The notion of Asian Canadian pan-ethnicity based on shared and converging racialization serves as the ground that my research builds on. Two major events within the past 20 years marked Canada's recognition of its role and responsibility in racial discrimination. In 1988, Prime Minister Brian Mulroney issued an official apology to Japanese Canadians for the Internment during World War II (Miki 2004). In 2006, Prime Minister

Stephen Harper issued an official apology to Chinese Canadians for the Head Tax imposed upon them from 1885 to 1923 (Dyzenhaus & Moran 2005). The public acknowledgement by the Canadian government for its human rights violation and unjust taxation was the culmination of decades of Asian Canadian grassroots organizing and political campaigns at local, provincial, and national levels. Scholars have documented the government policies and sociopolitical contexts of the Head Tax and the Internment from the late 1800s to the mid-1900s (Roy 1989; Walker 2008; Ward 2002). The media has also covered the momentous apologies in 1988 and 2006, thereby bringing the issue of racial injustice and reparation to a broad mainstream audience. However, what is missing in our scholarly analysis and popular understanding is what took place between the period of outright racial prejudice against people of Asian descent and the Canadian government's relatively recent formal apologies that were spurred by community mobilizations. Largely unexamined is the process through which Asian Canadians have turned their experiences and memories of racial discrimination into demands to the Canadian government to redress its historical transgressions. What I am calling the "public pedagogy of activism" by Asian Canadians is a story that remains untold in Canadian school and university curriculum.

To shed light on this neglected yet important aspect of Canadian history, my research asks the central question: How do subjects of discrimination turn their grief into grievance? By examining how racialized peoples in general, and Asian Canadians in particular, have organized for social justice, my research also inquires into: How have communities of color used their histories and memories of racial suffering to press demands to the government? How have history and memory authorized or discredited claims for reparation due to racial injustice? What have been the political and sociocultural effects of their organizing efforts? By pursuing such a line of inquiry, I have arrived at three research objectives: (1) to undertake the first historical and comparative study of Asian Canadians; (2) to develop a different way of theorizing race and racialization in Canada based on the history and activism of Asian Canadians through discursive, historical materialist, and psychoanalytic approaches; and (3) to investigate both governmental policies of discrimination and grassroots movements of resistance to shed light on the interplay of race, nation, and citizenship.

I am mindful of the critique that a focus on the pan-ethnic may efface ethnic-specific experiences and conditions or, put differently, that emphasis on "race" may supplant the "ethnic" as a relevant category of analysis (Espiritu 1992). Such a critique warrants further consideration, especially since the signifier "Asian" has been dominated by, or has become synonymous to, East Asian and more specifically, Chinese and Japanese. Who can make claims to, or is considered within, the term Asian Canadian is highly contested (Lee 2007). Some communities consider themselves a part of, yet apart from, the entity that coheres under the Asian Canadian category. For instance, South Asians and Filipina/os have raised issues regarding cultural differences, interethnic conflicts, and colonial trajectories between and within Asian ethnic groups (Bannerji 2000; Coloma et al. 2012; Espiritu 2003; Dua 1999). How to recognize and value the differences and convergences, as well as identify and advocate for ethnic-specific and pan-ethnic concerns is an ongoing negotiation among Asian Canadians and a significant issue to address for scholarly, policy, and educational discussions. While cognizant of the political strategy and numerical force of a collective, I also insist on disaggregating information and attending to the diversity within it. I emphasize for this analysis the tension between pan-ethnic and ethnic-specific approaches, and in turn, my research in this chapter investigates what constitutes not only "Asian" but also "Canadian." Hence, in my research on the history of Asian Canadian social movements, I juxtapose the more prominent case studies of Chinese and Japanese Canadian activism with the relatively lesser known advocacies regarding the Live-in Caregiver Program (LCP) and the *Komagata Maru* incident by the Filipina/o and Asian Indian Canadian communities, respectively (Buchignani, Indra, & Srivastiva 1985; Kazimi 2004; Pratt 2004; Stasiulis & Bakan 2005). The Filipina/o and Asian Indian cases will be discussed in greater detail in the sections to come.

INTERSECTIONAL FRAMEWORK

Another approach to researching and teaching about Asian Canadians is through an intersectional framework. This framework examines the ways in which race overlaps with, and is constituted by other indices of difference, such as class, gender, ability, sexuality, language, spirituality, migration, and generation (Coloma 2008). Developed and advanced primarily by feminists of color, it questions claims of a universal experience or perspective about and by a community, and foregrounds how unique specificities shed light on multidimensional conditions and broader issues. Challenging overdeterminations and generalizations, an intersectional approach underscores the "heterogeneity, hybridity, multiplicity," of not only individuals and communities, but also of academic fields (Lowe 1996, 60).

The intersectional framework is useful in analyzing Filipina/o Canadians and the LCP.[7] It is important to integrate the lives and conditions of Filipina/o Canadians in curriculum studies since my research indicates that, unlike the Chinese and Japanese Canadian communities that have received some, albeit limited and skewed, attention in the narration of Canadian history,

Filipina/o Canadians are virtually absent in Canadian history textbooks (Coloma 2012). I contend that analysis of the conditions of Filipina/os as abject beings, or as degraded and cast out entities in the historical account of the nation, can throw into sharp relief the representational power of racial inclusion, exclusion, and denial in Canadian curriculum studies. Using an intersectional framework to analyze and integrate Filipina/o Canadians in the curriculum, we can gain insights into the blurring of public and private spaces in domestic labor, and the development of Canadian economic capital and professional work-life balance on the backs of women of color. For instance, the University of Toronto holds informational sessions entitled "How to Find Reliable and Quality Home Care Services" to provide a venue for placement agencies and current employers of caregivers to help faculty, staff, and students find a "Nanny or a Caregiver who is 'the right fit for your family.'"[8] The LCP has received critical media attention in the province of Ontario in light of the flagrant human rights abuses experienced by the caregivers, and the recent provincial legislation geared to regulate recruitment agencies. The class, racial, and gendered exploitation of migrant women of color through the LCP has been well documented. Research indicates that over 95 percent of the caregivers in the LCP are Filipina/os, a highly educated and skilled, yet poorly treated and remunerated group, who are recruited from the Philippines (Pratt 2004; Stasiulis & Bakan 2005).

The LCP, which has been called a modern form of slavery, indentured servitude, and transnational trafficking, derived from the Foreign Domestic Movement Program in 1981 (Diocson 2001; Saywell 2010). The LCP has two draconian conditions that position caregivers as expendable and vulnerable workers. First, the recruited women arrive in Canada with a work permit that requires them to be employed for 24 out of 36 months with very limited status, benefits, and protection. Their treatment as recruited workers is very different from mine, as someone who came as a faculty member from the United States, since I can file for permanent residency immediately upon my arrival in Canada. The LCP workers must wait until the successful completion of their two- to three-year work term before they can file for permanent residency. Second, the LCP requires that caregivers live in the homes of their employers, consequently putting them in vulnerable conditions. Research indicates that many women caregivers suffer from verbal, physical, and even sexual abuse, yet find very few recourses due to the mandatory length of employment contracts, the live-in requirement, and their limited status under Canadian law (Diocson 2001; Pratt 2004; Stasiulis & Bakan 2005; Saywell 2010).

My university colleagues inform me of the emotional challenges faced by students, who were raised by Filipina nannies, when reading and discussing research on the exploitation of women of color through the LCP.

While many deny findings indicating that caregivers are abused and have limited recourses, others have difficulty recognizing their own participation and complicity. Confronting what Deborah Britzman (1998) calls "difficult knowledge" of one's complicity in processes of exploitation requires a commitment to teaching that pursues self-reflection, and to unlearning what one has taken for granted or previously learned as norm. Since imagining and enacting curriculum studies from antioppressive perspectives can engender strong affective responses, we need to create spaces for ourselves and students to work through these affective crises. To be sure, the unpredictability of affect requires a similarly vigilant commitment to working through its uncertain consequences, even in our hopes to redress marginality.

TRANSNATIONAL FRAMEWORK

My research on the history of Asian Canadian social movements and on the advocacy efforts of Filipina/o Canadians to scrap or reform the LCP not only sheds light on the increasing liberalization and privatization of healthcare in Canada, but also on Canada's immigration policies and Filipina/os' global diaspora. This points to the third framework of *transnational* in theorizing Asian Canada, which attends to issues of migration, globalization, and imperialism (Appadurai 1996; Cho 2007; Espiritu 2003; Grewal & Kaplan 1994; Parreñas & Siu 2007). My research builds upon the work of scholars who have noted the delineation in policies between the preferred economic immigrants, who bring in financial and human capital, and the less desired refugees and family-sponsored migrants, who are perceived as a drain on federal, provincial, and local resources (Cameron 2004). Filipina/o LCP workers occupy an ambiguous and vexed position between these two categories for three reasons. First, they have become integral in Canada's regime of care, as caregiving for children, the elderly, and the differently abled has become more privatized. While Filipina/os may not directly bring in economic capital, they play a crucial role in the work-life balance that supports the development of careers and capital in Canada. Second, the LCP was originally designed as a temporary labor initiative, and is not an official immigration program per se. Filipina/os who utilize it to become permanent residents and citizens are viewed with suspicion as using the system for their personal gain. Third, when they petition and have their family members join them in Canada, they are considered a drain to resources that should be provided to allegedly more deserving and proper Canadians (Coloma et al. 2012; Pratt 2004; Stasiulis & Bakan 2005). Thus, a combined intersectional and transnational analysis enables investigations into the complex and intertwined relationships of race, gender, economy, nation, and diaspora. A transnational perspective in curriculum studies, hence, demands that we view the lives and conditions of our students and their families as deeply imbricated in the interrelatedness of domestic and foreign policies, programs, and perspectives.

The growing migration and community formation of Filipina/os in Canada, like many immigrant communities, need to be understood within the broader dynamics of Filipina/o global diaspora that is structured by economic push and pull factors in the Philippines and receiving nation-states like Canada (Espiritu 2003; Li 2003). Human labor has become the largest export of the Philippines, making Filipina/os "servants of globalization," a phenomenon underpinned by foreign structural adjustment programs and national policies of economy and labor (Parreñas 2001). Poverty, high unemployment rates, and political instability in the Philippines cause many Filipina/os to seek opportunities as overseas workers. At the same time, their high educational attainment, linguistic proficiency in English, and reputation for diligence and collegiality make them desirable for global North countries like Canada (Coloma et al. 2012). With filial ties to their homeland, Filipina/os send money remittances to the Philippines, amounting to about 10 percent of the gross domestic product and shoring up the national economy (Espiritu 2003; Parreñas 2001). Hence, a transnational framework offers a lens through which to examine Asian Canadian subjectivities, material conditions, and psyches as indelibly shaped by global migrations, politics, and dynamics. Through such an analytical perspective we can understand, teach, and learn about not only the migration of Filipina/os to Canada, but also transnational activism, for instance, the recent protests by the Tamil community in Toronto regarding the devastating genocide, civil war, and human rights violations in Sri Lanka (Coutts 2009; Sriskandarajah 2002).

While the organizing efforts of the Filipina/o and Tamil communities are recent examples of Asian Canadian transnational social movements, the *Komagata Maru* incident presents a historical scenario (Kazimi 2004). In 1914, the *Komagata Maru* steamship carried 376 Asian Indian passengers, mostly of Sikh background, from India to Hong Kong and Shanghai, China, to Yokohama, Japan, and finally to Vancouver, Canada. The passengers were barred entry into Canada due to Canada's "Continuous Journey" policy, initially established in 1908, which mandated that only those who could travel directly from their country of origin to Canada would be allowed to emigrate (Buchignani, Indra, & Srivastiva 1985; Dua 1999; Li 2003). The policy functioned to limit Asian Indian migration to Canada due to the fact that it was impossible, at the time, for ships to travel from India to Canada without stopping at ports for fuel and food. It reflected and reinforced Canada's white supremacist laws and public sentiment to keep "White Canada forever" by excluding immigrants from Asia, yet keeping an open door for those coming from Europe (Ward 2002). That Asian

Indians were a part of the British Empire and were thus British subjects, like Canadians, did not save them from the discrepancies of Canada's racist immigration laws and the prevailing prejudice to exclude Asians from North America in the early twentieth century.

The transnational framework to theorizing Asian Canada challenges the dominance of the nation as the main unit of analysis in mainstream research and teaching. Transnationalism highlights the movements of peoples, materials, ideas, and cultures across geopolitical borders (Appadurai 1996), and calls into question scholarly fields like Canadian curriculum studies, whose prevailing interpretive parameters remain bounded within the nation-state. Our interpretive stance as scholars in Canada in general, and as Canadian curriculum studies scholars in particular, is underpinned by the realities of Asian migration to Canada, both from Asia, as well as from the Caribbean, Latin America, Africa, and Europe. It is also supported by research on globalization and imperialism that demonstrates diaspora between "developed" and "developing" regions as not merely unidirectional, but actually reciprocal, albeit in different degrees (Appadurai 1996; Cho 2007; Espiritu 2003; Sriskandarajah 2004; Parreñas & Siu 2007). Finally, this approach helps to rethink the position of Asian Canadians as a racialized community and as a minority field of study in relation to Aboriginal peoples in a settler nation. In *Exalted Subjects: The Making of Race and Nation in Canada*, Sunera Thobani (2007) argues that the exalted white citizens are positioned over and against migrants of color and indigenous peoples in the areas of law, welfare, and public services. What is intellectually and pedagogically provocative in Thobani's analysis is that the claims made by migrants of color, including Asian Canadians, for recognition, redistribution, and rights often occur, whether consciously or not, over and against the claims of indigenous peoples for rights, land, and sovereignty. In other words, the migrants of color's citizenship claims could also work against the claims of indigenous peoples. I contend that Thobani's insight on race, aboriginality, citizenship, and nation has enormous implications in theorizing Asian Canada, especially in regards to intellectual and pedagogical points of convergence and tension. Consequently, an inquiry into Asian Canadians from a transnational viewpoint can produce new ways of theorizing and teaching concepts of home, migration, belonging, and citizenship.

Theorizing race from a transnational curriculum framework highlights how Canadian racial formations and understandings are indelibly shaped by cultures and groups within *and* beyond the national border. Foregrounding local-global perspectives that draw from studies of diaspora, globalization, and colonialism, it argues for the denationalization of scholarly and curriculum projects in order to move analysis beyond the boundaries of Canada and demonstrate the historical and contemporary relations between Asia and Canada. Such an approach challenges the compartmentalized configurations of "area studies" that separate Canadian culture, history, and curriculum from what is Asian. It disrupts the commonsensical notion that Asia is "over there," outside of, and apart from, what is considered "Canadian"; rather, it locates them "here" as part and parcel of Canada. Simultaneously, if not paradoxically, a transnational framework needs to account for the ways in which Asian Canadians are implicated in the ongoing colonial dynamics of a settler nation. Heeding Celia Haig-Brown's (2008) call to "take indigenous thought seriously," teaching and learning about race need to address the trichotomy of Aboriginals, white citizens, and migrants of color, including Asian Canadians; a trichotomy that discursively and structurally configure racial formations and relations in Canada. This racial trichotomy certainly "reframe[s] and decentre[s] conventional scholarship," and pushes "educators to confront their epistemic and ontological assumptions about teaching and learning, as well as the established curriculum practices and interests that have been traditionally exercised in public schools" (Haig-Brown 2008, 12–13).

COMPARATIVE FRAMEWORK

The final framework that I put forward for theorizing Asian Canada is through a comparative lens. As part of larger scholarly and pedagogical discourses on minority studies, an inquiry into Asian Canadians can illustrate how research and teaching on racialized and ethnic peoples have emerged and developed in Canadian higher education. By using a comparative approach, I aim to move beyond its usual denotation of "the arbitrary juxtaposition of two terms in difference and similarity," and instead foreground "the recognition and activation of relations that entail two or more terms," thereby bringing "submerged or displaced relationalities into view" (Payne & Barbera 2010, 144). This has relevance and implications for the advancement of academic and curricular areas that address racialized, area/regional, and ethnic/cultural groups, such as Asian studies, Caribbean studies, francophone studies, Jewish studies, and Middle Eastern studies. An inquiry into Asian Canadians can also reveal the historical and political conditions that enable or constrain the formation of particular lines of inquiry. It provokes questions, such as: How do the various multicultural policies at the federal and provincial levels facilitate and/or limit the development of Asian Canadian studies as an intellectual, institutional, and curricular field? How does the absence of civil rights movements, such as those in the United States in the 1960s and 1970s, produce a different trajectory for the study and teaching of minoritized groups in Canada? How do Canada's shifts in immigration policies and changing demographics impact what is researched and taught in universities and colleges?

A comparative approach, therefore, insists that understanding Asian Canadians as a community and as a field of study needs to be contextualized to critically account for the ways in which their racialization both impacts and is impacted by other groups under particular historical, sociocultural, and political conditions (Mawani 2010; Raphael-Hernandez & Steen 2006). The LCP, for instance, can function as a significant index to scrutinize the comparative experiences of other peoples of color, such as Black Caribbean women who also served as domestics and caregivers, as well as Latina/os who are recruited into temporary work by agricultural and service industries. Analysis into the Foreign Domestic Movement, the LCP, and the Temporary Foreign Worker Program within the past 30 years can yield significant insights into the comparative historical continuity of governmental policies and economic practices in relation to race, gender, labor, and migration.

In spite of being the largest racialized minority group in this country, Asian Canadians remain in the margins of mainstream academic discourse. This has enormous consequences for the curriculum and pedagogy, not only for students, but also for educators working with them. Canada has not seen a historical and comparative analysis of Asian Canadians, in ways that groundbreaking scholars Ronald Takaki (1998) and Sucheng Chan (1991) have narrated the history of Asian Americans in the United States. My comparative research on the history of discrimination and social movements with four case studies on Chinese, Japanese, Filipina/o, and Indian communities works in the intellectual spirit of Takaki and Chan, and intends to provoke new ways of theorizing and teaching about race and racialization in the Canadian context. A critical mass of scholarly literature on critical race and antiracism studies is emerging in Canada (Bannerji 2000; Razack 2008; Thobani 2007), and it is my aim to contribute to that discussion by foregrounding the specificities of Canada's racialized history in relation to peoples of Asian descent.

From a comparative perspective, my research contributes to the scholarship on the history of peoples of color, and the analysis of social movements in Canada (Smith 2007; Walker 2008). It addresses major intellectual and pedagogical concerns regarding the ways in which history and memory are used in public policies and educational institutions (Sandwell 2006). In addition, it participates in the ongoing dialogues and debates on racial discrimination and governmental reparation nationally and internationally, including the boarding schools for indigenous students in Canada and the United States, the internment of Japanese Canadians and Japanese Americans, and the apartheid system in South Africa (Torpey 2006). Ultimately, my research grapples with the persistent questions of racial injustice, suffering, and reparation that, I contend, need to be addressed first before racial reconciliation and healing can occur.

CONCLUSION

In this chapter, I have offered four frameworks to theorize Asian Canada in order to expand and reconsider the ways in which race and racialization are studied and taught in the Canadian academe in general, and in curriculum studies, in particular. By analyzing the discursive terrains within which Asian Canadians can be construed, I foreground the logics and rationalities that enable and foreclose how inquiries on race, diaspora, and nation are undertaken (Foucault 1969). I include my research on the history of Asian Canadian racial discrimination and social movements, not only to provide an example of the various ways to theorize Asian Canada, but also to interweave the four frameworks of pan-ethnic, intersectional, transnational, and comparative. These four frameworks provide an interrelated set of approaches that, I argue, could broaden and deepen our study and teaching of Asian Canadian lives, representations, politics, and cultures. Collectively these frameworks of differences could help produce more robust and nuanced conceptualizations in theories, research, and curriculum of race in Canada.

ENDNOTES

1. Following Statistics Canada (2008), I use the term "Asian Canadians" to include people who derive from East, South, Southeast and West Asian countries and regions. The term "East Asian" denotes those from China, Japan, Korea, etc. "South Asian" denotes those from India, Pakistan, Sri Lanka, etc. "Southeast Asians" are from the Philippines, Vietnam, Thailand, etc. "West Asians" are from Iran, Afghanistan, etc. I use the term "visible minority," in relation to governmental categorization and in accordance with the Employment Equity Act, to refer to "persons, other than aboriginal peoples, who are non-Caucasian in race or non-white in colour" (Minister of Justice 1995, 2). I share Grace-Edward Galabuzi's concern and discomfort with the "visible minority" term "because it implies permanence of minority status that is imposed on the population." Like Galabuzi, I prefer the term "racialized" since it "denotes that process of imposition, the social construction of the category, and the attendant experience of oppression as opposed to the seemingly neutral use of the terms 'visible minorities' or 'racial minorities,' which have the effect of masking the oppressions" (Galabuzi 2006, xvi–xvii). Hence, I use "racialized minority" or "racialized peoples" when addressing nongovernmental contexts.

2. As of Fall 2011, faculty at the University of Toronto and the University of British Columbia have submitted proposals to establish a Minor in Asian Canadian Studies in their respective institutions. Approvals for these academic programs may come as early as Spring 2012.

3. For more information, see the following websites for the Asian Institute at University of Toronto (http://www.utoronto.ca/ai) and the Centre for Asian Research at York University (http://www.yorku.ca/ycar).

4. As part of faculty initiatives to further develop Asian Canadian Studies at the University of Toronto, I taught a new graduate seminar on "Theorizing Asian Canada" in Fall 2010 and a new undergraduate course on "Asian Canadian History" in Winter 2012. I also successfully proposed a new course for pre-service teachers in the Initial Teacher Education program on "Teaching Asian Canada for K-12 Educators."

5. Following Lily Cho, I consider "diaspora" as a "condition of subjectivity" that is "marked by the contingencies of long histories of displacements and genealogies of disposession. Diaspora is not divorced from the histories of colonialism and imperialism, nor is it unmarked by race and the processes of racialization" (Cho 2007, 14). See, also, Rhacel S. Parreñas and Lok C. D. Siu (2007).

6. For more information, see the following websites for the fu-GEN Company (http://fu-gen.org) and the Asian Community AIDS Services (http://www.acas.org).

7. According to Citizenship and Immigration Canada, The Live-in Caregiver Program (beginning in 1981 as the Foreign Domestic Movement) "is a special program whose objective is to bring workers to Canada to do live-in work as caregivers when there are not enough Canadians available to fill the available positions…. The [LCP] exists only because there is a shortage of Canadians to fill the need for live-in care work" (cited in Pratt 2004, 41).

8. One of the more recent sessions on live-in caregivers geared toward faculty, staff, and students at University of Toronto (UT) was held on February 18, 2009. On May 4, 2009, along with another UT professor, a UT student, and two community members, I met with Angela Hildyard, the UT Vice President of Human Resources and Equity, to address the LCP and the problematic message that the university is sending by hosting such sessions. As of July 1, 2010, a year after our meeting, the session information on "How to Find Reliable & Quality HomeCare Services" remains on the UT Family Care Office website (Accessed July 1, 2010, http://www.familycare.utoronto.ca/events/past.html#howtoReliableServices09). According to the website, "At the end of the workshop you will be familiar with: The Live-In Caregiver Programme which brings foreign Nannys/Caregivers to Canada, or employs people already living in the GTA; Interview techniques, reference checks and preparing a contract; The costs of this type of child/elder /special needs care in your home; Experiences of other people who hired a Nanny on their own."

REFERENCES

Althusser, Louis. 1971. *Lenin and Philosophy and Other Essays.* New York and London: Monthly Review.

Appadurai, Arjun. 1996. *Modernity at Large: Cultural Dimensions of Globalization.* Minneapolis: University of Minnesota Press.

Bannerji, Himani. 2000. *The Dark Side of the Nation: Essays on Multiculturalism, Nationalism and Gender.* Toronto: Canadian Scholars' Press.

Bélanger, Alain, & Éric Caron Malenfant. 2005. "Ethnocultural Diversity in Canada: Prospects for 2017." Accessed August 15, 2009, from http://www.stat can.gc.ca/pub/11–008-x/2005003/article/8968-eng.pdf

Britzman, Deborah P. 1998. *Lost Subjects, Contested Objects: Toward a Psychoanalytic Inquiry of Learning.* Albany: State University of New York Press.

Buchignani, Norman, Doreen Marie Indra, & Ram Srivastiva. 1985. *Continuous Journey: A Social History of South Asians in Canada.* Toronto: McClelland and Stewart.

Cameron, Elspeth, ed. 2004. *Multiculturalism and Immigration in Canada: An Introductory Reader.* Toronto: Canadian Scholars' Press.

Chan, Sucheng. 1991. *Asian Americans: An Interpretive History.* New York: Twayne.

Cho, Lily. 2007. "The Turn to Diaspora." *Topia: Canadian Journal of Cultural Studies* 17 (Spring): 11–30.

Coloma, Roland Sintos. 2006. "Disorienting Race and Education: Changing Paradigms in the Schooling of Asian Americans and Pacific Islanders." *Race Ethnicity and Education* 9 (1): 1–15.

———. 2008. "Border Crossing Subjectivities and Research: Through the Prism of Feminists of Colour." *Race Ethnicity and Education* 11 (1): 11–27.

———. 2012. "Abject Beings: Filipina/os in Canadian Historical Narrations." In *Filipinos in Canada: Disturbing invisibility*, edited by Roland Sintos Coloma et al. Toronto, ON: University of Toronto Press.

Coloma, Roland Sintos, Bonnie McElhinny, John Paul Catungal, Lisa Davidson, & Ethel Tungohan, eds. 2012. *Filipinos in Canada: Disturbing Invisibility.* Toronto, ON: University of Toronto Press.

Coutts, Matthew. 2009. "Major Tamil Protest Takes Place in Downtown Toronto." *National Post,* March 17. Accessed July 1, 2010, from http://news.globaltv.com /story.html?id=1394928

Diocson, Cecilia. 2001. "Filipino Women's Identity: A Social, Cultural and Economic Segregation in Canada." Accessed July 1, 2010, from http://pwc .bc.tripod.com/resources/RaceGen/speech.html

Dua, Enakshi. 1999. "From Subject to Aliens: Indian Migrants and the Racialisation of Canadian Citizenship." *Sociologie et Societes* 31 (2): 145–162.

Dyzenhaus, David, & Mayo Moran, eds. 2005. *Calling Power to Account: Law, Reparations, and the Chinese Canadian Head Tax Case.* Toronto, ON: University of Toronto Press.

Egan, Kieran. 2003. "What is Curriculum?" *Journal of the Canadian Association for Curriculum Studies* 1 (1): 9–16.

Espiritu, Yen Le. 1992. *Asian American Panethnicity: Bridging Institutions and Identities*. Philadelphia, PA: Temple University Press.

———. 2003. *Home Bound: Filipino American Lives Across Cultures, Communities, and Countries*. Berkeley and Los Angeles: University of California Press.

Foucault, Michel. 1969. *The Archaeology of Knowledge and the Discourse on Language*. New York: Routledge.

Fuss, Diana. 1995. *Identification Papers: Readings on Psychoanalysis, Sexuality, and Culture*. New York: Routledge.

Galabuzi, Grace-Edward. 2006. *Canada's Economic Apartheid: The Social Exclusion of Racialized Groups in the New Century*. Toronto, ON: Canadian Scholars' Press.

Grewal, Inderpal, & Caren Kaplan, eds. 1994. *Scattered Hegemonies: Postmodernity and Transnational Feminist Practices*. Minneapolis: University of Minnesota Press.

Haig-Brown, Celia. 2008. "Taking Indigenous Thought Seriously: A Rant on Globalization with Some Cautionary Notes." *Journal of the Canadian Association for Curriculum Studies* 6 (2): 8–24.

Kazimi, Ali. 2004. *Continuous Journey* [film]. Toronto: Peripheral Visions Film and Video.

Lee, Christopher. 2007. "The Lateness of Asian Canadian Studies." *Amerasia* 33 (2): 1–17.

Li, Peter S. 2003. *Destination Canada: Immigration Debates and Issues*. Don Mills, ON: Oxford University Press.

Li, Xiaoping. 2007. *Voices Rising: Asian Canadian Cultural Activism*. Vancouver: University of British Columbia Press.

Lowe, Lisa. 1996. *Immigrant Acts: On Asian American Cultural Politics*. Durham, NC: Duke University Press.

Mackey, Eva. 2002. *The House of Difference: Cultural Politics and National Identity in Canada*. Toronto: University of Toronto Press.

Mawani, Renisa. 2010. *Colonial Proximities: Crossracial Encounters and Juridical Truths in British Columbia, 1871–1921*. Vancouver: University of British Columbia Press.

Miki, Roy. 2004. *Redress: Inside the Japanese Canadian Call for Justice*. Vancouver: Raincoast.

Minister of Justice. 1995. *Employment Equity Act*. Ottawa, ON: Author. Accessed March 1, 2010, from http://laws.justice.gc.ca/pdf/statute/E/E-5.401.pdf

Ng-A-Fook, Nicholas. 2009. "Fourth Biennial Provoking Curriculum Studies Conference—An Uncommon Countenance: Provoking Historical, Present, and Future Perspectives Within Canadian Curriculum Studies." Accessed March 1, 2010, from http://www.education.uottawa.ca/assets/pdf/pcs-program-en.pdf

Omi, Michael, & Howard Winant. 1994. *Racial Formations in the United States*. New York: Routledge.

Parreñas, Rhacel Salazar. 2001. *Servants of Globalization: Women, Migration, and Domestic Work*. Stanford, CA: Stanford University Press.

Parreñas, Rhacel Salazar, & Lok C. D. Siu, eds. 2007. *Asian Diasporas: New Formations, New Conceptions*. Palo Alto, CA: Stanford University Press.

Payne, Michael, & Jessica Rae Barbera, eds. 2010. *A Dictionary of Cultural and Critical Theory*. Malden, MA: Wiley-Blackwell.

Pratt, Geraldine. 2004. *Working Feminism*. Philadelphia: Temple University Press.

Raphael-Hernandez, Heike, & Shannon Steen, eds. 2006. *AfroAsian Encounters: Culture, History, Politics*. New York and London: New York University Press.

Razack, Sherene H. 2008. *Casting Out: The Eviction of Muslims from Western Law and Politics*. Toronto, University of Toronto Press.

Roy, Patricia E. 1989. *A White Man's Province: British Columbia Politicians and Chinese and Japanese Immigrants, 1858–1914*. Vancouver: University of British Columbia Press.

Sandwell, Ruth. 2006. *To the Past: History Education, Public Memory, and Citizenship in Canada*. Toronto, ON: University of Toronto Press.

Saywell, Shelley, director. 2010, July 7. *The Nanny Business* (Television series episode). In *GlobalTV currents*. Toronto, ON: Global Television.

Smith, Miriam, ed. 2007. *Group Politics and Social Movements in Canada*. Peterborough, ON: Broadview.

Sriskandarajah, Dhananjayan. 2002. *The Migration-Development Nexus: Sri Lanka Case Study*. International Migration 40 (5): 283–307.

Stasiulis, Daiva K., & Abigail B. Bakan. 2005. *Negotiating Citizenship: Migration Women in Canada and the Global System*. Toronto: University of Toronto Press.

Statistics Canada. 2008. "Appendix C: Comparison of Ethnic Origins Disseminated in 2006, 2001 and 1996." Accessed March 1, 2010, from http://www12.statcan.ca/census-recensement/2006/ref/dict/app-ann003-eng.cfm

Takaki, Ronald. 1998. *Strangers from a Different Shore: A History of Asian Americans*. New York: Back Bay.

Thobani, Sunera. 2007. *Exalted Subjects: Studies in the Making of Race and Nation in Canada*. Toronto: University of Toronto Press.

Torpey, John C. 2006. *Making Whole What Has Been Smashed: On Reparations Politics*. Cambridge, MA: Harvard University Press.

Ty, Eleanor. 2004. *The Politics of the Visible in Asian North American Narratives*. Toronto: University of Toronto Press.

Walcott, Rinaldo. 1997. *Black Like Who?: Writing Black Canada*. London, ON: Insomniac.

Walker, Barrington, ed. 2008. *The History of Immigration and Racism in Canada: Essential Readings*. Toronto, ON: Canadian Scholars' Press.

Ward, W. Peter. 2002. *White Canada Forever: Popular Attitudes and Public Policy toward Orientals in British Columbia*, 3rd ed. Montreal: McGill-Queen's University Press.

Winant, Howard. 1994. *Racial Conditions: Politics, Theory, Comparisons*. Minneapolis: University of Minnesota Press.

Yu, Henry, & Guy Beauregard, eds. 2007. "Pacific Canada: Beyond the 47th parallel." *Amerasia Journal* 33 (2).

CHAPTER 7

PROVOKING CURRICULUM STUDIES IN MULTICULTURAL SOCIETIES

DENISE EGÉA-KUEHNE

NOWADAYS, MOST NATIONS MAY BE LABELED "CULTURALLY DIVERSE," since different ethnic, racial, and religious groups live together. In most cases, these societies turn to education, holding it responsible for both problems and solutions. Under political and ideological pressures, what should have been a choice has been presented as inevitable. The challenge is daunting since, as a result, educators have had to face a dual exigency: How is it possible for them to respond to the necessity of respecting, *at the same time*, the particularities of individual differences and singularities *and* the universality of majority law? What part does and can curriculum studies play in responding to the promise made by UNICEF of the right to "a quality education" for all?

In this chapter, I propose to address the persistent constraining and misleading dichotomy of particularism versus universalism in curriculum traditional responses to cultural diversity, stressing that the other and the different are inherent in a quest for knowledge. I discuss the right of access to education, and the predominant role that culture and language play. A reflection on double injunctions suggests a paradigm to help understand that the impossible task of education in the face of diversity is in fact *the very condition* for its possibility.

TRADITIONAL RESPONSES TO CULTURAL DIVERSITY

In the United States,[1] core curriculum and multicultural education are two major advocated approaches to respond to diversity. A combination of the rise of national sentiment and the discrediting of the notion of "bilingual deficit"—that is, the notion that knowing French would leave less room for learning English, or that being Hispanic in a US curriculum means being learning impaired—have led to some change in attitudes toward diversity.

The core curriculum approach corresponds to the fundamentalist official discourse advocating assimilation. In the United States, it comes largely from the humanities (e.g., Bennet on "cultural literacy"). Their critics call them "assimilationists." Actually, they are more concerned about the economical and technological status of the United Sates in international competitions than about assimilating culturally diverse groups into the mainstream culture. They call for "neutrality in education" and "teacher-proof curricula."[2] In practice, the realization of this agenda repeatedly proved to be an impossible assumption—that is, that the academic performance of children of both the minority and majority communities depend solely on what goes on inside the schools, and that all we need to do is "fix the schools." Although that policy had some positive but limited effects, the main drawback is that it does not address the nature of minorities' cultural diversity.

Multicultural education corresponds to the constructivist discourse, with an emphasis on diversity and differences. The current movement is led largely by the minorities. In the United States, it emerged primarily in the sixties, initially in response to the "cultural deprivation" theory, and to African Americans wanting to be like the whites. Now it is linked to cultural diversity, and concerned with minorities doing well, as well as those doing poorly. Although there is no clear definition of multicultural education, looking at the available literature, one can identify a number of goals and diverse "models," though rarely based on ethnographic or empirical studies of minority cultures. It aims at fostering pride in minority cultures, helping minority students develop new insights into their respective cultures, reducing stereotyping and prejudice, and promoting intercultural understanding. However, questions remain: To what extent is it successful? And to what extent does it improve the academic performance of minorities? The limitations of multicultural education stem from the following: it generally ignores minority students' own responsibility for their academic performance; its theories and programs are rarely based on actual studies of minorities' cultures and languages; and it fails to distinguish minority groups who are able to cross culture and language boundaries from those who are not able to cross those boundaries.

Neither the core curriculum nor the multicultural education responses in their various forms are satisfactory, for they both fail to recognize that minority children are influenced by complex social, economic, historical, and cultural factors, and by the relationship between the minority and the mainstream cultures.

Furthermore, as analyzed by Ogbu (1983, 1990, 1992), there are different types of minority groups and minority status. There are "autonomous minorities" (essentially religious in the United States—Amish, Mormons, Jews), immigrants or "voluntary minorities" (Vietnamese immigrants in the United States), "internal minorities" (migrants within the country, from rural areas to cities, for example), and "caste-like" or "involuntary minorities" resulting from slavery, colonization, conquest, or border shifting (in the United States: Mexican Americans in Texas or California; Native Americans, and African Americans descendents of slaves). Ogbu also made a distinction between primary culture differences before two groups come in contact (voluntary immigration), and secondary culture differences after two groups come in contact (involuntary immigration). Ogbu discussed how the relationship between minority cultures and mainstream culture generally affects minorities' schooling; but minorities are affected differently, and involuntary minorities exhibit the most frequent and greatest amount of difficulty.

It is of paramount importance to recognize that there are different kinds of cultures that carry differences in language and tradition; it is also of paramount importance to recognize that there are different types of minority groups; and it is equally important to recognize that all minority children face problems of social adjustment and academic performance in school because of these differences in culture and language and the differences in their relation to the dominant culture.

Therefore, teaching these students has traditionally presented major difficulties, often ignored, overlooked, or misdiagnosed. When confronted with *otherness*[3] and *difference*, several responses have traditionally been proposed: (1) it can be ignored; (2) it can be used to modify current understanding to incorporate new meanings; or (3) it can be mistranslated into meanings already familiar. While the first and second responses respect differences in the expression of otherness—though with unequal consequences—in the case of the third response, the difference is never even acknowledged, much less reflected upon as a source of knowledge. Yet, developing an ability to learn is essentially dependent on developing an ability to reconstruct an understanding of anything other than, different from, learners' prior knowledge and experience of self and the world. Therefore, education means including otherness and multiple, even conflicting voices, thus providing opportunities for critical reflection. Excluding these voices, that is neutralizing education, is tantamount to a decision not to educate (see Egéa-Kuehne 1997).

RIGHTS TO CULTURE, LANGUAGE, AND EDUCATION

Throughout history, throughout the world, examples abound, showing how one group can compromise or restrict educational rights in an attempt to gain control of the political and economic fate of a nation. In the United States, the agenda of organizations promoting the legislation of English as the official language (e.g., *US English, English First*) provides a striking example of hegemonic planning, and of its consequences for education. Phillipson (1992) investigated the use of languages and the hegemonic principles behind the promotion of a particular language. Since language has been argued to be constitutive of reality (see, e.g., Cicourel 1985 and Foucault 1979), it can be, and has been used as a mechanism of ideological control, to manipulate and shape the thinking and values of various groups. Through language control, access to education can be denied, and as a consequence, language minorities may be excluded from access to the language, culture, education, and the information they need to be socially and economically engaged. Aronowitz (1989) described how American schools can function "to strip away what belongs to the student," and how those who succeed in the institution sometimes "do so at the cost of their ethnicity, race and sex, all of which are stripped away" (200).

When such a situation occurs, the object of the interdiction is a fundamental interdiction, an absolute interdiction: the silencing, the obliteration of a voice. It may or may not be couched in legal terms, but, in any case, the interdiction is there. The imposed language and culture are supposed to be substituted for the home language and culture. However, the sources, the norms, the rules, the laws, and the history of the imposed language and culture are situated elsewhere, anywhere but in the homes of the minority students (Derrida 1998).[4]

In instances of linguistic and cultural hegemony, the distance between the home language and culture and the dominant norm may be no more than that between the countryside and the metropolitan area, reservation and "White man's world," inner city and suburbs, between home and the school where the child is bused. But in *every* case, this distance is between the reality of the context in which the dominated group lives, and the place of hegemonic power. Then the curriculum takes a form where the content taught as well as the teaching approach are literally foreign to minority students. These curricula offer them, Derrida (1998) writes, "the experience of a world without any sensible continuity with the one in which they actually live, almost without anything in common with [their] natural or social landscapes" (45).

Serious as this discontinuity may be, it has some even more dire consequences. In this process, the decisive agent is, wittingly or not, the school, and particularly the teacher, who plays the main part in promoting the dominant culture and in facilitating the assimilation to the dominant norms of the linguistically and culturally diverse children. Although conducted nearly 40 years ago, a study by Pfeiffer (1975) revealed the powerfully destructive effects of this type of policy, also masterfully represented in the film *Rabbit Proof Fence*. As they lost all connection with their families, their language, and their culture, the children forcefully enrolled in those schools struggled with confusion and the loss of markers, and eventually, the loss of identity.

The most tragic point, like for the Navajo children in chapter 5, is not just the indifference of the hegemonic culture toward such consequences, but rather, that it is in fact precisely the goal to be achieved: where language and cultural assimilation are sought, the devastation, the systematic obliteration of minorities follow.

In the United States, there has been a well documented tradition of "social control in the service of cultural homogeneity,"[5] from attempts at "cultural standardization" through "coercion" to absorb the waves of new immigrants at the turn of the century and respond to the problem of cultural diversity as a possible threat to the American democracy itself, to various "reformulated" versions of social control through "voluntarism, persuasion and democratic cooperation" to respond to the needs of corporate economy and preserve corporate capitalism (Franklin 1988). Currently, social control has not been eliminated from curriculum theory and practices; it has only changed name and focus according to trends, and political and economic needs. Muted and disguised, less easily detectable, its supporters nevertheless continue to view education as an instrument for ensuring cultural homogeneity, and the hegemony of the dominant language and culture.

Some measures have been proposed to minimize the damaging impact of imposing dominant norms through education. For example, the *United Nations Declaration on the Rights of Indigenous Peoples* and, in the United States, the *Proposed American Declaration on the Rights of Indigenous Peoples* both establish some fundamental rights, some that specifically address education, that is, the right to all forms of education, including right of children to education in their native languages and cultures, and right for minorities to establish, structure, conduct, and control their own educational systems and institutions.[6]

I have argued for the necessity of otherness and multiple voices before (Egéa-Kuehne 1997), so have others. For example, Sidorkin (personal communication October 30 1994) worked "on an attempt to go beyond the antinomy of universalism vs. particularism" based on "Bakhtin's understanding of dialogue." However, in previous research, I stressed that we must remain aware of the part that hierarchical dichotomies still play in the language, and how they are perpetuated in rationales to "go beyond." We need a paradigm that would enable us *not* to "go beyond" or *not* to "bypass" the difficulty of the antinomy universalism / particularism, one which would deconstruct the persistent hierarchy, and empower us to think *from within* such aporias.

THE DUAL EXIGENCY OF CURRICULUM

A very first step is to understand the nature of multicultural coexistence so as to minimize the glaring ignorance about the cultural other, keeping in mind that "I" is also "other." Part of this understanding implies a thorough grasp and knowledge of the history that engenders these cultural differences, which is why we cannot lump the many factors that cut across them into one monolithic entity. It is impossible to understand these differences without an analysis of ideologies and their relations with power and lack of power, across time and space.

It is impossible to hope overcoming oppression, discrimination, passivity, or rebellion without first acquiring a critical comprehension of the history within which these intercultural relations take place. They are part of a historical process; for as human beings, our actions construct history, but they are also historically conditioned. Through a historical perspective in which men and women are capable of assuming themselves as both objects and subjects of history, capable of reinventing the world out of an ethical and aesthetic mold of the cultural patterns that exist, Freire (1993) sees history as a time of possibility. And for him, "to think of history as possibility is to recognize education as possibility."

In particular, in *The Other Heading* and *The Specters of Marx*, Derrida discussed this condition of possibility in conjunction with the play of antinomies and aporias inherent in his notions of a cultural capital as memory (no repetitive memory yet no absolutely new) and as hegemony (no assimilation yet no dispersion). These double injunctions are, for Derrida, the very essence of responsibility. He has described and discussed extensively, and in most of his texts, how these dilemmas are inherent in his concept of responsibility, are in fact *the very condition* of its possibility. For "at a certain point, the promise and the decision, that is to say the responsibility, owe their possibility to the test of undecidability which will always remain their condition" (Derrida 1994, 126). He stressed repeatedly that, if there is an easy decision to make, there is, in fact, no decision to be made, therefore no responsibility to be taken, only a set of rules to follow, a program to implement.

Derrida links this concept to the notion of "messianism," to the experience of the promise. It is by opening a space for the affirmation of this promise, of the "messianic and emancipatory promise," of the impossible event (the only possible event as event) as a promise, that it will preserve its capital of possibilities, of dynamic ideal in-the-making, to-come. No doubt there is danger in settling for an easy consensus, for "transparency," since while "claiming to speak in the name of intelligibility, good sense, common sense, or [supposedly] the democratic ethic, this discourse tends, by means of these very things, and as if naturally, to discredit anything which complicates this model" (Derrida 1992, 55). However, as soon as we settle for a common space, we turn all possibilities into a program. Derrida has discussed his concept of "promise," in particular, when discussing democracy, and complicate it later on it with the notions of "as if" and "perhaps," analyzed at length in his various versions on the unconditional university (Derrida 2002, 213).[7] This same concept applies here: it can manifest itself only where there is disruption, upheaval, or uncertainty, where there exists a gap between the present state, and the ideal that one strives for. Thus, in curriculum, the apparent impossibility to respond to the dual exigency of cultural diversity is *a priori* characteristic of curriculum. In fact, it is in this very gap that curriculum is being shaped

> between an infinite promise (always untenable at least for the reason that it calls for the infinite respect of singularity *and* infinite alterity of the other as much as for the respect of the countable, calculable, subjectal equality among anonymous singularities) and the determined, necessary, but also necessarily inadequate forms of what has to be measured against this promise. (Derrida 1994, 65)

In this gap must be preserved heterogeneity "as the only chance of an affirmed, or rather re-affirmed future" (Derrida 1994, 37). Without this gap, without this disjunction, curriculum may simply believe, *in all good conscience*, that it has succeeded, that it has accomplished its duty, fulfilled its responsibility, and in thus believing, it may lose its "chance of the future, of the promise... (that is [the chance of] its very possibility)" (Derrida 1994, p. 28).

As educators, it may be easy to be attracted by the lure of making everything equal and equally accessible to all, apparently removing all sources of possible contention and conflicts. However, Derrida warns that under the pretense of "the univocity of democracy," a model that "coincides with certain institutional powers" may in fact be imposed (Derrida 1994, 55).

CONCLUSION

In this chapter, I addressed the challenge of managing cultural diversity in facing curriculum. Considering the aporetic nature of knowledge and the issues of rights to cultures and languages overlooked in all proposed models of curriculum, I argued that, as educators, we should not look to settle for easy consensus, to simplify, neutralize or translate diversity into a common ground. Rather, that we should value diversity, and strive to engage our students in a quest for knowledge that should take them beyond the boundaries of their immediate sociopolitical contexts, in space and time, and encourage them to take risks in learning and discovering the unfamiliar, the other— within and without themselves—while building a greater sense of responsibility toward themselves and other(s).

Understanding and accepting contradictions, double injunctions and aporias can help educators and the profession find means and ways to articulate more clearly the problems posed by curriculum in a culturally diverse society, and to move toward a more responsive and responsible approach to educating all children. For the true dilemma is not how to make a choice, but how to respect and assume our responsibility to, *both and at the same time*, welcome minorities, but also recognize, accept, respect, and learn from their diversity.

1. For the situation in Europe, see D. Egéa-Kuehne (2000).
2. On neutrality in education see D. Egéa-Kuehne (1997).
3. "Otherness" includes both "you" and "I," and otherness within same-name groups. It also refers to otherness within ourselves, such as described by S. Griffin (1982).
4. See also the example of the Cajuns in Louisiana.
5. While historical accounts of American curriculum and education had often represented them as politically, economically, and culturally neutral, "this view was discredited by the mid-1970s, largely as a result of the work of Michael W. Apple" (Pinar 1988, 80). Besides Apple and Franklin many other scholars worked towards a better understanding of the political and social aspects of American education, including, but not limited to: Anyon, Campbell, Caswell, Giroux, Kliebard, LaPiere, Macdonald, Norton, Raup, Rugg, Wexler. For a thorough review of the history of social and political text in education see Pinar, Reynolds, Slattery and Taubman (1995, 243–314).
6. See *Draft United Nations Declaration on the Rights of Indigenous Peoples*, Commission on Human Rights, Sub-Commission on Prevention of Discrimination and Protection of Minorities, Forty-fifth session, Agenda Item 14. Discrimination Against Indigenous People, Report of the working group on indigenous populations on its eleventh session. Chairperson-Rapporteur: Ms. Erica-Irene A. Daes. (Article 15). E/CN.4/Sub.2/1993/29 /Annex I—GE.93–85003 (E) (August 23, 1993). http://www.cwis.org /drft9329.html; *Proposed American Declaration on the Rights of Indigenous Peoples* (Approved by the Inter-American Commission on Human Rights

on February 26, 1997, at its 1333rd session, 95th regular session). Article IX. Education. http://www.cidh.org/Indeginous.htm

7. Derrida has spoken and published numerous times about "the university without condition." See for example the Stanford lecture written in 1999. Originally titled "The Future of the Profession; or, The University Without Condition (Thanks to the 'Humanities,' What *Could Take Place* Tomorrow), it was published under the shorter title "The University Without Condition," in *Without Alibi*, P. Kamuf, (ed.). With minor variations, the same lecture was delivered at the University of SUNY Albany on October 11, 1999, under the title "The Future of the Profession or the Unconditional University." Derrida can be heard delivering this lecture at http://www.albany.edu/history/derrida.html. Under its longer title "The future of the profession or the university without condition (thanks to the 'Humanities,' what *could take place* tomorrow)," Tom Cohen included this text in the collection he edited titled *Jacques Derrida and the Humanities: A Critical Reader* (Cambridge: Cambridge University Press, 2001), 24–57.

REFERENCES

Aronowitz, Stanley. 1989. "Working-class Identity and Celluloid Fantasy." In *Popular culture: Schooling and Everyday Life*, edited by Henri Giroux & R. Simon Granby, MA: Bergin & Garvey.

Cicourel, Aaron. 1985. "Text and Discourse." *Annual Review of Anthropology* 14: 159–185.

Derrida, Jacques. 1992. *The Other Heading. Reflections on Today's Europe.* Translated by Pascale-Anne Brault & Michael B. Naas, Bloomington and Indianapolis: Indiana University Press.

———. 1994. *Specters of Marx: The State of the Debt, the Work of Mourning, and the New International.* Translated by Peggy Kamuf, New York and London: Routledge.

———. 1998. *Monolingualism of the Other; or, The Prosthesis of Origin.* Translated by Patrick Mensah, Stanford, CA: Stanford University Press.

———. 2002. "The University Without Condition." In *Without Alibi*, edited by Peggy Kamuf, 202–237. Stanford, CA: Stanford University Press.

Egéa-Kuehne, Denise. 1997. "Neutrality in Education and Derrida's Call for 'Double Duty'." In *Philosophy of Education 1996*, edited by Frank Margonis, 154–163. Urbana, IL: Philosophy of Education Society, 1997.

———. 2000. "Paths to Integration and/or Multiculturalism: Cultural Crossroads and/of Education." In *The New Europe at the Crossroads II*, edited by Ursula Beitterr, 89–109. New York: Peter Lang Publishing, Inc.

Foucault, Michel. 1979. *Discipline and Punish: The Birth of the Prison.* Translated by Alan Sheridan. New York: Vintage.

Franklin, B.M. 1988. "Whatever Happened to Social Control? The Muting of Coercive Authority in Curriculum Discourse." In *Contemporary Curriculum Discourses*, edited by William F. Pinar. Scottsdale, AZ: Gorsuch Scarisbrick.

Freire, Paulo. 1993. *Pedagogy of the Oppressed.* New York: Continuum Publishing Company.

Griffin, Susan. 1982. "The Way of All Ideologies." In *Feminist Theory: A Critique of Ideology,* edited by Nannerl O., Kohane, Michelle Z., Rosaldo, & Barbara C., Gelpi. Chicago: University of Chicago Press.

Ogbu, John U. 1983. "Minority Status and Schooling in Plural Societies." *Comparative Education Review* 27(2): 168–190

———. 1990. "Minority Education in Comparative Perspective." *Journal of Negro Education* 59 (1): 45–57.

———. 1992. "Understanding Cultural Diversity and Learning." *Educational Researcher* 21 (8): 5–14.

Pfeiffer, Anita B. 1975. "Designing a Bilingual Curriculum." In *Proceedings of the First Inter-American Conference on Bilingual Education,* edited by Rudolph C. Troike & Nancy Modiano. Arlington: Center for Applied Linguistics.

Phillipson, Robert. 1992. *Linguistic Imperialism,* Oxford, England: Oxford University Press.

Pinar, William F. 1988. *Contemporary Curriculum Discourses.* Scottsdale, AZ: Gorsuch Scarisbrick.

Pinar, William F., William M. Reynolds, Patrick Slattery, & Peter M. Taubman. 1995. *Understanding Curriculum: An Introduction to the Study of Historical and Contemporary Curriculum Discourses.* New York: Peter Lang Publishing, Inc.

Sidorkin, Alexander. 1994. Personal communication October 30, 1994.

CHAPTER 8

A CURRICULUM OF THE STREETS THROUGH THE CAMERA LENS: MARGINALIZED CANADIAN WOMEN AND SMOKING

SHARON ANNE COOK

HOW DO WOMEN WHO LIVE ON THE MARGINS OF CANADIAN SOCIETY, or in any Western culture, learn the means of their survival? What is the nature of this "curriculum of the streets," what skills are associated with it, and how do these skills intersect with women's identity? Further, how is the researcher to learn about this women's curriculum, when academics are not typically part of that stratum of society? Using insights generated by Judith Butler, this chapter explores the importance of performing identity as a means of survival in difficult circumstances. This chapter uses photographs to provide insight into a curriculum of the streets as practiced by women in two major urban Canadian centers: Vancouver's Lower East Side and Toronto. It focuses especially on women's use of an important theatrical prop in performing self-identity as part of this curriculum: the cigarette.

For most of its history, smoking has been a countercultural practice used by women. The exception to this pattern was the relatively short period from 1940 to the 1980s, during which smoking was a normative and largely accepted practice across all classes and ethnicities and by both men and women in Canada (Cook 2012). Before that time, however, from the late nineteenth century and after, since the late 1980s, federal, provincial, and municipal restrictions have defined smoking as dangerous to personal and public health, and offensive as a cultural aesthetic. By the turn of the twenty-first century, almost a third of young women in Canada aged 20 to 24 smoked,[1] and this group remains the most resistant of any to smoking cessation programs.[2] By 2005, the rate had dropped to 18 percent for both sexes.[3] It remains at 18.5 percent for women of all ages in 2008 (Statistics Canada 2008). This slice of the Canadian population comprises all classes and includes many vocational identifications. Furthermore, far younger women have become devoted smokers earlier. The average onset age for young women is now about 14 years old. While smoking rates have steadily declined since the 1970s in most sectors of the Canadian population, smoking rates among marginalized women remain high, in many cases up to 90 percent of a given population. A recent study of young women living on the street in Toronto, indicated that 91 percent smoked,[4] while 87 percent used alcohol, and 60 percent took hallucinogens (Erickson, King & Ywit 2007).

In this study, by "curriculum," I refer to "the explicit cognitive and affective goals of formal instruction," as well as what has come to be known as the "hidden curriculum," the "unstated norms, values, and beliefs that are transmitted ... through the underlying structure of meaning" of a given site for learners (Giroux 1998, 23). None of the women at the center of this study were in a formal school setting, but all had negotiated the curriculum of the streets, where the lessons came in both explicit and implicit forms. In this learning site, younger women study the skills, habits, and behaviors of the more experienced practitioners, and then imitate their "teachers", often peers, adding to the skill base and making the act their own.

Judith Butler has enriched our understanding of the meanings of social exchange as instructional practice. Particularly sensitive to detecting counterdiscourse, Butler (1990) argues that stylized images and actions must be mined for meaning.[5] She suggests that repetitions of acts, both social and linguistic, eventually take on the power of ritual, creating a kind of "social magic" for the performer (Butler 1990, 29–48). Such repetitive acts have particular instructive meaning for the socially disenfranchised, creating behavioral codes that, she argues, constitute the person, and which can eventually take on hegemonic authority in cultural terms. Butler's insights are applied most often to social roles that are "transgressive" or boundary-breaking, and so are an ideal platform from which to decode and try to understand the curriculum of the streets in which marginalized women engage. The careful analysis of such practices can also be illuminating for the academic researcher who aims to make sense of the identity performance of these marginalized women.

The textual form that this analysis mines are photographs, some taken *of* young women, and others taken *by* the women themselves to represent the iconic authority of smoking to women in this age group (16 to 19) and in the main, a lower middle-class socioeconomic position. These photographs suggest how some young women have used smoking to negotiate life on the street, to learn from this curriculum site, and to interject their own agency into this visual record. In other words, they are creating their own "social magic." These visual sources create a "window" on the curriculum of the streets through which women demonstrate what must be learned to survive, and what can be altered to shape the social landscape to meet their own needs.

Let us begin with four examples from a much larger fond of photographs relating to women living in the Vancouver Lower East Side. All of these women would be defined by any official standard as "marginalized." For a woman, marginal living occurs outside the protected domestic space, possibly in someone else's home, or even on the streets and is managed with unstable resources. "Private" behaviors and habits, normally exercised in protected spaces are exercised in public by the marginalized woman. The public space is used differently by these women than, for example, middle-class men or women engaged in salaried or waged labor. Marginalized women do not often hold onto regular schedules. While they might not sleep on the street, they live good portions of their day in that context—visiting, arguing, exchanging money, or services for drugs. Very often, they meet their physical needs with an unstable income that is far below the national average, or even below poverty-line figures. Their learning according to this specific curriculum happens in this particular space with other like-minded people.

Many women living in marginalized circumstances choose to be smokers. Drug addiction has a particularly high correlation with smoking. A subset of this group of women who have been exposed to personal violence will be found later in life to be homeless and/or working in the sex trades (Erickson, Kin & Ywit 2007, 53) as well as battling drug addictions. Other research shows that childhood or adolescent experience with physical or sexual abuse is associated with a greater likelihood of early-onset smoking, drinking, illegal drug use, and self-medication during adulthood.[6] Higher rates of smoking and heavier use as well as greater difficulty in quitting later in adulthood has been linked in women with major childhood stressors and adversity, including a history of abuse, violence, and trauma (Haines 2008, 125). Finally, the coincidence between mental illness and smoking is also very high, though the debate continues as to the nature of the relationship (133–134).

Women "living on the edge" also often draw attention to their unconventional status and lifestyles through theatrical gestures enlivened by using the cigarette as a prop. Cigarettes can be used as a simple form of social exchange: if a woman has an abundance of cigarettes one day, she might share them with friends on the understanding that she will be treated the same way when she is out of cigarettes. Cigarettes are used to calm the nerves, to extend the finger and give emphasis during debates, to quell hunger and to replace meals when food is unavailable or unappealing, to provide pleasure when life is particularly difficult, and to signal to others that the smoker is at leisure or in distress. Smoking has multiple uses in different situations, often taking on the intensions of the smoker as an extension of that person's body or emotional range.[7]

Despite the ghettoized nature of both drug addiction and prostitution, women needing to find customers typically do so by visual displays of particular kinds that involve wearing enticing clothing and accessories, displaying skin and "attitude," all of which are intended to demonstrate something particular and identifiable about the women, and to present them as distinct and compelling individuals. However, while women living on the street seem ubiquitous in some areas, the limitations of the documentary record have made it difficult to record their motivations for this lifestyle and substance use.[8]

Since the 1980s, many women with this lifestyle have clustered in Vancouver's Lower East Side. Long known as "skid row," before the 1980s this neighborhood was the home of former seamen, loggers, miners, railway workers, and veterans down on their luck. Accommodation was mainly single-room occupancy hotels scattered around East Hastings.[9] First catapulted into public awareness in the 1970s by a campaign by the federal Central Mortgage and Housing Corporation to renew the inner-city urban housing, and by an early documentary by Alan King, "Skid Row," the area was soon again forgotten.[10] The trial of Robert Picton in 2007, after five years of investigation, and his eventual conviction of first-degree murder in the deaths of six women from the Lower East Side reignited interest in the occupants of this neighborhood. Further, the fact that many of the women who had disappeared were from First Nations' societies, both by Picton's hand and by other violent forces, has fed a growing recognition of this district as racialized, nonwhite and as especially threatening to members of the aboriginal community. The final galvanizing force in rediscovering the Lower East Side was preparations for the 2010 Winter Olympics in Vancouver. The need to "clean up" such areas for the expected influx of visitors was suddenly a major public concern.

In this context then, Lincoln Clarkes, a Vancouver photojournalist, took more than 400 portraits of the women of the lower Eastside over a period of five years. Situating his work in the long tradition of Lewis Hines and Jacob Riis, who used photography as a form of social commentary, Clarkes profiled the conditions of the neighborhood as much as he sought to document the women who lived within it, for the area was his home as well. Through a

Figure 8.1   Photograph by Lincoln Clark, The Worldly Traveler[18]

long and respectful process of inviting each woman to choose her location as well as her stance, gestures, clothing, and props, Clarkes sought to give these (mainly) heroin addicts voice and recognition. It is also arguable that he was honoring the "curriculum of the street," where the women determined their own performance through the details of these still images. It is striking how many of the women have chosen to pose with a cigarette. The collection has appeared as a photo display, a documentary (2001),[11] and a book (2002). At the same time, Clarkes carefully preserved the anonymity of each woman by recording only the location and date of the photograph shoot.

In this first image (see fig. 8.1), a young woman stands before the heavily barred door of the Hastings Medical and Dental Clinic. Wrapped in a rain-coat and jaunty straw Stetson, she holds her cigarette in the time-honored "flag" stance with her other arm wrapped around her waist and supporting the outstretched one. She chooses to face away from the camera, but her thin frame and pale face speak of exhaustion and illness. In holding her cigarette as she has chosen, she hearkens back to an earlier, glamorous age of the woman smoker, more movie siren than most other women shown in this set of photographs. The use of the cigarette is almost coquettish. Were this in a different place and a different time, we could easily imagine this young woman to be anyone's daughter or sister, standing in front of a public building somewhere, enjoying her cigarette and flirting with her boyfriend. Recalling Judith Butler's insights on the importance of ritualized performance in the constitution of identity, one can perceive the "social magic" created by the cigarette in this image as the woman invokes an easier time and age than the one in which she struggles to survive.

The second photograph depicts a woman choosing to avert her eyes from the camera (see fig. 8.2). This woman perches atop a graffiti-covered public porch, where even the graffiti has been defaced. A feathery chalk drawing graces the building wall immediately behind her head, adding a softening effect to her hair, which seems to blend with the drawing. Official architecture and illegal graffiti act as a frame and backdrop, invoking the woman's marginal position in society. The woman is ambiguously clothed: shorts bare her legs, while she wears mittens and a sweater under her leather jacket. The day must be cold, as she has also warm socks in her tasseled boots. She appears older than many of the women in Clarkes' collection, judging from her musculature, and her face and neck. Her highlighted hair suggests care in her appearance, and her necklace, barely peeking out from her shirtfront, adds to this impression. The cigarette hangs from the corner of her closed

Figure 8.2   Photograph by Lincoln Clark, The Combatant[19]

mouth as she stares off into middle space. Interestingly too, she holds drug paraphernalia in her hands, moving it enough to blur the image. Is she nervous, or drug addled, or just seeking a prop for this photographic session? This is beyond our capacity to know. One thing is certain, however: this woman is fully conscious of the identity she is projecting; she has coordinated her wardrobe and projects an image of control. And the cigarette that she holds with such practice in her mouth, adds to that general image of worldliness and control as a further construction of the curriculum of the street she wishes to inhabit.

A third young woman, dressed here in a delicate voile top, stares directly into the camera, but with her face slightly averted, eyeing the camera with a hint of rebellion, just a bit of a scowl (see fig. 8.3). Accessorized very carefully with matching silver bracelet, necklace, and rings, this young woman projects a conventional, even conservative image back to the camera. Her face is made up heavily and carefully with enhancements to her eyebrows, her eyes, and lips. Her sunglasses sit atop her head as would any high school girl's as she stands casually chatting with others. Her outfit is hyper-feminine, and she is thin, also in the prescription of the modern girl. She has loosely wrapped around her a leather jacket in the style developed by young women. And yet, she isn't just any girl in any setting. She stands in front of a site locally called "the old Buddha" with a tangle of pipes and bars framing

Figure 8.3   Photograph by Lincoln Clark, The Flirt[20]

the photograph. Her cigarette is central in the photograph, positioned like a pointer between her index and second fingers. Taken with her hostile expression, the cigarette looks almost like a weapon. The young woman's angry expression reminds us that she is engaged in a zero-sum game in her life, that her chances of ever escaping it are limited, and that every day requires a hard scrabble to continue at all. Her cigarette punctuates the stark realism that she faces daily. The curriculum she accesses is one where her cigarette gives her license to express anger amid confusion.

There are many reference points from popular culture from at least World War I to explain why this young woman adopts this look and this stance with her cigarette and her jacket. She situates herself in a long tradition of the female vamp as smoker. Who is caught in her gaze? Is she the one controlling it, or does the photographer determine her "look," despite his protestations about the agency he offered the women?[12] Is being immortalized by the photographer an act of empowerment, or one of diminishment?

The final image is of a woman, an apparently butch dyke sex worker, in the Lower East Side. Of the four photographs, this woman stares most directly, unflinchingly into the camera, her head slightly raised and her eyes downcast. The power of her gaze contrasts with her sisters' and one immediately gets the message: "Don't mess with me!" There is a regal and almost haughty turn of her head's position, which is belied by the provocative set of her legs. Even more expressive is her vest, unlaced as

Figure 8.4   Photograph by Lincoln Clark, The Provocateur [21]

far as she can manage, if the top is to actually stay on her extraordinarily thin body. As if to further draw attention to her thin arms, she sports several tattoos. Her boots, a cultural code for her butch status, are placed by the woman in the center of the frame. Her hair is short and swept away from her severe and unenhanced face. Her cigarette completes the composition: unlit, it is poised between her fingers in a relaxed grip. But one would misunderstand this pose to assume that it is one of leisure. With her alert, knowing stare, she seems ready to spring on anyone who might threaten her. Her seeming maturity lends dramatic effect to the photograph, as does her conscious performance as a butch sex worker. Here, the unlit cigarette advertises who she is; the cigarette is left to be smoked at her wont. As with the first image with the Hollywood-inspired pose, this woman also creates her own "social magic" of a curriculum through the brandishing of her unlit cigarette. However, here the curriculum is intended to mark her social authority and power, rather than create a vision of the "gal next door."

What can these photographs add to our investigation of a curriculum of the street as expressed in one time and place? The "texts" for these women's performances of identity are consistent with most prescriptive norms for all women in society. The women are thin, in fact, painfully thin, and some look ill. In an ironic twist on one of the most powerful reasons for women smoking—weight control—we see women who have achieved the societal prescription for slenderness, but little else. They remind us through their self-representation both of their normality, and their exceptional status. Cigarette smoking is the least of their worries in terms of a shortened life span. Of course, in addition to their smoking keeping them thin, their drugs almost guarantee it, but at a great cost.

In every case too, the cigarette is used as an expressive instrument, by the woman being photographed. We see here the cigarette used in a wide variety of accepted ways to support the identity performance of each woman as she shapes her own curriculum of the street: cigarette-user as flirt, cigarette-user as worldly traveler, cigarette-user as combatant, and cigarette-user as authoritative and tough dyke.

Other studies have investigated the importance of smoking for women in socially disadvantaged settings. In Canada, Lorraine Greaves has made important contributions to the literature in tracing the relationship between women's smoking and social disadvantage (Greaves 1996), while a study by Frohlich showed the importance of smoking as a shared social practice among Canadian teenagers.[13] The importance of female adolescent social hierarchies in interrupting or encouraging smoking has also been explored by Mitchell and Amos.[14] There is more and more recognition that adolescent society constitutes its own culture within which young women must find a place. Smoking can facilitate inclusion in this social framework,[15] although just how this occurs is still not well understood.[16] Several studies indicate the importance of smoking as an adolescent route to identity formation and re-formation (Haines 2008).

A second set of photographic records has been generated of young women in Toronto through the doctoral research of Dr. Rebecca Haines. Haines (2008) sought young women's narrative and visual explanations for smoking—theirs, their friends', and their families'. She used the Photovoice method to ensure that the young women "retain[ed] complete control over their images, the stories or captions they write about their imagery and how their photographs are shared with a broader public audience" (53). Young female smokers between the ages of 16 and 19 were interviewed and demographic data was collected about the participants. The women were provided with a digital camera and support in affixing captions to the photographs they took. Finally, a photo discussion group occurred, where the images and the captions were discussed by the whole group of 25 participants.

Haines' (2008) research helps to illuminate the world of the adolescent woman smoker. Many of her respondents were disadvantaged, and some had lived on the street. A number of her respondents self-defined as "tough" girls, having survived lives of disruption, abuse, and neglect. While a few were middle class in origin, most came from working-class families, where smoking was common. Most of the young women generated images of locations where smoking occurred, with whom, and under what circumstances. These self-generated records of youth smoking constitute a clear self-defined "curriculum of the streets," where the young women engage in both formal and hidden curricular messages to each other.

The images taken by the young women in this study are unremarkable in terms of the subjects surveyed, the locations, and the technical quality. The strength of the young women's photographs was the freedom with which they controlled how smoking would be represented, in terms of image and caption. The results of these young women's photographic project constitute a female-centered curriculum of the street for the uninitiated. In the final stage of the project, the young women argued among themselves about appropriate captions, or the legitimacy of the images, presented their photographs with passion and knowledge, and offered insider information about such matters as supply networks of cigarettes, cigarettes' value as social currency, and appropriate posturing with the cigarette for a girl wanting to telegraph her social power.

One of several results of this doctoral research design was to lay bare many of the assumptions held by young women smokers, as they constructed and supported a peer-based adolescent culture. Haines achieved an understanding of the cultural context within which adolescent women smokers circulate that helps to explain the importance of smoking within adolescent female culture. She did this by tapping into the female adolescent "curriculum of the street," not with a view to improve or alter this curriculum, but rather to recognize its authority as a knowledge-producer and disseminator. Haines' hope was to more effectively penetrate the socially formalized curriculum, as well as the powerful hidden curriculum for smoking, as a way to encourage these young women to interrogate and explain their smoking practices. Ultimately, she aimed to empower the learners in this adolescent subculture, by providing them with the opportunity to claim ownership of the forces that they recognized had shaped their identities as young women smokers.

Photographs produced by the young women explore a number of issues, among them, the appropriate poses for the smoker.[17] It seems irrelevant whether it is tobacco or marijuana is being smoked: the key pose required through the "formal curriculum" of smoking is that the arm be crooked, in ready reach of the mouth, as a "flag" pose. The photographs indicate that these gestures have achieved a form of social magic. The young women explain that smoking is triggered both by stress, and particular social activities. Some of the photographs critique the young women's self-presentation. One young woman for example, decodes her smoking stance as rebellious and embarrassing, reflecting on the message she sends by lighting up with her lurid nail polish in view. She argues that her nail polish color marks her as immature, while her smoking contradicts this as being a mature act. The latter message can be understood as another component of the "hidden" curriculum.

Taken as a whole, the photographs produced by Lincoln Clarkes and the young women smokers of Haines' Toronto's Photovoice project provide an insight into the formal and hidden curricula of the streets negotiated by women marginalized by family violence, drug addictions, or the vagaries and many social challenges of being an adolescent urban woman in Canada. For all of these women, the cigarette serves as a powerful symbol of authority and identity performance. For many too, it creates a means to draw on the stylized imagery of the gutsy woman smoker that has been a staple of popular culture in this country since the 1920s. It allows some women living on the margins to refashion this trope in ways that served their own identity needs.

The patterns that emerge through the photographic record discussed in this chapter show how a curriculum of acceptable practices, beliefs, and identities become available to young women by virtue of their membership in this society of the streets. They are thus invited to learn from others, and reinforce their own prescriptions of allowable acts and beliefs in forging an identity of the "woman smoker."

ENDNOTES

1. In 2001, 32 percent of this age group is estimated to have smoked. *The National Strategy*, 2001, 6.

2. See for example, *Mixed Messages*, Health Canada (1995a). *Smoking Interventions in the Prenatal and Postpartum Periods*, Ottawa: Minister of Supply and Services Canada; Health Canada (1995b). *Tobacco Resource Material for Prenatal and Post Partum Providers, A Selected Inventory*, Ottawa: Minister of Supply and Services Canada; Health Canada (1996a). *Francophone Women's Tobacco Use in Canada*, Ottawa: Minister of Supply and Services Canada; Health Canada (1995c). *Women and tobacco: A Framework for Action*, Ottawa: Minister of Supply and Services; Health Canada (1995d). *Smoking and Pregnancy: A Woman's Dilemma*, Ottawa: Minister of Supply and Services; Health Canada (1995e).

3. Health Canada (1996b, 2000, 2005, 2006). Canadian Tobacco Use Monitoring Survey.

4. Other studies have found a similar pattern, that between 80 and 90 percent of alcohol and drug users also smoke. Malmo, Gail. 2007. "Addressing Tobacco Dependency in Women's Substance Use Treatment", in *Highs & Lows: Canadian Perspectives on Women and Substance Use* edited by Nancy Poole and Lorraine Greaves, 324. Toronto: British Columbia Centre of Excellence for Women's Health.

5. For a complex and revealing argument around the functions and means of "performance" for women, particularly "transgressive" women bridging established norms of propriety, see Butler, J. (1990).

6. Vermeiren, R., Schwab-Stone, M., Deboutte, D., Leckman, D & Ruchkin, V. 2003.
   Violence exposure and substance use in adolescents: Findings from three countries. *Pediatrics* 111 (3): 535–540, as cited in Erickson, P.G., King, K. and Ywit. 2007. "On the Street: Influences on Homelessness in Young Women," in *Highs & Lows: Canadian Perspectives on Women and Substance Use*, edited by Nancy Poole and Lorraine Greaves, 52–53. Toronto: British Columbia Centre of Excellence for Women's Health.

7. Lennon, A., Gallois, C., Owen, N. And McDermott, L. 2005. "Young Women as Smokers and Nonsmokers: A Qualitative Social Identity Approach", *Qualitative Health Research*, 15 (10): 1345–1359; Nichter, M., Vuckovic, N., Quintero, G. and Ritenbaugh, C. (1997). Smoking experimentation and initiation among adolescent girls: qualitative and quantitative findings. *Tobacco Control*, 6 (4): 285–295.

8. There have been some significant advances in our knowledge within the past decade, however. Figuring importantly in adding to our understanding of how women see themselves are such collections as Poole, N. and Greaves, L., eds. 2007. *Highs & Lows: Canadian Perspectives on Women and Substance Use*. Toronto: British Columbia Centre of Excellence for Women's Health, and Haines 2008.

9. Canning, P. 2002. Photographer as Witness in Clarkes, L. *Heroines: Photographs*. Vancouver: Anvil Press.

10. King, A. 1957. *Skid Row*. Script by Ben Maartman, Narration by Art Hives.

11. Peace Arch Entertainment, *Heroines: A Photographic Obsession*, 2001.

12. Clarkes, introduction.

13. Frohlich, K.L., Potvin, L., Chabot, P. and Coring, E. 2002a. A theoretical and empirical analysis of context: neighborhoods, smoking and youth. *Social Science and Medicine, 54 (9), 1401–1417,* Frohlich, K.L., Potvin, L., Gauvin, L. and Chabot, P. (2002b). Youth smoking initiation: disentangling context from composition *Health and Place*, 8 (3), 153–166.

14. Mitchell, L. and Amos, A. 1997. "Girls, Pecking Order and Smoking." *Social Science and Medicine*, 44 (12): 1861–1869.

15. McCracken, G. 1992. Got A Smoke? A Cultural Account of Tobacco Use in the Lives of Contemporary Teens. Toronto, ON: Ontario Ministry of Health Tobacco Strategy.

16. Kobus, K. 2003. Peers and adolescent smoking. *Addiction* 98 (Suppl 1): s37–s55.

17. Unfortunately, permission to reproduce the photographs has been denied.

18. Clarkes, 13 January 2002, Hastings Medical and Dental Clinic, 50 East Hastings Street, Vancouver, p. 101. Permission to reproduce granted by Anvil Press.

19. Clarkes, November 21, 2000, Pigeon Park, West Hastings and Carrall Street, Vancouver, 9. Permission to reproduce granted by Anvil Press.

20. Clarkes, July 1, 2001, old Smiling Buddha, 109 East Hastings Street, Vancouver. Permission to reproduce granted by Anvil Press, 31

21. Clarkes, August 8, 1998, back door, The Only Seafood, 20 East Hastings Street, Vancouver. Permission to reproduce granted by Anvil Press.

REFERENCES

Butler, J. 1990. *Gender Trouble: Feminism and the Subversion of Identity*, London: Routledge.

———. 1996. "Performativity's Social Magic." In *The Social and Political Body*, edited by Schatzki, T. R. & Natter, W., 29–48. New York and London: The Guilford Press.

Clarkes, L. 2002. *Heroines: The Photographs of Lincoln Clarkes*. Vancouver. BC: Anvil Press.

Cook, S. A. 2012. *Sex, Lies and Cigarettes: Canadian Women, Smoking and Visual Culture, 1880–1990*. Kingston and Montreal: McGill-Queen's University Press.

Erickson, P. G., King, K. & Ywit. 2007. "On the Street: Influences on Homelessness in Young Women" in *Highs & Lows: Canadian Perspectives on Women and Substance Use*, edited by N. Poole & L. Greaves, 52–53. Toronto: British Columbia Centre of Excellence for Women's Health

Frohlich, K. L., Potvin, L., Chabot, P. & Coring, E. 2002a. "A Theoretical and Empirical Analysis of Context: Neighborhoods, Smoking and Youth." *Social Science and Medicine* 54 *(9)*: 1401–1417.

Frohlich, K. L., Potvin, L., Gauvin, L. & Chabot, P. 2002b. "Youth Smoking Initiation: Disentangling Context from Composition." *Health and Place* 8 (3): 153–166.

Giroux, H. A. 1998. *Teachers as Intellectuals: Toward a Critical Pedagogy of Learning.* New York: Bergin and Garvey, 23.

Haines, R. 2008. "Smoke, in My Eyes: A Bourdieusian Account of Young Women's Tobacco Use." PhD Thesis, University of Toronto.

Health Canada. 1995a. *Mixed Messages.* Ottawa: Minister of Supply and Services Canada.

————. 1995b. *Smoking Interventions in the Prenatal and Postpartum Periods.* Ottawa: Minister of Supply and Services Canada.

————. 1995c. *Francophone Women's Tobacco Use in Canada.* Ottawa: Minister of Supply and Services Canada.

————. 1995d. *Women and Tobacco: A Framework for Action.* Ottawa: Minister of Supply and Services.

————. 1995e. *Smoking and Pregnancy: A Woman's Dilemma.* Ottawa: Minister of Supply and Services.

————. 1996a. *Tobacco Resource Material for Prenatal and Post Partum Providers, A Selected Inventory.* Ottawa: Minister of Supply and Services Canada

————. 1996b.*Canadian Tobacco Use Monitoring Survey.* Ottawa: Minister of Supply and Services.

————. 2000. *Canadian Tobacco Use Monitoring Survey.* Ottawa: Minister of Supply and Services.

————. 2001. *The National Strategy.* Ottawa: Minister of Supply and Services.

————. 2005. *Canadian Tobacco Use Monitoring Survey.* Ottawa: Minister of Supply and Services.

————. 2006. *Canadian Tobacco Use Monitoring Survey.* Ottawa: Minister of Supply and Services.

Kobus, K. 2003. "Peers and Adolescent Smoking." *Addiction* 98 (Suppl 1): s37–s55.

Lennon, A., Gallois, C., Owen, N. & McDermott, L. 2005. "Young Women as Smokers and Nonsmokers: A Qualitative Social Identity Approach." *Qualitative Health Research*, 15 (10): 1345–1359.

Mitchell, L. & Amos, A. 1997. "Girls, Pecking Order and Smoking." *Social Science and Medicine*, 44 (12): 1861–1869.

Malmo, Gail. 2007. "Addressing Tobacco Dependency in Women's Substance Use Treatment." In *Highs & Lows: Canadian Perspectives on Women and Substance Use* edited by Nancy Poole and Lorraine Greaves, 324. Toronto: British Columbia Centre of Excellence for Women's Health.

McCracken, G. 1992. *Got A Smoke? A Cultural Account of Tobacco Use in the Lives of Contemporary Teens.* Toronto, ON: Ontario Ministry of Health Tobacco Strategy.

Nichter, M., Vuckovic, N., Quintero, G. & Ritenbaugh, C. (1997). "Smoking Experimentation and Initiation among Adolescent Girls: Qualitative and Quantitative Findings." *Tobacco Control,* 6 (4): 285–295.

Poole, N. & Greaves, L. eds. 2007. *Highs & Lows: Canadian Perspectives on Women and Substance Use.* Toronto: British Columbia Centre of Excellence for Women's Health, and Haines 2008.

Statistics Canada. 2008. *Youth Smoking Survery.* Ottawa: Minister of Supply and Services.

Vermeiren, R., Schwab-Stone, M., Deboutte, D., Leckman, D., & Ruchkin, V. 2003. "Violence Exposure and Substance Use in Adolescents: Findings from Three Countries." *Pediatrics* 111 (3): 535–540.

PART 3

CURRICULUM, INTERTEXTS, AND WISDOM TRADITIONS

CHAPTER 9

REVISITING AOKI'S "INSPIRITING THE CURRICULUM"

WILLIAM. E. DOLL, JR.

> *Now I a fourfold vision see,*
> *And a fourfold vision is given to me;*
> *'Tis fourfold in my supreme delight*
> *And threefold in soft Beulah's night*
> *And twofold Always. May God us keep*
> *From Single vision & Newton's Sleep!*[1]

"MAY GOD US KEEP FROM SINGLE VISION." RATHER than allowing the materialist vision that Blake attributes to Newton in this plea to overwhelm us, let it provide a vision that integrates the material with the intellectual, the emotional, and most of all, the spiritual. This vision is one that resonates well with a plea: Aoki, the "father" of Canadian curriculum theory, makes in his 1978 essay, "Toward Curriculum Inquiry in a New Key," in *Curriculum in a New Key*. In this essay, Aoki asks us to

> increase our *vision* of whatever we are viewing through the employment of as many perspectives as we can find appropriate... (96; emphasis added)[2].

Here Aoki recommends a multifocal perspective: one integrating the empirical-analytic, the situational-interpretative, and the critical-theoretical. The first two of these perspectives—the empirical-analytical (a scientific frame) and the situational-interpretative (a humanities frame)—I find akin to the scientific/rational and narrative/interpretative (or storied) perspectives of

Jerome Bruner, a major figure in educational psychology, philosophy, and cognitive learning theory. Bruner develops these perspectives in his essay, "Two Modes of Thought." Bruner, in this essay, does comment on the scientific (our usual, quantitative research procedure) in ways quite akin to Aoki's, and while his narrative or storied perspective (with its qualitative research approach) has strong phenomenological and cultural thrusts, again akin to Aoki's situational-interpretive perspective. However, Bruner does not mention a third mode or way, as Aoki does. He does not mention, in Blake's terms, a "supreme" or Spiritual way of being (1802, letter 40). Personally, I align myself with Aoki and with Blake, more than with Bruner, proposing that we approach life and our activities in life, including teaching and curriculum design, in a way that allows the spirit or soul of these activities and of ourselves to come forth. Such a vision helps, I believe, in understanding and appreciating Aoki's notion of "inspiriting" a curriculum (1987, 1996).

Before discussing Aoki's essays and his concept of *inspiriting* though, I would like to ponder just a bit about Aoki's critical-theoretical perspective, brought forth in his 1978 essay, "Toward Curriculum Inquiry in a New Key." In this essay, written for a particular academic conference on looking at art education from a phenomenological perspective, Aoki brings forth *the power of reflection* in helping us free ourselves from "hidden assumptions" (105). The "moral attitude of liberation" in this approach is colored by a particular, neo-Marxist, political framework (106). Acknowledging the contributions, this framework has helped us to see the hidden assumptions underlying our actions (often our teaching actions). Aoki makes a nod toward the spiritual in this 1978 essay when he talks of critical reflection or "critically reflective social theory" (107). For him, critical reflection not only brings forth the hidden, examining both human intentions and assumptions, it also makes "conscious the unconscious," and "leads to an understanding of what is beyond" (106). In these two comments, I believe that the focus of Aoki's critical reflection not only presages the spirituality he brings forth in his 1987 and 1996 essays, but is also allied with my own *reflexive reflection,* whereby one gains insight into not only that which is studied, but also into one's own method of studying, or indeed one's way of being. Such interpretative insight leads, I believe, into a wondering of "what is beyond"; and with this wondering comes a search for the spirit or soul of a subject. My framework for a third perspective then, is more theological than political.

On the next page is an image of what I call the 3 S's: Science, Story, and Spirit (fig. 9.1).[3] Each has its own mode of thought: analytic, interpretative, and intuitive. The three flow into, through, and with one another in that great mystery we call life and our experience of it. I believe curriculum,

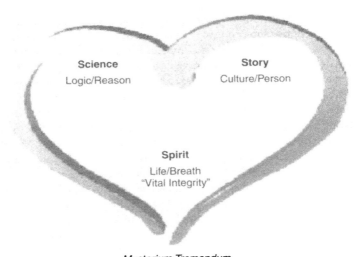

Science
Logic/Reason

Story
Culture/Person

Spirit
Life/Breath
"Vital Integrity"

Mysterium Tremendum

Figure 9.1   Mysterium Tremendum

especially as *currere*,[4] is infused with, indeed is permeated with, spirit. Such a curriculum is alive, vital, and dynamic.

The three S's displayed here[5] are intended to illustrate *multiple perspectives*, a framework prominent throughout Aoki's writings. Such a framework is also key for Gregory Bateson (1972, 1988), an insightful anthropologist, cyberneticist, educator, and sociologist. The phrase Bateson (1988) uses (akin to Aoki's term "bifocal" [1978, 106]), is "binocular vision" (73–74). In such vision, there is *both* unity and difference. Binoculars bring two separate lines of sight into focus, but each eye has its own vision. The depth that we see using binoculars is due to this act of bringing different perspectives into unifying (but not unified) relations. For Bateson, it is through *relations of difference* that learning, as the acquiring of new insights, occurs. In focusing on *relations among differences* (not just the differences themselves), Bateson is seeking to find "the difference which makes a difference" (105ff), the difference that helps us acquire a new perspective. Here, I believe Bateson to be in agreement with Aoki[6] who, borrowing a quote from Hans-Georg Gadamer, says that in a dialectical relationship between self and other, "the other world we encounter...has not only its own truth in itself, but also its own truth for us" (Aoki 1987, 242). This *truth for us* is a "deeper understanding," "a deeper awareness," of who we are; in a sense, a recursive coming to know ourselves for the first time, truly a difference that makes a difference.

In Bateson's view, the *really real of reality* (and of teaching and learning) focuses on relations, not on discrete facts, data, or objects. I believe Aoki would agree; for both Aoki and Bateson encourage us to adopt a *new vision* for curriculum design and instructional activity: one focusing on Relations, Rich in context, Recursive in design, and Rigorous in application.[7]

Focusing on the *relations among facts,* not on the facts themselves, is a challenge for us brought up to honor and respect facts as the foundational building blocks of knowledge. As Alfred North Whitehead (1967) points out, though, facts by themselves, in their discreteness, are "dead," "barren," "useless," and "lifeless". For him, it is what one does with the facts, how one relates to facts, how facts relate to each other, to the situation, environment, and the culture in which they are enmeshed that is important.[8] Bateson (1972) calls such a contextual framework, an "ecology of mind."

Those who have laid a foundation for my thinking about the power and importance of relations are, in addition to Ted Aoki and Gregory Bateson, Jacques Derrida, John Dewey, Hans-Georg Gadamer, N. Katherine Hayles, Stuart Kauffman, Bruno LaTour, François Lyotard, Martin Heidegger, Lynn Margulis, C. S. Peirce, Ilya Prigogine, Michel Serres, Alfred North Whitehead, and Ludwig Wittgenstein, among others. Those curricularists in Canada who I believe have done seminal work in helping us all see curriculum and instruction in a new (*relational*) light are—besides Ted Aoki—Brent Davis, Rita Irwin, David Jardine, Tom Kieran, Antoinette Oberg, William Pinar, Dennis Sumara, and Donna Trueit. My own work has, I hope, been of some help in furthering this relational perspective.

At this point, it might be of value to provide an instance of such a relational perspective. A number of years ago, Dennis Sumara and Brent Davis (2006) talked of (and still do talk of) having students use "stickies" when reading a story. On the stickies (commonly known as "Post-it-Notes") or in notebooks, the students write a short note about the word, phrase, or idea that attracts their attention. In recursive fashion, at a later time, the students read the story again, *and* the stickies. This act of *seeing again, yet for the first time*[9] occurs as the students read not only the story again, but also read their stickies. In effect, they reflect on their original reflections. Such *reflection on reflection* opens up a whole new world of thinking, that of *Reflexivity*. In this activity of recursive process, one comes to understand better not only the story, but also one's self reading the story. One's spirit, *vital integrity*, or soul (to use Aoki's word)[10] now comes in union with that which is being studied. Here one is studying self as well as text. Studying here goes beyond learning, a point William Pinar (2006) emphasizes, drawing on Alan Block and Joseph Schwab (114). In such studying, we delve into both the text and into ourselves as textual interpreters.

The notion of reflexivity, with its feedback loops where we might understand self as we understand text, enthused Gregory Bateson at the Macy Conferences and ultimately became the grounding for his educational epistemology (see Hayles, 1999). Indeed it was shortly after the conferences (1946–1953) that Bateson returned, for a second time, to reflect (1958) on his original reflection put forth in his novel *Naven*, describing his 1920's anthropological work with the Iatmul. The Iatmul are a head-hunting tribe in New Guinea, who manage to organize their rule-free society by utilizing an elaborate, cross-dressing ceremony.[11]

Leaving for future conversation the notion of a society organized not according to rules (hence "methodized") but around rituals, I'd like to (re) turn to Aoki's (antimethodizing) 1987 essay, "Inspiriting Curriculum." Here Aoki asks, indeed *implores*, us to be aware that even the most seemingly benign educational act, is a political act, one with strong ethical implications. Drawing on story, which Aoki does so well, he recounts his early years of teaching as the sole teacher in a one-room school (grades one to eight) in a Hutterite school in 1945. Following the set, methodized curriculum, he used reading primers: *We Work and Play,* and *We Think and Do.* In later reflections, he realized he was not merely having the students *do* reading, he was inadvertently "teaching an ethic—an ethic that separated work from play, that sublimated work and deemphasized play" (357). In our Calvinist oriented, North American culture such a hierarchal separation has encouraged us not only to frame learning in terms of hard work, but also to neglect the creativity that emerges from play (see Doll et al. 2005; Triche and McKnight 2004). In his reflection of the reading primer *Think and Do*, Aoki (1987) became aware of another dichotomous separation: *Think* first, *Do* second. A superficial reaction to this linear frame might well be—Of course! We do not wish to do without first having thought. Doing here, though, becomes derivative of thought: "thinking is primary, doing is secondary" (358). When we have thought well, we have "got it," "nailed it"—into a coffin, as Michel Serres might say (1997). This emphasis, I'd say overemphasis, on rationality leaves us blind to the possibilities that can emerge from being and living in the world, from experiencing our world. It is, as we all know, a lived curriculum not a planned (or methodized) curriculum that Aoki encourages us to develop. More accurately, he encourages us to find a useful, I'd even say an essential, tension between the lived and the planned (1986, 161). A curriculum that is only, or heavily, planned reduces the educational act to a series of skills and techniques, rendering it to a "half-life of what it might be" (Aoki 1987, 357). Moreover, I would say, a curriculum that is only or heavily lived as planned, renders our lived experiences null and void. What is needed, instead, is a curriculum infused with, inspirited with, "good" or "appropriate" tension: "To be alive is to be appropriately tensioned"; to be "tensionless, like a limp violin string, is to be dead" (360).[12] Educational language is filled with words and phrases such as balance, equality, and in-the-middle. These words and phrases are too often are filled with stasis. Life and education need not live in stasis, but should have just the right amount of *difference*, of tension. That Aoki brings out this point in the late 1980s, when the new sciences of chaos and complexity, with their sense of dynamic interaction, were just barely on the horizon of intellectual (let alone educational) thought, is a tribute to his foresight. In his lifetime, he has seen what we are still struggling to see.

To inspirit a curriculum (Aoki 1987, 1996)[13] is to bring life to it, to infuse it with a soul; indeed, to bring its deadness back to life, as it were. The word spirit—over 160 definitions in the *Oxford English Dictionary Online*—literally means, "to give breath to," to animate, bring life to, infuse with being. It is synonymous with soul. In the Christian theological sense, spirit is Holy: it caused John to leap in Elizabeth's womb, it impregnated Mary so that Jesus might be born, it visited the disciples and *activated* them, indeed infused them with the *power* to preach the gospel of Jesus, which became the Christian message.[14] There are, of course, unholy spirits, those to be exorcised: the devil, evilness, the "unclean spirit," who finding no rest in waterless places, returns home and finding it empty, brings into it "seven other spirits more evil than himself" (Matt.12:43 Oxford Annotated Bible). In a nontheological frame, spirit is a force that animates, infusing a situation or entity (team, school, organization, movement) with a *power*, essentially the power-to-do that shapes the quality or mode of a situation or entity. There are also blithe and playful spirits, as well as those who inhabit the pages of Shakespeare and Dickens and other writers from the misty isles. For Aoki (1987) though, spirit is a sense of hope, one that can help us as educators and curricularists "reclaim the fullness of body and soul" (359). To inspirit curriculum is to open it to the fullness of possibilities inherent in a situation through relations with the world at large, to acknowledge *more-ness* (Huebner, 1999), the ineffable, the stochastic, that which is greater than, and beyond control of, our human selves.

In advocating we build a curriculum around the concept of relations that we infuse curriculum with the spirit of "dwelling aright in thoughtful living with others" (Aoki 1987, 365), Aoki wisely asks us to look closely, deconstructively if we will, at the notion of relations. He asks us to develop a "notion of relationship...that *breaks* with the notion of application" (364, emphasis added). That is, to break with the traditional relation of practice to theory, where *practice is only* an application of theory. This is not the sort of curriculum vision Aoki advocates. Nor, do I believe, is it the sort of vision any of us should advocate, for such a misguided vision leads to the "teaching-as-telling" model both Donna Trueit and Sarah Pratt (2006) decry. *Living with*, instead of learning about, is the *New Key* Aoki offers us.

Playing, almost anthropomorphically, with curriculum as a concept, Aoki asks us to conceive of curriculum as "containing" an invitation: "an invitation to teachers and students to enter into it", "to find [in it] a live tension that will allow the teachers and the students to say, 'We live curriculum'" (Aoki 1987, 362). Such an invitation is akin to John Dewey's exhortation that we consider curriculum as an activity into which we "plunge" (Dewey 1958/1934, 53), feeling the situation with "passion" and "affection" (Dewey 1917, 10) of being immersed, of "surrendering ourselves" to the situation, in order to experience the fullness of the situation and the development of our own abilities.

There are, of course, many differences among Aoki, Bateson, Dewey, Whitehead, and the new science of complexity—differences that have inspired my wandering reflections written here. In Aoki's own vast and deep reflections on curriculum, reflections that I hope I have in some small way honored in this chapter, there is much that I have not touched on. Beside the Japanese/Canadian connection about which Aoki (1992) writes movingly (263–277), I am fascinated by what might be called his Heideggerian turn, toward spaces of possibilities, spaces inhabited by silence, ponderings, and questing. This, though, is another topic for another chapter, written some other time. For now, I am happy to reflect on Spirit and its aesthetic companion, the Sacred, supreme among Blake's visions, the epitome of Ted Aoki's "Curriculum in a New Key."

ENDNOTES

1. William Blake, an early nineteenth century visionary and mystic, worried (mistakenly) that the visions Isaac Newton had in his sleep would lead our Western culture into a universalizing, *materialistic* frame. For more, see *The Letters of William Blake, 3rd ed.* (Letter No. 40), Geoffrey. Keynes ed., (Oxford University Press, 1980). Single vision refers to this materialistic frame; twofold vision brings in the intellectual; three fold the emotional and imaginary; fourfold (supreme) the spiritual (43–46). For an interpretation of Blake's symbols see *A Blake Dictionary*, Samuel. Damon ed., (Brown University Press, 1965).
2. All page references to Aoki's statements are from the Pinar and Irwin book (2005); the year references are to when Aoki's essay were written.
3. The 3 S's, along with the 5 C's and 4 R's, are my (playful) way of envisioning a curriculum appropriate for our post-modern age. See, Doll et al. 2005.
4. The concept of curriculum as *currere* can be found in William Pinar et al. 1995; and in his 2004 book.
5. I am indebted to Brent Davis for the particular form of this image. Thanks.

6. Aoki's own comments about the importance of difference—"it is the differ-ence that really matters"—come in his 1987 essay, "Notions of Leadership and Identity" (Ch. 21, in Pinar & Irwin, 354).

7. These 4 R's are my alternative to Ralph Tyler's 4 steps to developing a good curriculum. See Doll, Chapter 7 1993.

8. A common view of scientific activity is that it consists essentially of collect-ing facts/data. Lately though, there is a movement to consider the role con-versation plays in the development of scientific thought. As Joseph Vining says, "Against the statics of knowledge" (gathering of facts) there arises the view that the "essence of scientific life [lies] in the 'dynamics of prac-tice' "(2004, 275), with the heart of this practice being *conversation*. Donna Trueit is working on the role of conversation in teaching (2009).

9. T. S. Eliot, in "Little Giddeon," the last poem in his "Four Quartets" 1944, expresses this thought poetically when he says:
   We shall not cease from exploration,
   and the end of all our exploring,
   will be to arrive where we started
   and know the place for the first time.

10. Aoki, Ted. 1987. "Inspiriting the Curriculum" in *Curriculum in a new key* 2005, edited by Pinar & Irwin, 362. (New York: Peter Lang Publishing, Inc).

11. *Naven* is a complicated, transvestite ceremony, often performed when a male youth makes his first (sometimes human) kill. Laura Jewett (in Doll et al., 2005) layers some of her interesting reflections on Bateson's reflections.

12. The notion of "dynamic tensionality" (Pinar & Irwin 2005, 33, 61, 161, 232) is a key theme throughout Aoki's work. Again he presages the new sciences of chaos and complexity. For an introduction to these sciences and their educational implications see B. Davis and D. Sumara 2006; W. Doll et al. 2005; M. Mason 2008.

13. The 1996 essay, "Spinning Inspiriting Images" takes a tack—that of the 3rd space—different from the 1987 essay. I will not go into this notion of a 3rd space where possibilities abound but will recommend those inter-ested to read Hongyu Wang 2004, 2006, and Sean Buckreis 2010. Again, Aoki's bringing forth the notion of such a space "where newness can enter"; "spaces of possibilities," those "ambivalent spaces between life and non-life, between the known and the unknown, between universals and particulars, even between possibilities and impossibilities where inspiriting newness is ongoingly constituted and reconstituted" (1996, 422) is a tribute to his farsightedness.

14. The O.E.D. 2008, online talks of Spirit infusing life into, "actuating" I, 3, c. In the second set of definitions, it talks of Spirit as "the active essence or essential power of the Deity, conceived as a creative, animating, or inspir-ing influence" II, 6, a. This sense of life having a vibrancy to it, a certain dynamic integration which *inspires all* who look at it, is what motivates Stuart Kauffman, then living in New Mexico (the Land of Enchantment), to write his *Reinventing the Sacred* 2008.

REFERENCES

Aoki, Ted. 1978. "Toward Curriculum Inquiry in a New Key." In *Curriculum in a New Key* edited by William Pinar, William & Rita Irwin, 89–110. [2005]. New York: Peter Lang Publishing, Inc.

———. 1986. "Teaching as Indwelling Between Two Curriculum Worlds." In *Curriculum in a New Key* edited by William Pinar, William & Rita Irwin, 159–165. [2005]. New York: Peter Lang Publishing, Inc.

———. 1987. "Inspiriting the Curriculum," In *Curriculum in a New Key* edited by William Pinar, William & Rita Irwin, 357–363. [2005]. New York: Peter Lang Publishing, Inc.

———.1992. "In the Midst of Slippery Theme-Worlds: Living as Designers of Japanese Canadian Curriculum." In *Curriculum in a New Key* edited by William Pinar, William & Rita Irwin, 263–276. [2005]. New York: Peter Lang Publishing, Inc.

———. 1996. "Spinning Inspiriting Images in the Midst of Planned and Live(d) Curricula." In *Curriculum in a New Key* edited by William Pinar, William & Rita Irwin, 413–423. [2005]. New York: Peter Lang Publishing, Inc.

Bateson, Gregory. 1972. *Steps to an Ecology of Mind.* New York: Ballantine.

———. 1988. *Mind and Nature: A Necessary Unity.* New York: Bantam. (Original publication, 1979).

Blake, William.1802. Poem, "With happiness stretched…." In *The Letters of William Blake, 3rd edition revised* (No. 40) by Gregory Keynes. New York: Oxford University Press.

Bruner, Jerome. 1986. *Actual Mind, Possible Worlds.* Cambridge, MA: Harvard.

Buckreis, Sean. 2010. "Reflections on Teaching: Searching for a Third Space." Louisiana State University Dissertation.

Damon, Samuel. 1965. *A Blake Dictionary.* Providence, R.I: Brown.

Davis, Brent, & Dennis Sumara. 2006. *Complexity and Education.* Mahweh, NJ: Erlbaum.

Dewey, John. 1917. "The Need for a Recovery of Philosophy." In *Creative Intelligence*, 3–69. New York: Holt.

———. 1958. *Art as Experience.* New York: Capricorn. (Original publication, 1934)

Doll, William, M. Jayne Fleener, DonnaTrueit, & John St.Julien, eds. 2005. *Chaos, Complexity, Curriculum, and Culture.* New York: Peter Lang Publishing, Inc.

Eliot, T. S. 1944. "Little Gidding," Verse 5 in "The Four Quartets," in *Collective Poems, 1909–1962, of T.S. Eliot.* New York: Harcourt, Brace.

Gray, W. S. (1946). Ed. *We Work and Play and We Think and Do.* Toronto: W. J. Gage and Co.

Kauffman, Stuart. 2008. *Reinventing the Sacred.* New York: Basic Books.

Keynes, Geofrey. 1980. *The Letters of William Blake, 3rd edition.* New York: Oxford University Press.

Hayles, N. Katherine. 1999. *How We Became Posthuman.* Chicago: University of Chicago Press.

Huebner, Dwayne. 1999. *The Lure of the Transcendent*, Vicki Hillis, ed. New York: Peter Lang Publishing, Inc.

Jewett, Laura. 2005. "Minding Culture." In *Chaos, Complexity, Curriculum, and Culture,* edited by William Doll. New York: Peter Lang Publishing, Inc.

Mason, Mark. 2008. *Complexity Theory and the Philosophy of Education.* Chichester, UK: Wiley-Blackwell.

Oxford English Dictionary (OED online, 1989 edition). Oxford: Oxford University Press.

Pinar, William. 2004. *What is Curriculum Theory?* New York: Peter Lang Publishing, Inc.

———. 2006. *The Synoptic Text Today.* New York: Peter Lang Publishing, Inc.

Pinar, William, William Reynolds, Patrick Slattery, & Peter Taubman, eds. 1995. *Understanding Curriculum.* New York: Peter Lang Publishing, Inc.

Pinar, William, & Rita Irwin, eds. 2005. *Curriculum in a New Key.* New York: Peter Lang Publishing, Inc.

Serres, Michel. 1997. *Troubadour of Knowledge.* Translated by Sarah Glaser & William Paulson. Ann Arbor, MI: University of Michigan Press. (Original French publication, *Le Tiers- Instruit,* 1991)

Sumara, Dennis. 1997. "Reading is an Interpretive Activity." *Update: The Journal of the British Columbia Teachers' Association* 39 (1): 4–10.

Triche, Stephen, & Douglas McKnight. 2004. "The Quest for Method: The Legacy of Peter Ramus," *History of Education* 33 (1): 39–54.

Trueit, Donna. 2009. "Thinking Complexly: *Being*-in-Relation." Paper presented at the Third International Association for the Advancement of Curriculum Studies (IAACS) Tri-Annual Conference, Capetown, South Africa.

Trueit, Donna, & Sarah Pratt. 2006. "Complex Conversations in Education: Moving Away from   Teaching-as-Telling." Paper presented at the Second IAACS Tri-Annual Conference,   Tampere, Finland.

Vining, Joseph. 2004. *From Newton's Sleep.* Princeton NJ Princeton University Press.

Wang, Hongyu. 2004. *The Call From the Stranger on a Journey Home: Curriculum in Third Space.* New York: Peter Lang Publishing Inc.

———. 2006. "Speaking as an Alien: Is a Curriculum in a Third Space Possible?," *Journal of Curriculum Theorizing* 22 (1).

Whitehead, Alfred North. 1967 [1929]. *The Aims of Education and Other Essays.* New York: The Free Press.

CHAPTER 10

WABI SABI AND THE PEDAGOGICAL COUNTENANCE OF NAMES

JACKIE SEIDEL AND DAVID W. JARDINE

> *Wabi Sabi is a way of seeing the world that is at the heart of Japanese culture. It finds beauty and harmony in what is simple, imperfect, natural, modest, and mysterious. It can be a little dark, but it is also warm and comfortable. It maybe be best understood as a feeling, rather than as an idea.*
>
> Reibstein and Young 2008, n.p.

I

These considerations began with our discovery of a new picture book entitled *Wabi Sabi*, written by Mark Reibstein with stunning artwork ("collages" made from "a collection of timeworn human-made as well as natural materials" [cited from the inside back cover]) by Ed Young.

The book begins with a description of the meaning of the concept of *Wabi Sabi*, and a Zen proverb:

> *Kosho Hanaya Wo Danzu.*
> An old pine tree can teach you the sacred truths. (n.p.)

We then turn the page and are ushered into the book's mysteries and exquisite beauty. Oriented as if a scroll, opening not left to right but top to bottom, four texts inhabit each page simultaneously: the narrative text of the story, an English haiku, a Japanese haiku (by Basho and Shiki, in Japanese

Kanji, with English translations provided at the end of the story) and the collage illustrations.

Between these multiple texts, we enter the story of Wabi Sabi, a cat in Kyoto, Japan.

Near the beginning of the tale, strangers appear, "visitors from another country" (n.p.), who ask Wabi Sabi's master about the meaning of the cat's name. Her master responds, with an intake of breath, "That's hard to explain." The rest of the story unfolds from this moment, as Wabi Sabi experiences a profound unsettling of her identity: "It had never occurred to her before that *wabi sabi* was anything more than her name" (n.p.). Curious, she asks her animal friends about the meaning of her name. They, too, say that it is hard to explain. A passing bird tells her that a monkey named Kosho can help her:

A wise old monkey
living among the pine trees
knows *wabi sabi*. (n.p.)

Wabi Sabi sets off on a journey, through the dazzling, shining city and then to the woods of Mount Hiei, where she falls asleep beneath an old pine tree. She awakens to the sounds of the monkey Kosho preparing tea nearby. To her query about her name, the monkey also responds with "That's hard to explain," and invites Wabi Sabi to "Listen. Watch. Feel" (n.p.).

The monkey makes tea as if dancing, holding wooden and clay objects as if gold, and speaks to her in haiku. Wabi Sabi notices the designs of life in the woods and realizes that everything is "alive and dying" at once. Finally, Wabi Sabi upon seeing a reflection of herself in her tea whispers, "Now I understand." On her way home, "because she did not hurry," she finds Ginkakuji, the "Silver Temple" (n.p.). Inspired by the simple beauty, she composes three haiku before continuing on her journey. When she arrives home, Wabi Sabi curls up on her straw mat in the kitchen, warm, content, still smelling "the wind in her fur" and feeling her "journey's steps deep in her bones" (n.p.).

Her master is happy to see her: "Wabi Sabi!" she cries, "Where have you been?"

Wabi Sabi purrs, "That's hard to explain" (n.p.).

II

Seventeen years ago now, driving my ten-year-old son to school, deep winter days of overhead grayness. Suddenly: "Dad, what would have happened if we had called trees 'weekends' and weekends 'trees'?"

Part of the pedagogical countenance of teaching is to love such moments, since they can open up, for teachers and students alike, a whole, wild, living territory in which much is to be taught and learned, for all concerned. Even if this is not literally one's own child speaking, it is still one's kin, and this boy's words are still about words, about the very thing we teachers continuously teach with and about. There is so much here for a teacher to experience, to explore, to *enjoy*, in this happenstance question, "What would have happened?" Here is a young boy innocently flirting with the slippage between names and things, foreshadowing all the Saussurean arguments of postmodernism about how signs signify more signs, and always slip sideways away from the things we once so innocently thought they simply named.[1]

But, perhaps here is the rub, that something like this insightful Saussurean slippage is the source of the journey to find the calling of one's name. It is the impetus to find out what is called by *all those things* seemingly simply named in what was meant, from its name, to be a curriculum *guide*. Differently put, without this slippage, the name is just the name, pinned on the thing named, nailing it down, finishing it—something to be "covered." Without the slippage, the name loses something of its *calling* and becomes, like Wabi Sabi's thought at the beginning of the tale ("it had never occurred to her" [n.p.]), nothing more than a name. Without the slippage, names don't need to be *heeded*. They don't beckon, and we don't need to *follow* that beckoning (what the name is calling us to, what it is calling us for, what our calling might be in being called by this name).

There is a story in this name.

Wabi Sabi discovered something hard to explain: to be so named might be a provocation, calling (in Latin *vocare*) something "forth" (Latin *pro-*), which, when elided, also means a "challenge" (Latin *provocare*). That is why she journeyed, because her name beckoned. Within such a slippage, there is teaching and learning to do—a "journey's steps deep inside [our] bones" (n.p.).

III

In the earliest times the intimate unity of word and thing was so obvious that the true name was considered to be part of the bearer of the name. In Greek... onoma means... especially "proper name"—i.e., the name by which something is called. A name is what it is because it is what someone... answers to.
                                                       Gadamer 1989, 405

Wabi Sabi experiences this intimacy because her name becomes not just what she is called, but that *by which* she is called, that which *calls her*.[2] Her name is a lure, asking for her to venture through worlds of experience in order to be understood. Little wonder that those who she meets along the way—and she herself, after she returns home—consistently answer the question of "What does Wabi Sabi mean?" with "That's hard to explain."

This is why Gadamerian hermeneutics moves away from the phenomenological fetish with the lived experience (*Erlebnis*) that one "has," to a sense of experience as something you "go through," something undergone or suffered (Gadamer 1989, 256–257). The German term *Erfahrung* ("experience") indicates something of a journey, a traversing (German> *Fahren*, "to travel"). Becoming experienced (German> *Erfahren*) becomes understood as the very sort of thing Wabi Sabi is undergoing. There is even a clue in the roots of the English term "experience":

> To become experienced means "to learn your way around," that is, to have ex-*peri*-ence (Gk. *ek-* means "out of," *peri-* means "around, as in the term "perimeter"—the "measure" [*metron*] of "around" [*peri-*]). (Jardine, Friesen & Clifford 2006, 207)

Names—even the ordinary word "experience," which everyone already understands and whose meaning "goes without saying"—have sometimes hidden or occluded motion and agency to them, something to show and teach, some path set out that needs to be *taken* in order to be *understood*.

All of the figures Wabi Sabi meets along her way, all of the places that she visits, are moments that keep the sojourn going. None of them define the name and end the movement. The name remains alive, a living part of a living world.

Even when Wabi Sabi herself returns home and is asked, "Where have you been?" she answers, "That's hard to explain" (n.p.).

IV

There is a dialectic to the word, which accords to every word an inner dimension of multiplication: every word breaks forth as if from a centre and is related to a whole, through which alone it is a word. Every word causes the whole of the language to which it belongs to resonate and the whole world-view that underlies it to appear. Thus, every word, as the event of a moment, carries with it the unsaid, to which it is related by responding and summoning. The occasionality of human speech is not a casual imperfection of its expressive power; it is, rather, the logical expression of the living virtuality of speech that brings a totality of meaning into play, without being able to express it totally. All human speaking is finite in such a way that there is laid up within it an infinity of meaning to be explicated and laid out.

Gadamer 1989, 458

No word, no name, arrives alone. Not only do words have motion and movement in them. Every word summons up and responds to the world within which it calls, sometimes myriad worlds, "interweaving and criss-crossing" (Wittgenstein 1968, 33) like the layered texts of this children's book. "Only in the multifariousness of such voices does it exist" (Gadamer 1989, 284). Sometimes incommensurate, sometimes antagonistic worlds can be called up all at once through the very mention of a word.

Every word calls up a world. To understand any word is a worldly venture. It is this "worlding" (Heidegger 1962) that provides the imaginal territory or terrain for the ensuing venture. Becoming experienced in the meaning of her name is possible only once her name, Wabi Sabi, is experienced as an opening into a world to be ventured out, into and through, a world that calls her forth (one etymological root, by the way, of the Latin *educare*, education). To understand Wabi Sabi, then, is to venture through the world of its calling and thus venture to become experienced in that world. It is a pedagogical calling, full of learning, and teaching to come.

v

> not "this is that" but this is a story about that, this is like that.
>
> *Clifford 1986, 100*

This storied order of language denotes a deeply ecological order: these pine siskins at the birdfeeder live in a place in which pine grosbeaks are summoned up, and certain winters and rains. They do not properly exist as themselves and only then have relations of kin and kind and place:

> Seeds from pine cones are food for many songbirds such as the pine siskin, the pine grosbeak and the crossbills. Because the pine seeds are naturally shed through the winter months, the pine seeds are also food to many mammals in barren areas. (Beresford-Kroeger 2003, 110)

It is not just that the pine siskins are "surrounded." There is a more difficult truth here that Wabi Sabi is discovering: the pine siskins, like her, "are" their surroundings. They are empty (Sanskrit> *Sunyata*) of a self-existence (Sanskrit> *Svabhava*) separate from their abode. This is why venturing through the abode[s] of one's name is required to understand "myself":

> One sees ones own self in all things, in living things, in hills and rivers, towns and hamlets, tiles and stones, and loves these things "as oneself." (Nishitani 1982, 280–281)

This is "the self in its original countenance" (Nishitani 1982, 91). It is Wabi Sabi's "self" she is traversing through, contours of her living, gatherings of her own countenance, steps inside her own earthly bones.

Thus, too, the name pine siskins "breaks forth," as Gadamer (1989, 458) puts it, "as if from a centre," just as these birds outside the window swoop and flit down in large flocks from the Lodge-Pole pine, just like these Old French (*loge*, "arbour" or "hut"), Latin (*laubia*) and German (*Laube*, "arbour") bloodlines flits around the edges of that name.

"It's hard to explain."

This is the tough insight that Wabi Sabi slowly happens upon: she, like the siskins, like the Lodge-Pole, is the center of a breaking-forth world of relations and, at the same time, "*the center is everywhere.*" Each and every thing becomes the center of all things and, in that sense, becomes an absolute center. This is the absolute uniqueness of things, their reality" (Nishitani 1982, 146). This is why, as the tale proceeds, Wabi Sabi can become so composed. She isn't lost or failing to be elsewhere. Home is everywhere, life is everywhere; the pine siskins matter as much (and as little) as the cones. They simply follow their ways in great concert with each other. This is the simplicity that Wabi Sabi seeks and means.

VI

This is also part of the sacred truth that the old pine tree teaches, and that it teaches us about teaching. It, like all things, "breaks forth".[3] The Latin name for Lodge-Pole Pine is *Pinus contorta*. And this form of naming:

> presume[s] the great "Father of Taxonomy," Carolus Linnaeus (1707–1778), whose work, the enormous *Systema Naturae* (with its own bloodlines traceable back to the work of Aristotle before him), and his unfolding of the whole of creation into the grand typologies of Kingdoms and Genera and Species and Sub-Species and Families, that are still taught, in supplemented and modified forms, in our schools. From Linnaeus' binomial naming of these typologies in the One Universal Language of Latin, we have Latinate names that call back into a long colonial history which is not the one out of which this invitation had come to us. In a chilling parallel, and as was commonplace in his time, Carole Linne translated his own Swedish name to Carolus Linnaeus. Without such translation, one was not considered "a citizen of the world". (Reston 2005, 127; Friesen, Jardine, & Gladstone, 2010).

There is another haiku by Matsuo Basho (1644–1694) about the pine tree that teaches about teaching:

> From the pine tree
> learn of the pine tree,
> And from the bamboo
> of the bamboo.

"Everything around us teaches impermanence" (Tsong-ka-pa [1357–1419] 2000, 151), and, to learn of *this* site of opening—the pine tree, the siskins, the calling of the name Wabi Sabi—it is to this site that one must go, and each of us must go there for ourselves, no one can spare us this venture of experience (Gadamer 1989, 356).

Wabi Sabi must go herself and no one can go for her.[4]

VII

The community is an order of memories preserved consciously in instructions, songs and stories, and both consciously and unconsciously in ways. A healthy culture holds preserving knowledge in place for a long time. That is, the essential wisdom accumulates in the community much as fertility builds in the soil.

                                                                    Berry 1983, 73

Because she did not hurry, [Wabi Sabi] found a place called Ginkakuji, the "Silver Temple."

                                                        Reibstein and Young 2008, n.p.

There is/are another dimension of the wor(l)d(s) that open(s) up for Wabi Sabi in the calling of her name: not only a lure to venture, not only surroundings that open, but an opening of time back into the ancientness that sounds in one's surroundings. This venture that Wabi Sabi takes is intimate to her, how she herself is called and yet, at the same time, it is intergenerational. She herself stands before those who have gone before, traces and tracks of paths through the city, through the woods, up to the old Temple full of the ghosts of those who have gone, and these are her teachers. Her venture is thus inherently pedagogical—in fact, early on, a bird hears Wabi Sabi's cries for help and says "there is someone who can help you" (n.p.). Not only does Wabi Sabi meet The Monkey, an ancient figure of a teacher, but this teacher teaches, not by telling her the meaning of her name but by making tea—a space and slow-time in which Wabi Sabi can compose herself and appropriate the experiences she has undergone.

This intergenerational character of the "breaking forth" of the name is again found in the language of Gadamer's hermeneutics. Becoming experienced (*Erfahrung*) is linked to a journey (*Fahren*), and these are both linked etymologically to those who have traveled here before us, our ancestors (*Vorfahren*). This is another dimension of the wor(l)d(s) that open up in the calling of a name: not only a lure to venture, not only a surrounding which opens, but an opening of time back into the ancientness that sounds in one's surroundings. Paradoxically, the futurity that we experience when a name breaks open (that we have opening "ahead" of us multifarious ways that is yet-to-be-ventured) is at once also experienced as full of the echoes of ancestral voices, ventures taken before, signs on paths, old texts, old stories, old figures. Basho Matsuo's (1644–1694) haiku appears as the pages turn, as do those of Masaoka Shiki (1867–1902), coiner of the term "haiku," just like we have left traces of H. G. Gadamer (1900–2002) here in this writing. All these names give an intergenerational meaning to these tales. These, then, just like The Monkey in the Wabi Sabi story, are teachers who are invoked, those who have been on this sort of venture before us, teachers who are "kind," and "kin." The ecological insight here is that we must also include those very pine siskins, who are themselves great teachers and who occasion an opening into ways that are themselves folds of "that anciently perceived likeness between all creatures and the earth of which they are made" (Berry 1983, 76).

Time cuts across this intergenerationalness in another way as well. Wabi Sabi meets The Monkey, an ancient figure of a teacher who teaches, not by telling her the meaning of her name but by making tea—an open, inviting space and slowing of time in which Wabi Sabi can, shall we say, collect herself. Because she did not hurry, [Wabi Sabi] found a place called *Ginkakuji,* the "Silver Temple." This lack of hurry allowed her to while away the time (Jardine, 2008). In fact, the old temple entices Wabi Sabi, not only to compose herself, but also compose three haiku about yellow bamboo stalks, dark buildings, and streams and leaves on a raked Zen garden. The writing of this children's book, the writing of this chapter that is taking its own venture through the world opened up by Wabi Sabi—it seems like composition, composing oneself, is part of the journey-work that is being done to find the meaning of the name.

And thus, for us, is beckoning the gesture of writing. What might we tell our student-teachers about this book, if we ourselves have not taken the time to compose ourselves in the midst of the wor(l)d(s) it breaks open? We write, in some small way, in order to become experienced. But this sense of "being experienced" has the blush that Gadamer adds:

> "Being experienced" does not consist in the fact that someone already knows everything and knows better than anyone else. Rather, the experienced person proves to be, on the contrary, someone who, because of the many experiences he has had and the knowledge he has drawn from them, is particularly well equipped to have new experiences and to learn from them. Experience has its proper fulfillment not in definitive knowledge but in the openness to experience that is made possible by experience itself. (1989, 355)

VIII

To begin a story, someone in some way must break a particular silence.
                                   Wiebe and Johnson 1998, 3

*One day, visitors from another country asked Wabi Sabi's master what her
name meant. It had never occurred to her before that wabi sabi was anything
more than her name.*
                              Reibstein and Young 2008 (n.p.)

There is not simply an opening of time back into the ancientness that sounds
in one's surroundings. There is as well, an opening to a future yet to be.

The arrival of strangers can interrupt all those hard-to-utter familiarities
that define one's "home," one's "place," one's surroundings. As in this tale,
the stranger can often ask the question of those very things that are beyond
question and taken for granted by those who have become complacently at
home in their surroundings. There are myriads of tales of strangers arriv-
ing and saying "goes without saying." The stranger often puts back into
motion that which has atrophied, opens up what was a closed case, helps us
remember something that was forgotten, awakens the life in something that
seemed dead and forgotten.[5] We even have in Genesis 17 an instance where
the three strangers who visit Abraham are in fact heralds of the coming of
new life, Sarah's impending pregnancy and the whole great line of ancestral
surroundings that follows upon it. The strangers thus herald the intergen-
erationality of what once seemed barren. As go many old sayings, with the
arrival of the new, the old becomes young again (just like Wabi Sabi's just-
a-name seemed to wake up and become a new and fresh calling through
a now-living world) and the fervency of the young—like Wabi Sabi's at-
first-restless journey through this book—slowly comes to be held, comes
to "find itself" and its calling—in the comfort of the world and its ways
(which world, through the arrival of the new, as Hannah Arendt [1969, 193],
can now be "set right anew"). The ancestral thus becomes *answerable to* the
questions that the young pose to it, and ancestry is called to remember, to
reawaken, to open, to enliven anew its own wisdoms in such answerability.

The strangers thus prompt Wabi Sabi's journey by opening up the question of what Wabi Sabi means, a question that now gives her name, so to
speak, a "future" that has yet to arrive. Something opens, like a "horizon of...still undecided future possibilities" (Gadamer 1989, 112). This
estrangement from simply "being at home" (the estrangement from deaden-
ing thinking that it is just a name) induces the task of becoming experienced.
It induces, that is, a pedagogical sojourn, full of deeply Earthly, incarnate,
sensual learning and teaching. It induces the need for new experience. And,
as Heidegger (1962, 233) noted so well, the interruption by the strangers of

the homely, "goes without saying" comfort of "it's just a name" gives way to what he called an experience of *unheimlichkeit*—literally "unhomelikeness." Instead of "home" being a given that is simply familiar, home has become opened up to the question of its countenance and continuance, what makes it alive and susceptible to a yet-to-be-determined future. The three who appeared to Abraham were not just strangers, but *heralds*. They came with *news* of something *yet to come* (just like the experiences yet to arrive when Wabi Sabi first leaves her home). Home—like Abraham's bloodline—is thus held "open towards its future" (Gadamer 1989, 119) and Wabi Sabi becomes a calling which the strangers (the unhomelike ones, if you will) have helped "keep open for the future" (340) (notice how this places "diversity" and "difference" right at the heart of the health and well-being of "identity").

And this is not just "keeping myself open." The arrival of the openness of the young bespeaks the possibility of "keeping the world open" (Eliade 1968, 139) to the possibilities of venturing. This is a great pedagogical secret: there is no sense keeping myself open to a world which itself has no openings, no future, no possibilities, a world that doesn't call for my openness, my venture. Every student understands in their own way what it is like to be in a classroom where his or her presence cannot possibly make any difference, where everything is already decided, names ready to be memorized, no memorable ventures to be taken.[6]

The arrival of the openness of the young bespeaks the possibility of "keeping the world open" (Eliade 1968, 139) to the unforeseen possibilities of venturing.

IX

Literalism is the enemy. Literalism is sickness.

Hillman 1983, 3

The pine is first and foremost a tree of medicine. All over the global garden this knowledge is ancient. The pharmacy of the pine is as common in Turkey as it is in the Balkans, as it is to the Chinese, as it was to the ancient Picts of Scotland and now, as it is to us.

Beresford-Kroeger 2003, 105

Throughout the ages, the most popular use for pines was in the treatment of respiratory diseases. This included colds, coughs, laryngitis, chronic bronchitis, catarrh, sore throats, and asthma. This is because the pine exerts a dilatatory or opening action on the bronchi of the lungs. Since ancient times even a walk through a mature pine woods in summer was considered to be beneficial to one's general health. The fresh leaves exert a stimulant effect on breathing with the addition of mild anesthetic properties. There is possibly some mild narcotic function also in pines. In warm air, the pine sweats a natural monomythyl and dimethylester of pinosylvin, which are both aerosols. (109)

This is the pedagogical countenance of names. Just as the world helps Wabi Sabi understand the calling of her name, so too Wabi Sabi, in her world-opening ventures, saves the world of her name from being a "closed book"—she, like the strangers before us, asks the question which "breaks open the being" (Gadamer 1989, 360) of her name into its living world of living relations. Youthful, inexperienced, openness with no open world of ancient venture to take care of such exuberance, afflicts the young with puerility. A "closed world" of already foreclosed expertise is afflicted with senility, where Wabi Sabi's venture becomes little more than a bother. The pedagogical countenance of names is healthy and whole only in the properly pedagogical meeting of old and young, established and new, ancient and immediate. Without each other, each becomes ill, monstrous, and distorted.

(Back in that car ride, with "weekends" and "trees," Wabi Sabi helps me understand why this speculative question of "what would have happened" is not an error requiring correction. It is a revealing of a difficult truth about words, an opening up of a way of words that is beautifully "hard to explain").

Healing is not a final state but attending after the possibility of continuance, able to face what comes, not imperviously finished with the venture but ready for it, not as a stale expert but rather as one experienced in its ways.

From the Pine Tree learn of the pine tree, that it is a site where such haleness can be found, but it is not just healing *for us*:

> *Propolis* is collected from pines, among other species. The honeybee can be seen tearing at the resin with her mandibles. It takes her a quarter of an hour to load this *propolis*. When she arrives back at the hive, other worker bees help to unload. This is why spots of *propolis* are found around hive entrances. Bees mix *propolis* with wax and this becomes a fungicidal, antiseptic, and antibiotic wallpapering for the inside of the beehive. The fact that *propolis* is an old folk medicine in northern European forested areas is not surprising. (Beresford-Kroeger 2003, 109)

X

[It] compels us over and over, and the better one knows it, the more compelling it is. There comes a moment in which something is there, something one should not forget and cannot forget. This is not a matter of mastering an area of study.

Gadamer 2007, 115

The lure of the name *increases* as the journey proceeds, and there comes a moment in such ecological educative movement "when something is *there*." We all understand this experience: the more I have come to know a work of art, a piece of music, a track of forest, a bird's call, the meaning of a name like Wabi Sabi, quadratic arcs, or the beauty of a beloved novel—the more I experience such things, the *more* compelling they become, the more they are experienced as "standing there," over and above my wanting and doing, there, in the midst of the world. The more I know about such worlds, the increasingly incommensurate is my own knowledge to the ways of that world. *It* gets better and bests my ability to outrun it with my knowing. *This* is what it means to become experienced. *This* is the pedagogical countenance of the name broken open.

Wabi Sabi? It's hard to explain.

ENDNOTES

1. See the Online Etymological Dictionary for this and other etymological references (www.etymonline.com).
2. This beautiful play on the world "call" in H. G. Gadamer's *Truth and Method* (1960/1989) has some of its origins in Martin Heidegger's *What is called thinking?* (1968, originally published in German in 1954). In this text, Heidegger inverts an old German philosophical line of thought that extends back in its modern form to Immanuel Kant's (1963/1787) *Critique of Pure Reason*, and, from there, back to the Cartesian "I think" as the foundation of truth-as-clarity-and-distinctness. This line is fixated on the epistemological question of how to properly portray "thinking": what are the characteristics, forms, methods and criteria of knowledge? The hermeneutic tradition wants to interrupt this philosophical line of thought and its obsession with epistemology including the ways that part of its own heritage, Husserlian phenomenology, remains stuck in this line of placing human agency, human "wantings and doings" (Gadamer 1989, p. xviii), at the center of philosophical investigation (one could say that Husserlian phenomenology is the "last straw" in this line with its desire for "lived experiences" [Erlebnisse]). In Heidegger's text, the question is reversed: What is it that *calls for* thinking? This places thinking back into the world and asks after that which beckons it, that which needs thinking, that which makes thinking thus possible. It places the call of thinking beyond the agency of the "I" who thinks: "understanding begins when something addresses us" (1968, 299).
3. In Sanskrit, the term here is *pratitya-samutpapda*, "dependent co-arising." This means, simply put, that every thing is empty of a permanent and separate existence. Everything exists only in and *as* interdependent worlds of relations, and therefore, every thing has the potential to teach this sacred truth.
4. This beautiful play on the world "call" in H. G. Gadamer's *Truth and Method* (1960/1989) has some of its origins in Martin Heidegger's *What is*

called thinking? (1968, originally published in German in 1954). In this text, Heidegger inverts an old German philosophical line of thought that extends back in its modern form to Immanuel Kant's (1963/1787) *Critique of Pure Reason*, and, from there, back to the Cartesian "I think" as the foundation of truth-as-clarity-and-distinctness. This line is fixated on the epistemological question of how to properly portray "thinking": what are the characteristics, forms, methods and criteria of knowledge? The hermeneutic tradition wants to interrupt this philosophical line of thought and its obsession with epistemology including the ways that part of its own heritage, Husserlian phenomenology, remains stuck in this line of placing human agency, human "wantings and doings" (Gadamer 1989, xviii), at the center of philosophical investigation (one could say that Husserlian phenomenology is the "last straw" in this line with its desire for "lived experiences" [Erlebnisse]). In Heidegger's text, the question is reversed: What is it that *calls for* thinking? This places thinking back into the world and asks after that which beckons it, that which needs thinking, that which makes thinking thus possible. It places the call of thinking beyond the agency of the "I" who thinks: "understanding begins when something addresses us" (1968, 299).

In Sanskrit, the term here is *pratitya-samutpapda*, "dependent co-arising." This means, simply put, that every thing is empty of a permanent and separate existence. Everything exists only in and *as* interdependent worlds of relations, and therefore, every thing has the potential to teach this sacred truth.

This is the irreducible paradox of this way of experiencing things, that the center is everywhere and that, therefore, "none is the fundamental entity" (Hahn 1988, 70) while, at the same time, any thing can be experience as the center of all things. Nishitani Keiji (1982, 149) elaborates:

> To say that *a thing is not itself* means that, while continuing to be itself, it is in the home-ground of everything else. Figuratively speaking, its roots reach across into the ground of all other things and help to hold them up and keep them standing. It serves as a constitutive element of their being. *That a thing is itself* means that all other things, while continuing to be themselves, are in the home-ground of that thing. This way that everything has being on the home-ground of everything else, without ceasing to be on its own home-ground, means that the being of each thing is held up, kept standing, and made to be what it is by means of the being of all other things; or, put the other way around, that each being holds up the being of every other thing, keeps it standing and makes it what it is.

Versions of this sort of understanding abound. Linneaus's work attempted to map out a certain family-tree-like images of proximities and distances between things based, not on surroundings but on physical resemblances. Grouping pine trees together makes a certain kind of sense, but its sense is not the kind of sense that places the Lodgepole Pine with Pine Siskins. And these two morphologies of interdependence are not the same as the post-modern version of Linneaus found in the Human Genome Project that sorts relations according to genetic orders. Each of these, in its own way, breaks open the self-containedness of that which it explores and shows the impermanence of such containedness and the deep dependencies that belie such containedness.

Wabi Sabi, in particular, has an ecological, experiential character, bespeaking "that anciently perceived likeness between all creatures and the earth of which they are made" (Berry 1983, 76) mixed, of course, with a near-untranslatable cultural and ancestral character that makes things Zen so at-least-initially harsh to the Western ear. The Western tradition is rooted in the ancestry of Aristotle (circa 3rd century BCE) and his belief, coined by Descartes (circa 1640/1955, 255) that the reality of things, their "substance is that which requires nothing except itself in order to exist." The pine tree is the pine tree; the Siskins are the Siskins. In Western ontology, the relations between such things are ontologically subsequent. In the worlds evoked by the name Wabi Sabi, they are ontologically constitutive of the things thus related.

It is no accident, then, when Gadamer (1989) talks about how experience (*Erfahrung*) is playful in nature and in such playfulness, we do not begin with two separate players who are then subsequently in a relationship of play, but begin, rather with "the primordial sense of playing" (103) which is a "medial one" (103) in which there are "no subjects who are behaving 'playfully' " (102). There is, rather, play—interrelatedness, interdependence— out of which precipitates a sense of individual subjects who are "in play." Out of the *Spiel* of this woods precipitates the noticing: "look, there, Pine Siskins." But even here, *what is being noticed* is not some separate entity but a node in the web of interdependence, this one, *that* Siskin, there, leaving the feeder back to the pine branches. As such a node, this Siskin is experienced as a non-self-existent "opening" into a world, and my experiencing of this Siskin is experienced as of the same flesh as that which is experienced. All this noticing falls upon an eye that is itself noticeable.

It makes sense, then, too, why Gadamer says that coming to understand "breaks open the *being* of the object" (1989, 362, our emphasis) into a way of being that denotes topographical openness and possibilities, "places" of possible sojourn. In this, he follows the work of his teacher, Martin Heidegger, in critiquing the *metaphysics of substance*. Not incidentally, Nishitani Keiji (1900–1990), as well as his teacher, Nishida Kitaro (1870–1945), were both greatly influenced by Heidegger's (1889–1976) later meditations (see Nishitani, 1991; Nishitani studied with Heidegger from 1937–39). See also Heidegger's (1954/1971) "A dialogue on language between a Japanese and an inquirer" in which he directly references Shuzo Kuki (1888–1941), another student of Kitaro's who "died too early" (1). Kuki studied phenomenology with Edmund Husserl in Freiburg and then went on to study with Heidegger in Marburg and gave lectures at Kyoto University on Heidegger's work in 1939.

5. These three portends of the stranger (opening what was closed, enlivening what was dead and remembering something that was forgotten) are the three threads in the hermeneutic definition of truth as *alethia*—a line inherited by Gadamer from his teacher, Martin Heidegger (see Jardine, 2000).

6. "The West lives in a kind of frozen futurism in which what was expected to be revealed *has* been revealed, and what the revelations discloses is that the future will always be...more and more of this. The details may vary over time, but the essential grammar remains the same: Education seems like a preparation for something that never happens because...it has *already happened*. Teaching...freezes.... There *is* no future because the future *already is*. [Teachers] are the bearers of a verdict that, in the name of the future, the future is now closed. It is easy to see how frozen futurism is a recipe for despair for students as well as for teachers" (Smith 2006, 25–6).

REFERENCES

Arendt, Hannah. 1969. *Between Past and Present: Eight Exercises in Political Thought.* New York: Penguin Books.

Beresford-Kroeger, Diane. 2003. *Arboretum America: A Philosophy of the Forest.* Ann Arbor: The University of Michigan Press.

Berry, Wendell. 1983. *Standing by Words.* San Francisco: North Point Press.

Clifford, James. 1986. "On Ethnographic Allegory". In *Writing Culture: The Poetics and Politics Of Ethnography*, edited by J. Clifford & G. Marcus, 99–106. Berkeley: University of California Press.

Eliade, Mircea. 1968. *Myth and Reality.* New York: Harper & Row.

Friesen, Sharon, Jardine, David, & Gladstone, Brenda. 2010. "The First Thunderclap of Spring: An Invitation into Aboriginal Ways of Knowing and the Creative Possibilities of Digital Technologies." In *Teacher Education Yearbook XVIII: Cultivating Curious and Creative Minds: The Role of Teachers and Teacher Educators.*, edited by Cheryl Craig & Louise F. Deretchin, 179–199. Landham MD: Scarecrow Education.

Gadamer, H.G. 1989. *Truth and Method.* New York: Continuum Books.

———. 2007. "From Word to Concept: The Task of Hermeneutic Philosophy." In *The Gadamer Reader: A Bouquet of Later Writings*, edited by Richard Palmer, 108–122. Evanston IL: Northwestern University Press.

Hahn, Thich Nhat. 1988. *The Sun My Heart.* Berkeley: Parallax Press.

Heidegger, Martin. 1962. *Being and Time.* New York: Harper and Row.

———. 1968, originally published in German in 1954. *What is Called Thinking?* New York: Harper and Row.

Hillman, James. 1983. *Healing Fiction.* Barrytown NY: Station Hill Press.

Jardine, David. 2000. "Even There The Gods Are Present". In *"Under the Tough Old Stars": Ecopedagogical Essays* by David Jardine, 205–214. Brandon, VT: Psychology Press / Holistic Education Press.

Jardine, David, Sharon Friesen, & Patricia Clifford. 2006. *Curriculum in Abundance.* Mahwah NJ: Lawrence Erlbaum and Associates.

Jardine, David. 2008. "Translating Water." *Journal of Curriculum Theorizing* 24: 11–19. Accessed January 12, 2009 at: http://journal.jctonline.org/index.php/jct/article/viewFile/JARTRA/5.

Nishitani, Keiji. 1982. *Religion and Nothingness.* Berkeley: University of California Press.

Reibstein, Mark, & Ed Young (Illus). 2008. *Wabi Sabi.* New York: Little, Brown and Company.

Reston, John. 2005. *Dogs of God: Columbus, the Inquisition and the Defeat of The Moors.* New York: Doubleday.

Smith, David G. (2006). *Trying to Teach in a Season of Great Untruth: Globalization, Empire and the Crises of Pedagogy.* Rotterdam: Sense Publishing.

Tsong-ka-pa. 2000. *The Great Treatise on the Stages of the Path to Enlightenment.* Ithaca NY: Snow Lion Publications.

Wiebe, Rudy, & Johnson, Yvonne. 1998. *Stolen Lives: The Journey of a Cree Woman.* Toronto: Alfred Kopf Canada.

Wittgenstein, Ludwig. 1968. *Philosophical Investigations.* Cambridge UK: Blackwell's.

CHAPTER 11

AUTO/ETHNO/GRAPHY AS CONTINENTAL DRIFTWORK: A FRAGILE WEATHERING OF ICEBERGS DRIFTING AND STORIES SHIFTING...

PATRICIA PALULIS

> *Poststructuralist geography is a driftwork...*
>
> Marcus Doel 1999, 3

> *Driftworks in the plural, for the question is not of leaving one shore, but several, simultaneously; what is at work is not one current, pushing and tugging, but different drives and tractions.*
>
> Jean-François Lyotard 1984, 10

> *Education must become like textus, like a text, a story whose telling is not yet over.*
>
> David Jardine 2006, xii

A story always begins somewhere in the middle. This one began in the summer of 1976. I was co-instructor of an Inuit classroom assistants' course in Iqaluit on Baffin Island. I had lived in the Arctic for five years and, having just completed a two year teaching assignment in Pangnirtung, was preparing to depart for Japan in search of another teaching adventure. An unexpected opportunity to visit Greenland presented itself mid-summer. It was impossible to resist. I flew from Iqaluit on Baffin Island to Kangerlussuaq or Søndre Strømfjord in Greenland (Grønland). We embarked on the M.S. Disko, a passenger ferry, and traveled north along the west coast of Greenland. We docked at Jakobshavn, now Illulissat, where we disembarked from the ferry for scenic tours by smaller motor boats to drift slowly alongside Ilulissat Icefjord, a UNESCO Heritage Site with an active glacier. We witnessed the birth of an iceberg as an arche-texture of wonder to cadences of ice music. We had been drifting within the splendor of icy passageways for some time but now this was to be the ultimate ice show. It would be decades later, in a classroom in Vancouver, that a story book would arrive at my door to begin a series of recollections as an evocative event in an auto/ethno/graphic journey; a traveler's tale transforms itself with a series of close reading events. This time, an iceberg named Lulie, newly calved, embarks on a journey to the Antarctic in search of the Elders. The story follows me to my teacher preparation and graduate classes in the Nation's capital. And reminds me to remember the wisdom of my Elders.

DRAWING ON CONCEPTIONS OF POST-STRUCTURALIST GEOGRAPHIES as *drift-work*, Marcus Doel (1999) contends that "geography is an act, an event, a happening" (11). Sometimes a storybook becomes an event. A story happens as a geographical event. As a teacher of English Language Arts, I want to engage the reader in the story of *Lulie the Iceberg* (Takamado 1998) as geo-literacy[1] as eco-literacy[2]—as *an act, an event, a happening*—drawing from a teaching life as auto/ethno/graphy, and from a teaching praxis within the conceptual space of a/r/tography. Working out on the slope [/] de-stabilizes the text and those working nearby. I want to work with David Jardine (2006) as he weaves his words like *textus*—with a story *whose telling is not yet over.*

As a gift extended from a parent of one of my students, a children's book takes on a life of its own. As a teacher who engages with arts-based literacy and literature at the interstices of theory and practice, a/r/tography becomes a habitus for dwelling with students and stories. My travel notes and narratives are interwoven with those of multiple scholars as I draw from conceptions of auto/ethno/graphy (Reed-Danahay 1997; Russell 1999) and a/r/tography (Irwin & de Cosson 2004; Springgay, Irwin, & Kind 2005).

AUTO/ETHNO/GRAPHY AS DRIFTWORK...

As Gough and Gough (2004) contend: "Research is a textual practice, a process represented in language and performed through acts of writing, textual production and reading" (410). Textual practice becomes *drift-work*. Catherine Russell (1999) contends that "[a]utobiography becomes ethnographic" at the point where personal history becomes "implicated in larger social formations and historical processes" (276). Working out "on the Aokian (2003) slope [/] in-between the 'auto' and the 'ethno' and the 'graphy'...offers intervals for breaks and gaps and swerves" (Morawski & Palulis, 2009, 9). Metonymic moments as articulated by Aoki (2003) perform doublings—blurring boundaries and cracking clarity. The texts that I inhabit begin to do their performative work on me as reader. My "self" as a text shifts into the spaces at-work in the gaps and intervals of intertextuality. Readings are always already at-drift. I find my textual production at-work in the in-between spaces of geo-literacy, eco-literacy and post-structural geography. As a reader reads, geography is destabilized. And stories shift as they begin to do their work.

As a textual practice, I draw from Reed-Danahay's (1997) definition of autoethnography "as a form of self-narrative that places the self within a social context" (9). My self-narrative as a teacher places my "self" in the social context of storied praxis—of engaging with students in arts-based activities about environment and place inspirited through children's literature. From teacher as traveler to teacher as activist, from aesthetics to sustainability, my storied subjectivities shift at the intersections of geographic dislocations and historical narratives. Reed-Danahay (1997) works with "schooling stories," as she writes about the complicated relationships of leaving home and becoming educated.

Lulie the Iceberg breaks off from the Greenland Ice Sheet to meet the Elder Icebergs in Antarctica: A journey filled with wonder adrift through multiple ecosystems and geographical dislocations. A teacher breaks off from the continent and journeys from a teaching assignment on Baffin Island to a passenger ferry along the West Coast of Greenland *drifting with icebergs* to the coastal site of *Ilulissat* and beyond. A detour prior to taking a passage on a freighter to Japan as a *driftwork* in search of another teaching post. My auto/ethno/graphic teaching journey is interwoven with the story of the journey of an iceberg. Presented as a bricolage of recollections, teacher narratives are juxtaposed with textual fragments of a/r/tography as living pedagogy in primary school, teacher education classes, and graduate classes. Returning to the West Coast as a transposition, a classroom works at becoming a living site for wonder to thrive.

A/R/TOGRAPHY AS HABITUS...

When a story arrives, listen:

> Then one day, with sharp crackling noises and a deafening roar, Lulie slowly broke off. First the sea swallowed him into its depths, then he rose, faster and faster, till at last he burst through the surface. There followed much popping and crackling of air bubbles. And there he was—Lulie the new Iceberg! (H. I. H. Princess Takamado 1998, n.p.)

Lulie the Iceberg is a beautifully narrated and exquisitely illustrated story of the adventures of a Greenlandic iceberg journeying to Antarctica in search of Elders. The storybook was introduced to me by a Japanese parent whose daughter, as an international student, was in my primary classroom in an elementary school in Vancouver. The story, written by Her Imperial Highness Princess Takamado, and illustrated by Warabé Aska, was being performed by a Japanese Theatre troupe in collaboration with a Canadian Theatre company. An invitation was extended for my class to attend the performance. I welcomed this generosity as a Pacific Rim exchange to open a dialogue for transcultural meeting places and conversations on ecological concerns. Student response to the dramatic performance of *Lulie the Iceberg* was so filled with wonder that we continued with the themes of the storybook through arts-based literacy and research projects for several weeks. Peter de Bolla (2001) refers to aesthetic experience as "fragility"—as "an architecture of wonder" (129). He encourages us to engage in a "practice of wonder" (130). We worked with the themes of *Lulie the Iceberg* as an arche-texture of wonder evoking aesthetic reader response to the habitats and inhabitants of diverse environments. A/r/tography provides a habitus for students working with wonder: artists, researchers, teachers at one with another and always more than one.

One material event drifts into another. And once again, recycled cardboard box covers from school-based fund-raising activities become a quilted collage of our research activities on species of penguins. Our cardboard quilt as a/r/tography consumes the corridor wall outside our classroom. Giant murals teeming with sea life encircle the landings of the stairwell. Climbing up three flights of stairs we enter a papery exhibition of a sea-world reconstructed from a dramatic performance and a storied text. The light from windows facing out to the Pacific create a shimmering palimpsest of icy worlds. We enter through the classroom door for another layering of Lulie's worlds...

Beth Olshansky (2008) contends that through "placing art and the study of quality picture books at the center of literacy learning" students gain access to "multiple modes of thinking" (xii). I could not have predicted the excitement that was evoked through our engagement with text, image, and drama. Responding to an invitation to attend a dramatic performance of the story, our *driftworks* take on a series of diffraction patterns.

Rainbow cellophane sparkles from sun-drenched images—ice music as improvisation with students popping air pockets in packer's bubble plastic—resonating with the cadences of belly giggles—recycled cardboard, glitter glue, tissue paper in multiple hues overlapping as translucent shimmerings—and species of penguins emerge in their topographical habitats as the wonder of Antarctic icy reaches—sliding into pools of icy water—resplendent in black and white on trails blazed with shimmerings of silver metallic paint—in pursuit of virtual worlds and researched words—accordion pleated tagboard bound with masking tape in brilliant primary colors—and young researchers as info-kids and artists are immersed in critical inquiry and artistry juxtaposing virtual images and painted re-presentations with humorous riddles and serious environmental concerns—as expositions of their textworking. Warabé Aska's images become the inspiration for a research project on penguins. What draws a student to a specific species of penguin—chinstrap, macaroni, king, and emperor—and so many more? Students are drawn to specific species as curiosity and wonder provoke the work of research. Portfolios emerge and are shared with parents in student-led conferences.

Reading Barratt Hacking, Barratt and Scott (2007) on engaging children and environment, I am reminded that geography is one of the several topographies through which children connect with environmental learning. As Lulie drifts with the winds and the ocean currents in between continents, our classroom adventures shift as *driftworks* in multiple modalities. For De Bolla (2001) an "aesthetic experience is made out of its own singularity" (137). Students chase after aesthetic adventures sharing affinities and excitations with classmates. And I chase after mine, drifting into yet another text, on architecture. I am reading Mohsen Mostafavi (2007) reading Guattari on "dissident subjectivities" necessary for a social and political ecology (164). Mostafavi draws our attention to Guattari's call for a "collective production of unpredictable and untamed 'dissident subjectivities' rather than the mass movement of like-minded people" (164). I track the words to Guattari's (2000) essay "The Three Ecologies." From a multitude of voices, words begin to stir anew—to do their work. I don't know what they are up to. They become an invocation to work in messy spaces.

DIFFRACTIONS ON A WRITER'S DIARY: A TRANSLATION THAT STARTLES...

Donna Haraway (1997) suspects that, as a critical practice, "reflexivity, like reflection, only displaces the same elsewhere" (16). She suggests working with diffraction to open spaces for difference. "Diffraction patterns" she contends, "record the history of interaction, interference, reinforcement, difference" (273). Haraway (1994) insists that "textual rereading is not enough; through the trope of reading we do not swerve decisively enough" (60). I find myself seeking these spaces of difference. Sometimes to swerve decisively takes time. Your topographies shift. You don't know when it's going to happen. But when it does happen, "[i]t's like plugging into an electric circuit" (Deleuze cited in Roy 2003, 178). The interference of one "read" with another creates an electric current/cy. Working with my primary students, I had not tracked the connection between Lulie and *Ilulissat*. In my teacher education classes, translating *Ilulissat*, I am startled to locate an ice field that I had visited decades ago. I had been unaware of the connection in my first encounter with Lulie's story. In the busyness of everyday life, translation is neglected. An embodied experience emerges as evocative recollection.

Reading Patricia Clough (2000) on reading Haraway, I am drawn to diffractions as "rhizomatic writing, a composing and recomposing that cuts into and cuts away from genres, technologies, images, and scenes so that movement is never simply narrative or life story" (184–185). Rhizomatic writing evokes the possibilities for chance meeting places with writers and readers, with researchers and artists, with students and teachers.

DIFFRACTIONS ON ACOUSTIC HYBRIDITY: ACCENTED ENGLISHES...

The dramatic performance of the story was an invocation into research and/ as arts-based projects, an evocation of our interest and excitement. My recollections begin with that initial experience of wonder and excitation. One of the adults who had accompanied us to the performance commented on the difficulty of understanding Kiki's accented English—an accent marking membership in a Japanese theatre troupe. An accent marks an othering— an interference. Palulis and Low (2001) drawing from Beckett, write about porosity of textures and acoustic hybridities as in-between spaces. Accented englishes as diffracted acoustics open spaces for one language to dwell within another—to maintain a tenancy—to interfere with the hegemony of English. Listen to Trinh (2005) on the status of multilingualism within English:

> Language is not only an exercise of power or of resistance; it is also an act of creativity. Differences developed within the same language can be infinitely rich. In public or working situations, I often felt that although those of us involved all spoke English, we profoundly spoke different languages. (121)

We listened to Kiki, the Arctic Tern, chattering, twittering, and chirping in accented excitations around and about the *driftworking* of Lulie the Iceberg. Best friends were adrift in animated conversations. Articulations of accented English marking the hybrid are seen as more startling than anthropomorphic speech patterns of sea mammals and winged creatures chattering at sea with an iceberg. We have not yet learned to listen to the wonder of accented englishes. To welcome interference and/as difference.

Working now at the University of Ottawa, I share this storybook with my teacher education students. With Joseph and Paul (2004) we work with "handmade literacies...in an age when children are being suffocated and smothered by the emptiness of the timeless present of standardized tests and standardized prose" (v–vii). We work with the singularity of collective murals with the doublings of the aesthetic and the not so aesthetic. Doublings draw us into the tensions of eco-literacies and geo-literacies, working with and against the grain of the hegemonies of ministry dictations, packaged corporate literacies and faculty-mandated templates. We work with art as activism and shift into eco-criticism as theoretical discourse. Sometimes forgetting to listen to the reads and the trailers. And the unsaid stories drift past us. Unnoticed. I begin to search for the unseen and for the missing voices. From the intertexts of science and the arts the wonder of curiosity lives on.

A story begins to write itself as a traveler's tale. An auto/ethno/graphic journeying on land and sea through text and image. IceStoneWaterBlue. A mélange of juxtapositions. As I return to catch up on the transformations, Greenland votes for home rule. Place names are translated once again from Danish to Greenlandic from Jakobshavn to Illulissat. Painted fishing boats are docked nearby the red and blue and yellow houses perched on rocky precipices by the sea. Icelandic horses and young children roam together through the villages. Elders pensive seated with us in the small boats; we are tourists captivated by the splendor of icy architecture.

In his foreword to *A Reading Diary,* Alberto Manguel (2004) reminds his readers that every book dwells within a state of possibility "until the hands that open it and the eyes that peruse it stir the words into awareness" (ix). And through the wonder of awareness, a reader must not forget to pay attention. As Barthes (1979) contends: "The Text is experienced only in an activity, a production. It follows that the Text cannot stop, at the end of a library shelf... the constitutive movement of the Text is a *traversal*: it can cut across a work, several works... " (75–76). Like the little iceberg whose story it narrates, a book as text continues to tell its story as *driftwork*—as a *traversal*—cutting across the theoretical spaces of eco-literacy, geo-literacy, and transcultural dialogues to evoke possibilities for rereadings of environmental experiences and social responsibilities. A storybook at-work draws its readers into the issues and concerns of global warming in Arctic and Antarctic regions, sustainable communities and ecosystems. A storybook as text, rich with possibilities, provokes research as arts-based activism (Barndt 2006) within the discourse of eco-criticism (Glotfelty 1996). Eco-criticism (Dobrin & Kidd 2004) begins its work in the intersections of geo-literacy and eco-literacy as "interconnections between nature and culture, specifically the culture artifacts of language and literature... as a theoretical discourse" (Glotfelty 1996, xix). A storybook becomes a worksite for shaping and being shaped by environment and place. A worksite for wordworking in spaces of complexity as readings collide with multiple forms of storied praxis.

*A story travels from a primary classroom on the West Coast to take up resi-
dence in pre-service classrooms in the Nation's Capital. Students delight in the
texts and images of Lulie's journey. In papery passages wet with painted characters, once again the representations of water and ice—of dark blue skies and
mirrored glimmerings—as thumbprints become miniature penguins with paint
dabbled beaks gathering clustering chattering on Antarctic ice flows to the crack-
ling soundscapes of musical ice notes. Excitations abounding in multitudes of
words and images. Tissue paper crumpled as multidimensional constructions of
iceberg architecture. Shimmerings of silver metallic residue perform as gouache
one layering over another. Barefoot artists with painted faces—excitations from
live(d) experiences in practicum placements—evocations for the holidays that
are approaching...*

DIFFRACTIONS ON A VOID: FATEFUL
STORIES AND MISSING PEOPLE...

It is only later, in a graduate class on education and cultural studies, that
the intertext at-work begins once again the process of deconstruction. One
text drifts toward another as a praxis of intertextuality. From the wonder of
fantasy to the recollections of live(d) experience. In a transposition, something else happens—another diffraction. Another swerve with Haraway. I
introduce a series of articles by Inuit writers following the newly formed
territory of Nunavut in 1999. And then I relocate a book purchased during
one of my frequent excursions into the University of Ottawa Bookstore:
Lutz's (2005) *The Diary of Abraham Ulrikab.* Here is the context: Hartmut
Lutz shares the "fateful" stories that produced his edited "little" book. An
archive of Inuit manuscripts and the diaries of Abraham Ulrikab emerge
from their midst. I read about a group of Inuit recruited to be exhibited in
the "Volkerschauen" or ethnographic "peoples shows" in Europe. The Inuit
voices in the text remind us that our tendencies move toward voyeurism or
exclusion in our encounters with other cultures. Between spaces of absence
and presence, where are the people? Between voyeurism and erasure—constituted as nowhere to be found. How can we bring texts and authors into
conversations with one another in a curriculum of ecological diffractions?
    Listen to Iyola Kingwatsiak, in interview, responding to the experience of
printmaking at a Conference on Inuit Art.

> The non-Inuit at the conference spoke as much as they pleased about their own
> lives and how they lived like Inuit. But they never gave us a chance to speak or
> asked questions about our work. The white people dominated as usual.
>   We're just like part of the showpieces; they treat us like carvings. The
> white people never seemed to be interested in talking with us. We work hard

to make a living with our art and nobody asked us to talk about how we make our carvings and prints and what kind of tools and other things we use. (cited in Ipellie 2005, vii)

I am startled once again, as I recognize fragments of my "self" as non-Inuit in their dialogue. My humiliation transforms as humility into humus reminding me of a lesson taught by one of my Elders—Aoki. And then, *an act, an event, a happening* takes place in class. A graduate student informs her Inuit student in Nunavut that we are reading a paper written by her father. He passes on his approval. He is pleased when the teacher of his daughter tells him that we are reading his writing in our graduate class. One textual experience spins and swerves into another. A site-specific locality and the intertext begins again its work. From a children's story book to an Inuit diary. I want to bring Northern curricula into our Southern classrooms. So that we can work in education with *textus*—with stories—*whose telling is not yet over.* I look again at Warabé Aska's splendid artistry of Lulie's story and the images embedded in the icy textures of an enormous glacier: penguins disguised in the play of light and shadow in the icy fissures of a glacier. I am rereading the images seeking Greenlanders missing in action. No images texts names signatures voices—once again. An architecture of wonder splinters into shards and sets off another pattern of diffractions.

My auto/ethno/graphic journey draws on storied praxis from my years of teaching in Nunavut. We would make our tea from the ice chipped off the local iceberg locked into the sea ice over the long winter months. The very best tea, according to the Inuit, was made from the water of melted iceberg heated in a teakettle. Classroom teacher always adrift, university professor at-work with drift I introduce my students to Michael Kusugak with Northern Lights and the Soccer Trails where Inuit words dwell side by side with English words. Where a girl whose name is Kataujaq rides with her mother and grandmother in a big canoe on a creaking sled. I met Kusugak in Rankin Inlet during my first two years in the Arctic. Rankin Inlet is situated on the West Coast of Hudson Bay. His mother made my parka. Now I read Kusugak's stories with my students.

> They travelled on the sea ice. Kataujaq sat with her mother and her grandmother in the big canoe on the sled.
> Sometimes they had to go over big cracks in the ice. Kataujaq's father threw the dogs into the water and made them swim across. As they climbed out of the water, the dogs shook their fur, throwing tiny droplets of water everywhere which sparkled in the bright sunlight. Then Kataujaq's father made the dogs pull the sled across with the canoe and the people in it. Kataujaq and her mother screamed, "Aaiee!!" and hugged each other really hard because the water was dark and ominous looking. (Kusugak 1993, n.p.)

The people at-work with working dogs at-work with ice and water condi-tions—geo-literacies critical for survival. Blue water is safe. Black water is deep and dangerous. From the intertextual spaces, weaving one read into another, we can journey with students to begin in the middle of the work that must be done. Working the intertext from story to story becomes a two-way flow. Working with the architecture of wonder and the movement of a sled traversing over open water in the cracks in the sea ice. Literacy for survival is about reading ice conditions. Lulie heeds the messages from his friends on the ocean currents and survives to meet the Elders in Antarctica. The sled dogs heed the guide. Listen to the cadences in Kusugak's story:

> It was very rough and there was a lot of water on the ice. The dog's paws went "Slosh, slosh, slosh, slosh..." and the sled creaked. Kataujaq's father ran along beside it, holding onto the bow of the canoe, pushing this way, pull-ing that way, guiding the sled. "Hut, hut, hut," he said to the dogs, and they turned left. (Kusugak 1993, n.p.)

Furry paws and metal runners over water and ice. The literacies of place have their own lived/living cadence(s). WaterIcePawsMetal. We are speaking here of discourse as a two-way flow. *Hut, hut, hut*... As non-Inuit researchers, we work toward learning respect for another's *unuusiq,* or way of being a person. The work is not one-sided. Bennett and Rowley (2004) in their collections of the oral history of Nunavut structured their text to resemble a *qamutiik* with two runners—a book with two parts.

In a series of recollections, a writer risks entanglement in reflexivity and seeks to resist, attending, rather, to Haraway's (1997) diffractions. Diffracted reading patterns invite rereadings in-between readings as *driftwork*—destabilizing prediction.

> Since Lulie is an iceberg—and Lulie's name comes from the Greenlandic word that means iceberg, *iluliaq.* When an iceberg calves, it sounds at first like ice cubes cracking, then becomes a rumbling, roaring sound like thunder. When it crashes into the ocean, it drags a lot of air down with it... Together all these sounds are called ice music. (H. I. H. Takamado 1998, 37)

Can we learn to listen to the ice music? An anthropomorphic rereading happens in-between two sets of scripts. In the dramatic production, humans take on the roles of sea mammals and birds. In the storybook, these crea-tures have voices and take on human attributes. Between the two sets of inscriptions, Greenlandic peoples are absent. A message that there is work to be done. My traveler stories shift from one continent to another transform-ing into a reading diary as a journeying in-between texts.

Anthropomorphizing nonhuman elements alerts us to Abram's (1996) more-than-human world, and at the same time makes absent the voices of Arctic peoples. I query my responsibility as a teacher. How can I bring the voices of Northern peoples into my courses? Aglukark (1999) reminds us of the bond between the Inuit and the land. Kublu and Mallon (1999) remind us of the connection between the Inuit and their language. They further contend that if Inuktitut is to be the working language in Nunavut then non-Inuit must be instructed in the language. How can we begin to deconstruct the arrogance of English? Destabilize the standardized curriculum?

Opening to wonder and curiosity, Aglukark (1999) shares a story with his readers as he leaves a classroom for the world of living pedagogy. And we leave our classroom site through the reads. Listen:

> The snow was melting on the streets of Arviat. I got excited whenever the school bell rang, in hopes that my father was preparing the sleds for a goose hunt. Sometimes, through the window of your classroom, you would watch the geese sailing through the clear, blue sky. As usual, the teacher couldn't understand your love for the season at hand, or your inner voice screaming at you to be out on the land as the geese cried out, flying in perfect formation in their annual migration north for the summer. (n.p.)

DIFFRACTIONS ON A POSTSCRIPT: A TEXT AT-WORK...

H. I. H. Takamado (1998) acknowledges:

> A word of appreciation to the scientists, researchers, organizations, institutes and project teams from the Arctic to the Antarctic who, through the Icebridge Forum, generously gave of their time in contributing information and photographs on ice and ice sheets, polar seas and ocean currents, as well as the archives, distribution and habits of birds, marine mammals, fish, retiles and other animals. (n.p)

I want to acknowledge those who incited my dissident selves. A delightful children's story journeys toward the wisdom of the Elders in the wake of ocean currents and in the company of friends at sea. A teacher as reader works at learning how to listen to the void. In my auto/ethno/graphic journeying, I am called upon to remember my Elder as mentor, curriculum scholar Ted T. Aoki, (2003) who teaches us about the metonymic doublings of presence and absence. Having lapsed into inattentiveness through the busyness of the everyday, I begin to pay attention.

> Reading and listening to the events of everyday life as Nunavummiut...And it is the children who count. Visit a community and listen to the children

playing.... What language are the children using? The first sign of decay is when the children play in English. (Kublu & Mallon 1999, 5)

What happens when we read Kublu and Mallon with Linda Tuhiwal Smith?

The decolonization project in research engages in multiple layers of struggle across multiple sites. It involves the unmasking and deconstruction of imperialism, and its aspect of colonialism, in its old and new formations. (Linda Tuhiwal Smith 2005, 88)

What are the losses when we lose a language that is closely tied to the land? Cynthia Chambers (2008) speaks of a wayfinding as/in a curriculum of place. Geo-literacies that are on the move. Chambers draws from Collignon (2003) on wayfinding as "living your geography" (123). Lulie the Iceberg lives his geography as *driftwork* as he journeys toward the Elders. Sedentary now in the nation's capital, I live my geography in the texts and textures of teaching responsibilities. How can we open spaces for our students to live their geographies? Glotfelty (1996) contends "ecocriticism takes an earth-centered approach to literary studies" (xviii). As an academic vagabond, I want to write *à pied* around and about the text (Palulis, 2009). To write *à pied* is perhaps to be in exile, to circle the text, *to create anew*. To exile my "self" through the swerve of a diffraction pattern.

Attending to Smith (2005) in the work of decolonizing our projects, how can we engage with "multiple layers of struggle across multiple sites" (88)? Smith focuses on the signification of a "pause" as a hopeful sign when the Western hegemonic gaze "pauses even momentarily to consider an alternative possibility. Indigenous research actively seeks to extend that momentary pause into ... alternative ways of seeking to live with and in the world" (103). Many of us in academia are waiting for that "pause" and, in the meantime, we are willing to risk working with alternative ways of seeking.

I returned to Baffin Island in May 2006 to begin the process of establishing research connections with the community of Pond Inlet. From the moment of arrival at the Airport in Pond, conversations that began at the Airport in Iqaluit take on momentum. I was surrounded by children with whom I had a connection through their parents some decades ago. The Inuit language is a spatial language and in the temporality of spatial events, speaking words work at recognition and reconnecting in multiple sites of interaction: the airport, the Co-op café, the school staff room, the library/archive centre bordering on the sea. Pond is also located within the global environment—a stopping point for cruise ships visiting the High Arctic. A local/global doubling of spatial praxis. An Inuit friend arrives at the small airport just before my departure with a contact written on a piece of torn-off brown wrapping paper: a contact for a tourist orga-nization that offers trips by land and sea; I am reminded of my role as a tourist outsider in this act of kindness.

From Qitsualik (1999), I locate and draw on the wisdom of the Inuit word—*pijariiqpunga*—because this is where the most difficult work must be done. We must learn to listen deeply when we learn to stop so that another can speak. Qitsualik speaks of *isuma*—of respect for another's *isuma*—"A fundamental tenet of Inuit society was the sacred nature of isuma: that another's mind was not to be intruded upon" (n.p). Listen to the words.

> The word "pijariiqpunga" has no English equivalent. In traditional Inuit cul-ture, each speaker is allowed his or her own isuma. Others won't interrupt until a speaker is allowed his or her own isuma. Others won't interrupt until a speaker indicates that they've said all they needed to. There is no time limit: a speaker can sit in silence for quite a while, yet no one will speak until he or she ends with "pijariiqpunga." It means that they're finished, and someone else can have a turn to speak. (Qitsualik 1999, n.p.)

As we engage with Lulie's story, we are reminded of another path in way-finding—as a diffraction pattern—as an acoustic dissonance. Working with the wisdom of the Elders and the wonder of children. Barratt Hacking, Barratt and Scott (2007) support a shift from "research *on* children to research *with* children" (540) expressing concern with "an adult-managed childhood" and lamenting the loss of childhood (531). We need to learn how to pay attention to the voices of children and to their concerns. Attending to Luke (1996) we need to rework the body literate opening to movement and the wonder of curiosity—disrupting mandated discourse and stilled inscrip-tions. Guattari (2000) calls for dissident subjectivities in ecological spaces. As Haraway reminds us, the swerve needs to swerve decisively. And listening to Lyotard we are working with "[d]riftworks in the plural, for the question is not of leaving *one* shore, but several, simultaneously; what is at work is not one current, pushing and tugging, but different drives and tractions" (10). Guattari's *dissident subjectivities* are at-work with Lyotard's *driftworks in the plural*. Resonating with Smith's multiplicities of sites and struggle. To my readers, I offer a pause of silence. And now—listen: ice bridges are shat-tering; ice is rupturing; ice shelves are drifting; permafrost is melting; the ocean is suffering from seasickness.

A passenger on the ferry along the west coast of Greenland, I become seasick caught up in the swell of the sea—disoriented equilibrium. I am already dread-ing the prospect of another sea journey by freighter to Japan. I spend the interval recovering on a sofa bed in a friend's apartment in Montreal. A flight to Seattle and I am on my way once again. During the sea voyage to Japan, a storm mid-Pacific threatens to break the freighter in half. As I sit with friends in the top deck library, I am so caught up in the momentum of fear-becoming-wonder that I am ready to go out in a torrent of waves. Soundscapes of a death toll. But the sea calmed and we lived on. And now, in the Sunday paper, I read as Alanna Mitchell writes about another kind of seasick—the global ocean is in crisis—the global ocean is seasick—and rereading is not enough—the swerve must swerve decisively—with a story whose telling is not yet over.

...pijariiqpunga...

ENDNOTES

1. Geo-literacy will be conceived as reading the earth, drawing from earth scientists (Clague, J., Turner, R., Bates, J., Haidl, F., Morgan, A. & Vodden, C. 2001). The Canadian Council for Geographic Education encourages understanding relationships between the physical environment and society.
2. Eco-literacy draws from the work of Capra (1996) and Orr (1992) on sustainable communities and ecosystems. Capra and Orr are co-founders of the Center for Ecoliteracy.

REFERENCES

Abram, David. 1996. *The Spell of the Sensuous: Language in a More-than-human World*. New York: Pantheon Books.

Aglukark, Brian. 1999. "Inuit and the Land as One." *Nunavut'99*. Accessed August 18, 2005. http://www.nunavut.com/nunavut99/english/inuit_land.html

Aoki, Ted. T. 2003. "Locating Living Pedagogy in Teacher 'Research': Five metonymic moments." In *Curriculum Intertext,* edited by Erika Hasebe-Ludt & Wanda Hurren, 1–10. New York: Peter Lang Publishing, Inc.

Barndt, Deborah, ed. 2006. *Wild Fire: Art as Activism*. Toronto, ON: Sumach Press.

Barratt Hacking, Elisabeth, Robert Barratt, & William Scott. 2007. "Engaging Children: Research Issues around Participation and Environmental Learning." *Environmental Education Research* 13 (4), 529–544.

Barthes, Roland. 1979. "From Work to Text." In *Textual Strategies: Perspectives in Post- structuralist Criticism,* edited by Josué V. Harari, 73–81. Ithaca, NY: Cornell University.

Bennett, John, & Susan Rowley. 2004. *Uqalurait: An Oral History of Nunavut*. Montreal and Kingston: McGill-Queen's University Press.

Capra, Fritjof .1996. *The Web of Life: A New Scientific Understanding of Living Systems*. New York: Anchor Books.

Chambers, Cynthia. 2008. "Where Are We? Finding Common Ground in a Curriculum of Place." *Journal of the Canadian Association for Curriculum Studies* 6 (2): 113–128.

Clague, J., R. Turner, J. Bates, F. Haidl, A. Morgan & C. Vodden .2001. "Geoliteracy Canada, A National Geoscience Education Initiative." *Geoscience Canada* 28 (3): 143–149.

Clough, Patricia T. 2000. *Autoaffection: Unconscious Thought in the Age of Teletechnology*. Minneapolis: University of Minnesota Press.

De Bolla, Peter. 2001. *Art Matters*. Cambridge, MA: Harvard University Press.

Doel, Marcus. 1999. *Poststructuralist Geographies: The Diabolical Art of Spatial Science*. Lanham: Rowman & Littlefield Publishers, Inc.

———. 2000. "Un-glunking Geography: Spatial Science after Dr. Seuss and Giles Deleuze." In *Thinking Space*, edited by Mike Crang & Nigel Thrift, 117–135. London and New York: Routledge.

———. 2004. "Poststructural geographies: the essential selection." In *Envisioning Human Geograph*, edited by Paul Cloke, Phil Crang, & Mark Goodwin, 146–171. London, UK: Oxford University Press.

Dobrin, Sidney, & Kenneth Kidd, eds. 2004. *Wild Things: Children's Culture and Ecocriticism*. Detroit, MI: Wayne State University Press.

Glotfelty, Cheryll. 1996. Introduction: Literary Studies in an Age of Environmental Crisis. In *The Ecocriticism Reader: Landmarks in Literary Ecology*, edited by Cheryll Glotfelty & Harold Fromm, xv–xxxvii. Athens: University of Georgia Press.

Gough, Annette, & Noel Gough. 2004. "Environmental Education Research in Southern Africa: Dilemmas of Interpretation." *Environmental Education Research* 10 (3): 409–424.

Guattari, Félix. 2000. *The Three Ecologies*. Translated by Ian Pindar & Paul Sutton. London and New York: Continuum.

Haraway, Donna. 1997. *Modest_Witness@Second_Millennium.FemaleMan©_ Meets_ OncoMouse™*. New York: Routledge.

Hasebe-Ludt, Erika, & Wanda Hurren, eds. 2003. *Curriculum Intertext: Place / Language / Pedagogy*. New York: Peter Lang.

Ipellie, Alootook. 2005. Foreword to *The Diary of Abraham Ulrikab: Text and Context*, edited by Hartmut Lutz, vii–xv. Ottawa, ON: University of Ottawa Press.

Irwin, Rita L., & Alex de Cosson, eds. 2004. *A/r/tography: Rendering Self through Arts-based Living Inquiry*. Vancouver, BC: Pacific Educational Press.

Jardine, David 2006. "Foreword: Dreaming of a Single Logic." In *Trying to Teach in a Season of Great Untruth: Globalization, Empire and the Crises of Pedagogy*, edited by David Geoffrey Smith, ix–xvii. Rotterdam: Sense Publishers.

Joseph, Michael, & Lissa Paul. 2004. "Praise for Handmade Literacies in an Age of the Standardized Kind." *The Lion and the Unicorn* 29: v–vii.

Kublu, Alexina, & Mick Mallon. 1999. "Our Language, Our Selves." *Nunavut'99*. Accessed August 18, 2005. http://www.nunavut.com/nunavut99/english/our.html

Kusugak, Michael. 1993. *Northern Lights: The Soccer Trails*. Toronto: Annick Press.

Luke, Allan. 1996. "The Body Literate: Discourse and Inscription in Early Literacy Training." In *The Communication Theory Reader*, edited by Paul Colby, 384–395. New York: Routledge.

Lutz, Hartmut, ed. 2005. *The Diary of Abraham Ulrikab: Text and Context*. Ottawa, ON: University of Ottawa Press.

Lyotard, Jean-François. 1984. *Driftworks*. Cambridge, MA: Semiotext(e)

Mitchell, Alanna 2011. *Sea Sick*. Toronto, ON: McClelland & Stewart.

Morawski, Cynthia & Palulis, Patricia. 2009. "Auto/ethno/graphies as Teaching Lives: An Aesthetics of Difference." *JCT: Journal of Curriculum Theorizing* 25 (9): 6–23.

Mostafavi, Mohsen. 2007. "Ecological Urbanism." In *Intervention Architecture*, edited by Aga Khan Foundation. London and New York, I. B. Tauris & Co. Ltd.

Olshansky, Beth. 2008. *The Power of Pictures: Creating Pathways to Literacy through Art*. San Francisco: Jossey-Bass.

Orr, David W. 1992. *Ecological Literacy: Education and the Transition to a Postmodern World*. Albany, NY: State University of New York Press.

Palulis, Patricia. 2009. "Geo-literacies in a Strange Land: Academic Vagabonds Provoking *à Pied*." *Educational Insights* 13 (4). Accessed January 30, 2010. http://www.ccfi.educ.ubc.ca/publication/insights/v13n04/articles/palulis/index.html

Palulis, Pat & Low, Marylin. 2001. "Messy (W)rites of Passage: Disrupting Circumscriptions through Doublings of Difference." *JCT: Journal of Curriculum Theorizing* 17 (3), 39–58.

Qitsualik, Rachel Attituq. 1999. "Living with Change." *Nunavut '99*. Accessed August 18, 2005. http://www.nunavut.com/nunavut99/english/change.html

Reed-Danahay, Deborah, ed. 1997. *Auto/Ethnography: Rewriting the Self and the Social*. Oxford, UK, and New York: Berg.

Roy, Kaustuv. 2003. *Teachers in Nomadic Spaces*. New York: Peter Lang Publishing, Inc.

Russell, Catherine. 1999. *Experimental Ethnography: The Work of Film in the Age of Video*. Durham and London: Duke University Press.

Smith, Linda T. 2005. "On Tricky Ground: Researching the Native in the Age of Uncertainty." In *The Sage Handbook of Qualitative Research Third Edition*, edited by Norman Denzin & Yvonne Lincoln, 85–108. Thousand Oaks: Sage Publishing Inc.

Springgay, Stephanie, Irwin, Rita., & Kind, Sylvia 2005. "A/r/tography as Living Inquiry through Art and Text." *Qualitative Inquiry* 11 (6): 897–912.

Takamado, Hisako. 1998. *Lulie the Iceberg*. New York, Tokyo and London: Kodansha

Trinh, Minh-ha T. 2005. *The Digital Film Event*. New York: Routledge.

CHAPTER 12

POACHING IN THE CHORDS OF READING: DWELLING IN THE MURKY SPACES OF THE LITERARY LANDWASH

DAVID LEWKOWICH

WHETHER IMMERSED IN THE FOLDS OF A BOOK, GAZING at a landscape, or remembering our childhood encounters, the experience of reading is a messy activity, through which the tendrils of stability and absolute coherence inescapably leak. As with every encounter in a social world, our thoughts move in a dialogic way, and as they take shape through myriad associational collisions, they emerge through what Mikhail Bakhtin refers to as *heteroglossia*, the integration of, "*another's speech in another's language*" (1981, 324; italics in the original). As with Ted Aoki's (2005) notion of the productive nature of "properly tensioned chords" in educational practice, I view the dialogues of learning that are performed in reading as through a space of sometimes discordant and sometimes harmonious textual engagement and conflict—a process of generative and often difficult conversation. The question of what these chords of reading work to generate is what I will be looking at here.

In this chapter, I discuss the perilous yet liberating nature of social reading, where reading itself is accomplished in the public space of a book club. In the field of curriculum studies, I also position this chapter as an inquiry into the relational significance of curriculum, whose meaning, as I understand it, is always potentially and socially performative. As Madeleine Grumet (2006) remarks, in relation to the worlds of literature and shared meaning: "The romance of reading invites us to recuperate our losses. As we enter into the fictive world and emerge from it, we experience the opportunity to reconsider the boundaries and exclusions that sustain our social identities" (221). This chapter, then, looks at the ways that readings leak interminably across boundaries of discipline and curriculum; and more specifically, across the margins of medicine and literature.

This chapter emerges out of a larger study (Lewkowich 2008), as part of Dr. Judith P. Robertson's *Saltwater Chronicles*[1], in which I worked with a reading group in the medical humanities out of Memorial University's faculty of medicine, located in Newfoundland and Labrador. Named the *Humanities, Arts & Medicine Interest Group*, (known henceforth as HAM,) their mandate, as expressed publicly and succinctly on their website, is "to discuss art that engages themes of health and illness." They meet about once a month in *Bitter's*, the graduate student on-campus pub. It's a bit of a raucous space for a book club, what with the pouring of pints of Guinness, exclamations of reunions between old friends, and soccer matches serving as the backdrop to a discussion about issues of literature and representation, death and the dying, the writing of poetry and the practice of medicine. As students and faculty who view the arts and medicine as complementary fields, insufficient unto themselves, they engage in a process of naming what their curricular environment lacks, and, in so doing, connect with a freedom only available to those who seek and name their restrictions (Greene 1988, 6–7).

Here, it is worth noting the humorous qualities of the group's title—HAM—through its relation to the jocular madness of children's author Dr. Seuss, and an overall tendency towards "hamming it up" in the slippages of humor. Since the appearance of the word HAM on the page, and as enunciated in dialogue, is slightly jarring in its colossal capitalization, these promptings to chuckle can never be overemphasized. While working with HAM, I observed the group's reactions and interpretive practices as applied to two diverse pieces of literature. The first, *Paula*, by Isabel Allende (1996), can be described simultaneously as an act of mourning, a confessional, a journal, and an autobiographical work of magical realism. The second is *Quick*, a collection of poetry by Anne Simpson (2007), whose principal themes are death, the body, the natural world, transubstantiation (the conversion of a given substance into another), and the ways in which thresholds and borders manifest themselves in the liminalities of everyday life.

My initial foray and pursuant analysis into how this group speaks of their space of reading is framed by two key metaphorical concepts: that of *poaching*, and that of the *landwash*. As with Maxine Greene (1995), I find it advantageous to dwell in "the domain of imagination and metaphor" (99). The use of metaphor is here enabled in the manner encouraged by Homi Bhabha and again by Greene, as it "produces hybrid realities by yoking together unlikely traditions" (Bhabha 1990, 212) and encourages "an ability to take a fresh look at the taken for granted," without which we might drown and "remain submerged in the habitual" (Greene 1995, 100).

The idea of poaching as a literary endeavor, and the conceptualization of reading group members as poachers in a space over which they cannot claim sole ownership, is employed in reference to Michel de Certeau's *The Practice of Everyday Life* (1984), where reading itself is seen as an act of poaching and appropriation, and where "everyday life invents itself by poaching in countless ways on the property of others" (xii). De Certeau regards the act of reading as one of clandestine labor, where the meaning that emerges—and which in its dynamic relations remains emergent—is accomplished through a hidden struggle of unceasing inventiveness and translation. Claims of meaning are staked as the reader engages the possibilities of place through acts of dispersion and association, themselves motivated by a series of secret desires. Such a concept also works to emphasize "the exploratory and productive *action* required of the reader or participant in the arts" (Greene 1995, 96; italics in the original), wherein a text is a meeting place, from a vantage subverting the supposedly systematic impulses to completion.

Acts of poaching, whether spontaneous or deliberative, are like the insensible plodding and plotting of footsteps—they come to pass whether or not we sit around and take the time to think about them first—yet they're always involved in the string of a reader's decisions, where the choices made determine where they go and what they poach, "to be personally present to what they see and hear and read" (Greene 1995, 104). Also, as "the action itself closes off alternatives" (Greene 1988, 5), *where* I poach is *where* I choose to value, for as "place is a pause in movement...the pause makes it possible for a locality to become a centre of felt value" (Tuan 1997, 138), and from there, to move on. In this, I am reminded of Grumet's observation—in her discussion of curriculum and textual selection—about the risks of colonizing the pleasures and desires of others, indicating that, "The task of pointing out the world is dangerous" (2006, 218). The movements and rhythms of collective reading, however, as fractal, typically messy, and purloining impulses of the "extraordinarily ordinary instances of life" are themselves also subject to another transformation—from the banal to the criminal and scandalous (Nafisi 2003, 6). In acts of reading, as we claim and produce a meaning for ourselves from texts we did not create, there is always an interwoven sense of stealing in a land of chance and gambling. Just as a poacher hunts for game on a land that is not her own, the reader treads for meaning on ice that could crack at any moment.

The second metaphor that has helped me to frame my understandings of reading in a social space is from the phenomena of tidal flow and regeneration, the movements of which encourage an impermanent space of natural flux, known in Newfoundland and Labrador as the *landwash*, and which is, "The sea-shore between high and low tide marks, washed by the sea" (Story et al. 1990, 297). George Story (1997), a principal editor of the Dictionary of Newfoundland English, writes how, in Newfoundland, the space of the landwash "has long been recognized as a rich, productive area. It is a margin, and now in other places the margin is increasingly gaining recognition as a site of change and progress. In Newfoundland, they knew that all along" (vi). Dwelling in the murky and shifting spaces of the landwash, as in the context of collective reading, depends on acknowledging the fruitful nature of liminal and potentially messy activities as methods for intellectual and affective pedagogical uncoverings; to, as Greene puts it, "break with the 'cotton-wool' of habit, of mere routine" (Greene 1988, 2), and in so doing, to look for openings. Like the landwash, what matters most in reading is not what you find, but what you build with what you find; for instance, how the chance encounter of whale bone, rusted-out motor and driftwood inspire and realign into a personally constituted work of sculptural art, or as a landscape of topographical poetics—an impetus through which to think. When we occupy a text, or sit as a member of a reading group, we read with one foot on the melting beach and the other on seemingly solid land.

The landwash, as I see it, functions in three related ways: (a) as a reprieve, and a predictable moment of pause. There is peace in looking out at the open ocean and knowing what will be there, as there is also a trust that transpires in meeting with other readers in a shared social circumstance; (b) as a space of adventure and questioning, where what is washed up by the waters is never known beforehand. While in Newfoundland, I witnessed chunks of an iceberg, thousands of years old, floating into the shore; chisel-wielding families hunkered down to chop a piece of the beast. When readers meet with each other, conflicts are crucial to the development of their conversation, erratic and sporadic as they might be; (c) as a space of danger, and a place you must leave, throwing certainty into disarray, and demonstrated by the violence of the Newfoundland shoreline. We all have lives to lead and to read outside of books, and at the end of a meeting surrounding a book we all must take our leave, and for the members of HAM, this means stepping back to a space where the validity of the arts might not be so appreciated. In drawing a distinction between a *visit* and a *tour*, Cynthia Chambers (2006) symbolizes the former as "a viewing with no obligations," while the latter, which is where I locate the productive nature of the landwash, and its potential for the field of curriculum studies, "is a form of renewal, a way of renewing and recreating people, places and beings and their relationships to one another" (35).

The space of HAM is thus in a landwash site, *tours* that "become sites of inquiry and pedagogy" (ibid.), spurring a space of adventure where rocks are overturned in the hope of finding scurrying and scuttling crabs of acuity, but a space which also must be abandoned to find safety from the crashing waves of the natural world—an awareness of overarching discipline. The imperatives of poaching in this space are thus made obvious; as poaching implies treading on land that is not one's known, it is an active seeking out of resistance and acting out of freedom—breaking through "the persisting eitherors" (Greene 1988, 8)—and since the blending of the categories of reading and knowing brings, to HAM, an awareness of this transgressive fact, there will always be a relative lack of safety that arises from, as Newfoundland satirist Ray Guy (1975) puts it, "arsing around down in the landwash" (13). Though organized out of an academic setting—which might be understood as a place of privilege and cultural influence—HAM's status, as a forum for engaging the uses and implications that literature brings to medicine, is also one tinged throughout by marginality. This is a contradictory and productive space, through which resistance to established conceptual norms is an inevitable consequence of reading as a form of vigorous questioning, and also, of "working though" knowledge, understood by the readers in HAM as always more than simply that which is given.

In approaching the articulations of readers, it is important to recognize how "every literary description is a view" (Barthes 1974, 54), and "that the speaker stands at the window, not so much to see, but to establish what [s]he sees by its very frame" (ibid., 10). As Elizabeth Long (2003) notes, in her fine work on women's book clubs, we "move back and forth between using people's remarks as windows into the text…and using the text as a window into people's lives or various aspects of the cultural and social lives we live together" (145). Framed in the litter of driftwood and bleached bones, then, writing here on reader's reading experiences, I'm in the landwash as much as they (though perhaps of a different cove).

Though looking at a literary text from the social vantage of a reading group can serve a plethora of purposes for its readers, from the vaguely therapeutic to the seeking out of community, I will here look briefly at one purpose that the members of HAM enunciate in their conversations: *Drumming in and drumming out; spaces of continuity in collective reading*. In approaching the words of HAM's readers, I look at the ways that language is used to describe their encounters in the manner that de Certeau speaks of everyday experience, as "an 'art' which is anything but passive" (de Certeau 1984, xxii). Each of HAM's members insist on the informal and casual nature of the group, and that the group's activities are inextricably marked by difference; from mainstream medicine, from book clubs, and what Karen—the group's self proclaimed "instigator"—calls the overall, "dailyness of things"

(K, I-1)[2]. This latter challenge is illustrated by one reader through the prevalence of what she calls a "get yourself through the day, and do what needs to be done" sort of attitude (B, I-2). This "participatory involvement" with the arts, in which difference is marked from the outset, enables those in HAM to, in the words of Greene, "*hear* more on normally unheard frequencies, to *become conscious* of what daily routines have obscured, what habit and convention have suppressed" (Greene 1995, 123; italics in the original).

Since the pleasures that she derives from HAM's readings are many, both in the realms of intellect and affect (not mutually exclusive), Karen—a medical student, a journalist, a seabird biologist originally from Alberta, and an award-winning author of fiction and poetry—envisions the reading group as a site for troubling, in the broader sphere of medical education, what Bill Ashcroft identifies as "the trope of boundary" (Ashcroft 2001, 128). For the group's readers, who for the most part were students and staff at the faculty of medicine, the curriculum they had been engaged with in medical school was most frequently directed towards a purely rational (and linear) model for understanding the human body. In such an atmosphere, being an artist marks you as subversive almost *by accident*, as what Robertson notes is "a public sign of recognition not only of [a] virtuous... identity, but also of the burden imposed by being special" (Robertson 2002, 201). And like other marks (cuts and bruises, scabs, scars, tattoos, the lightning rod on Harry Potter's forehead), such indications of difference, while sometimes extolled as necessary expressions of autonomy, are also and simultaneously felt as marks of idiosyncrasy and isolation, viewed at times as an unnecessary quirkiness that can lead the marked to a space of marginality.

HAM can thus be construed, as Long notes, "as one form of cultural constitution or cultural resistance" (2003, 145), and though sometimes such marks remain hidden, this is not always the case. Karen, the instigator, relates, "We're not trying to be... anti-establishment, or anything like that. It's just kind of an accident" (K, I-1). Out of such "accidents" emerge a subjective use-value for HAM's readers—a form of public affirmation and resistance in a practice of subversive artistic conservation, through which, as Karen again puts it, "If you played piano before medical school, to keep playing piano in medical school" (K, I-2). But this task is not simply a matter of wishing it so, and as Karen regretfully remarks, "You have to look like a human being in order to get in, but then as soon as you start medical school, those things are *drummed* out of you" (ibid.). Among the members of HAM, there is sometimes a shared and disorienting nostalgia, "a common experience of feeling trapped in an educational script [they] did not write" (Robertson & McConaghy 2006, 7).

The concept of *drumming* here takes on qualities beyond those of the simply rhythmic, and moves instead into the territory of violence, coercion, and regulation, since "subjectively," as human geographer Yi-fu Tuan (1977) recognizes, "space and time have lost their directional thrust under the influence of rhythmic sound. Each step...is striding into open and undifferentiated space" (128). The place of drumming is one where the waves of the ocean are giant handclaps, and not the slight whisper of trickling raindrops. It's also such a drumming that reduces the multiplicity of writerly performances, in Roland Barthes' characterization of what the writerly is, as a practice (and praxis) of discomfort, wherein texts are successfully diverted away from succumbing to the static and solitary fate as "objects of easy consumption" (Boler 1999, 169). For as, to steal a phrase from Barthes, "the writerly text is ourselves writing, before the infinite play of the world," in the face of the sharply driven barrel beat of a discipline's internal norms and regulations, mistaken for the heart beat of a living thing, such a text is again, and continuing with Barthes (1974), "traversed, intersected, stopped, plasticized by some singular system...which reduces the plurality of entrances, the opening of networks, the infinity of languages" (5).

When Bridget, another reader in HAM, and a medical student originally from St. John's, speaks of attempts to reflect artistically on her medical practice and the inner workings of human physiology through engaging poetry in her classes, she relates that "I was trying, but I got beat down a little bit. I got tired. It was hard for anyone who's a sensitive soul, and it beat me down pretty hard. The people are so cruel...to their patients" (B, I-2). The incidence of such beating distracts from reflections on life and death, as, and to quote again from Tuan (1977), "soldiers who march to military music tend to forget not only their weariness but also their goal—the battlefield, with its promise of death" (129).

Such cruelty is one of the unofficial attitudes of medical school referred to by curriculum theorist Delese Wear (2006), who writes that "if the formal curriculum doesn't deal with them directly, take up residence in the hushed (but often informally sanctioned) corridor talk among many students and residents, in the shorthand jargon they use to categorize particular kinds of patients...unlike themselves" (93). Military drumming transforms the fractures of a collective into a single entity: the plush mallets of the bass drum bring about, and sustain, a single cadence of worn footsteps, and with a constant, recurring beat, everyone eventually falls in step. "Such repetitions," note Robertson and McConaghy (2006), "beat at the heart of catastrophe" and, as they observe in the writings of Sylvia Ashton-Warner, uncover "a wound released in prosody that is a form of address, whose crying out asks us to witness a truth" (6). Bridget says of the medical school environment, that "It's all very (hit) (hit) (hit)," as she taps her knuckles on the table, indicating a force, a sharpness, a regularity, and a nowness to thoughts, *as breath*, a pulsating narrative that "commands others (then, now, and always) to awaken to its imperative demand" (Robertson 1999, 164).

There is a semiotic trauma here in witnessing, a difficulty in making a language speak in a space that is not its own, and as Robertson (1999) asks:

> When language is used in times of social and psychological crisis, how does that language always contain silences, struggles, and representations that may appear to be incoherent by very virtue of the fact that writers are attempting to assimilate or depict what is, in fact, an unassimilable experience (massive suffering, fear, and death)? (163)

A confession can be beaten out of someone; if one can drum something into you, one can also drum something out. For Karen, this military essence of medical school is at odds not only with her life as an artist, but also with her scientific nature. In her words:

> It's very militaristic, and it's all about evidence-based medicine, professional protocols, all this kind of thing, and I didn't really come from this. I studied evolution, where it's all about diversity, and strength in diversity, so to come from that background to go into professional school, where you're aspiration is to be just like the next guy is soul destroying. So to counter that with a group of people, and medical students, who see the value of *looking* at things, and not just getting sucked into this biomedical model...is just so refreshing. (K, I-1)

Remarkably, and as it emerges from a dwelling in the positive elements of collective projects, the regularity of drumming as a unifying force (for there is power in such a surge) is applied directly to HAM's organization, a caustic power turned onto its reiterative head. Karen relates to me: "To do that once a month, it's like 'Oh, right, this is important. Oh, I'm not just hallucinating, like other people think this is important too'" (ibid.). In conversation over books, where readers can, in the words of Greene, "plunge into subject matter in order to steep themselves in it...it is never enough simply to...recognize certain phenomena...there has to be a live, aware, reflective transaction if what presents itself to consciousness is to be realized" (Greene 1995, 30).

For HAM's readers, their space of collective reading functions as more than just a recognition that medicine can be represented in artistic terms, but that such reading itself, in a shifting and messy landscape populated by countless interpretive acts, challenges the notion that one line of interpretation is ever enough. What's more, and just like the movements of a rhythmic refrain, or the waves of a properly tensioned chord, revolving around the variances of a single repeated gesture, the landwash, in its mess and its absolute unpredictability, has a clearing quality as well; the laps of the waves, though violent, can also lull you to sleep. In this way, too, the readers in HAM "choose in a fundamental way...between a desire or harmony along with the easy answer and a commitment to the search for alternative possibilities" (Greene 1995, 129). Even though Karen realizes in the "beat" a destructive force, she also sees in the space that this beat creates a productive potential, understanding the impulse on which it preys: that of dependability, and the internalized stolidity of the visible. She says:

> So now [HAM] is an activity of the medical school, even though very few medical students come to it. At least it is there to say that this is important in practice, not just in principle, and here, look, we do it every month. That's why it's so important that we do it every month. (K, I-2)

And like the carving of an ocean's edge, through purposely veering into the stride of these multifarious beats of textual encounter, there is a moment of pause thus carved out of, and into, these spaces of reading. And, though messy, it offers to its readers what we can call an authentic choice, however fleeting.

ENDNOTES

1. This study is part of Dr. Judith P. Robertson's SSHRC-funded research project: *Saltwater Chronicles: Understanding Reading in the Regional Book Club of Newfoundland and Labrador,* (2003) Grant # 0401 213 03.
2. In this chapter, I identify two of HAM's primary participants. Karen (HAM's Instigator), and Bridget, one of the rare class of medical students whose academic background, before medicine, is strictly in the arts. Karen was my initial contact in HAM, and though not the group's 'leader,' she does organize the meetings and sometimes steer discussion. Though originally from St. John's, I actually met Bridget in Montreal, where she was working as a resident in adolescent health. The transcriptions are referenced in the following manner: (1) The respondent's pseudonym, and (2) The data source (i.e., Group meeting: GM-1 or GM-2, Interview: I-1 or I-2).

REFERENCES

Allende, Isabel. 1996. *Paula.* New York: Harper Perennial.
Aoki, Ted T. 2005. "Teaching as Indwelling Between Two Worlds." In *Curriculum in a New Key: The Collected Works of Ted T. Aoki,* edited by William F. Pinar & Rita L. Irwin, 159–165. Mahwah, New Jersey: Lawrence Erlbaum Associates.
Ashcroft, Bill. 2001. *Post-Colonial Transformation.* New York: Routledge.

Bakhtin, Mikhail M. 1981. *The Dialogic Imagination*, trans. Caryl Emerson & Michael Holquist. Edited by Michael Holquist. Austin: University of Texas Press.

Barthes, Roland. 1974. *S/Z*, trans. Richard Miller. New York: Hill and Wang.

Bhabha, Homi. 1990. "The Third Space." In *Identity: Community, Culture, Difference*, edited by Jonathan Rutherford, 207–221. London: Lawrence & Wishart.

Boler, Megan. 1999. *Feeling Power: Emotions and Education.* New York: Routledge.

Chambers, Cynthia. 2006. "'The Land is the Best Teacher I Ever Had': Places as Pedagogy for Precarious Times." *JCT: Journal of Curriculum Theorizing* 22: 27–37.

de Certeau, Michel. 1984. *The Practice of Everyday Life*, trans. Steven Rendall. Berkeley: University of California Press.

Greene, Maxine. 1988. *The Dialectic of Freedom.* New York: Teachers College Press.

———. 1995. *Releasing the Imagination: Essays on Education, the Arts, and Social Change.* San Francisco: Jossey-Bass.

Grumet, Madeleine R. 2006. "Romantic Research: Why we Love to Read." In *Love's Return: Psychoanalytic Essays on Childhood, Teaching and Learning*, edited by Gail M. Boldt & Paula M. Salvio, 207–225. New York: Routledge.

Guy, Ray. 1975. *You May Know Them as Sea Urchins, Ma'am.* Portugal Cove, Newfoundland: Breakwater Books.

Lewkowich, David. 2008. *Poaching in the Landwash: An Interrogation of Cultural Meaning in a St. John's Newfoundland Collective Reading Group.* MA Thesis, University of Ottawa.

———. 2009. "Landwash Readers: A Space of Collective Reading in the Medical Humanities." *Journal of the Canadian Association for Curriculum Studies* 7: 85–110.

Long, Elizabeth. 2003. *Book Clubs: Women and the Uses of Reading in Everyday Life.* Chicago: The University of Chicago Press.

Nafisi, Azir. 2003. *Reading Lolita in Tehran: A Memoir in Books.* New York: Random House.

Robertson, Judith P. 1999. "Teaching the *Holodomor* (Ukraine Famine): Issues of Language, Literary Pedagogy, and Learning." In *Teaching for a Tolerant World: Grades 9–12, Essays and Resources*, edited by Carol Danks & Leatrice Rabinsky, 152–173. Illinois: National Council of Teachers of English.

———. 2002. "What Happens to our Wishes: Magical Thinking in Harry Potter." *Children's Literature Association Quarterly* 26: 198–211.

———. 2003. *Saltwater Chronicles: Understanding Reading in the Regional Book Club of Newfoundland and Labrador.* SSHRC, Grant # 040121303.

Robertson, Judith P., & Cathryn McConaghy, eds. 2006. *Provocations: Sylvia Ashton-Warner and Excitability in Education.* New York: Peter Lang Publishing, Inc.

Simpson, Anne. 2007. *Quick.* Toronto: McClelland & Stewart.

Story, George. M. 1997. *People of the Landwash: Essays on Newfoundland and Labrador.* St. John's: Harry Cuff Publications.

Story, George M., William J. Kirwin, & John D. A. Widdowson, eds. 1990. *Dictionary of Newfoundland English.* Toronto: University of Toronto Press.

Tuan, Yu-Fi. 1977. *Space and Place: The Perspective of Experience.* Minneapolis: University of Minnesota Press.

Wear, Delese. 2006. "Respect for Patients: A Case Study of the Formal and Hidden Curriculum." In *Professionalism in Medicine: Critical Perspectives,* edited by Delese Wear & Julie M. Aultman, 87–101. New York: Springer.

CHAPTER 13

UNCOMMON COMPOSURE: BECOMING A TEACHER

MAXX LAPTHORNE AND DEANNE LOMHEIM BARRETT

THE UNCOMMON COUNTENANCE OF CANADIAN CURRICULUM studies is contested among academics who teach and write at Canadian Universities, *and* Canadian curriculum studies is also negotiated with students in public schools and their teachers. In this case, uncommon countenance does not refer to the arrangement of the teacher's face as she stands at the front of the classroom, peering imperiously at her students as she "delivers" the prescribed government curriculum. We wouldn't offer such a thin trick as a legitimate example of teacher composure, although one look at the offerings of many teacher handbooks, and it appears as though it is these kinds of "Monday morning ready" tips and tricks that teachers desperately need. It may be true that an occasional imperious glare is effective in redirecting a student's attentions, however, the disproportional amount of workshops and resources offered in this logistical vein suggests that as educators, our attentions are also in need of redirection. Where curriculum comes from, what it is, and who it is for are questions that come to bear in every classroom. Do we really have to study Shakespeare, again? Why do we need to know Pythagorean theorem? Who cares about colonialism? These questions may be taken as merely the plaintive cries of adolescents, however, they can also be taken as powerful questions about what we are doing together in schools. What *are* we doing together in schools? What are public school teachers, and scholars, and youths doing *together* in Canadian schools? Who are we *becoming* together?

As beginning teachers in the same high school and students who ventured into graduate work together, Maxx and I (Deanne) offer our intersecting stories and historicity as examples of an uncommon possibility within Canadian curriculum studies. Our many conversations and drafts and questions through the process of writing together has mirrored our shared struggle to compose ourselves as women, as teachers, and as scholars in the face of our unfolding understanding of the complexity of our profession. The work of becoming, in the Gadamerian sense of *bildung* (Gadamer 2004, 8), is ongoing, compositional work, as we continue to arrange together the ideas, the examples, the voices, and the questions that provoke us, compel us, and give us life.

The dialogic space was initially created during our discussions with Dr. David Jardine, Kai Kleinitz, and Tim Skuce at the 4th Biennial Provoking Curriculum Conference. When we face each other, and begin to speak our tentative understandings into the topics that so provoke us, we become composed together, as we rely on each other to fill in the gaps in our memory, and to flesh out the theoretical understandings that we have cultivated, with stories of students who have lived the curriculum. We begin to need the words of others, like Maxine Greene (1995), to remind us that, "No one of us can see the whole or sing the whole. Since I was a little child, I have known that all perspectives are contingent, that no one's picture is complete" (82).

What follows are our contingent, incomplete perspectives, woven together in a *métissage* inspired by the same intent that drives the work of Cynthia Chambers, Erika Hasebe-Ludt, and Carl Leggo (2009). Like them, "...our intent is to create a métissage of texts, which calls for new wor(l)ds with the transformative power of restor(y)ing us more wholly to the world." Where we "wish...to suggest that images and stories of the kind [we are] involving here do function as bearers of value" (12).

MAXX

Shortly after returning to teach my second year in the autumn of 2004, a teacher-mentor, Tim Skuce, was assigned to our high school. Our principal was worried about the turnover rate of the 25 newly hired teachers at our large, urban school that sits amid Calgary's least desirable neighborhoods and thus hosts Calgary's newly immigrated and least economically advantaged families. This mentor, instead of holding our hands through an idiot's guide to photocopiers or lecturing us on a myriad of cutting-edge classroom management techniques, interviewed each of us and simply asked if we had thought about what kind of teachers we wanted to become and how he might help us do that.

DEANNE

What kind of teacher do I want to become? I wanted to be the kind of teacher whom I encountered during my school experiences, the teacher who showed me a world of possibility, and who taught me how to be a part of that world. I wanted to be the teacher who could inspire her students to love books as I have loved them. I wanted to be the teacher who helped her students develop the skills they needed to become good writers. "Youth demands images," Gadamer (2004) tell us, "for its imagination and for forming its memory" (19). The images that I could draw upon to answer this question were images from my experiences as a student, as well as Hollywood versions of triumphant teachers. I had a few encounters with models of teaching that looked different from what I experienced, but these images retreated under the oppressive overhead lights of my first classroom.

MAXX

Despite what drew me to teaching in the first place: my love of studying, reading, and writing about politics and society, in my first teaching year, I quickly determined what I thought school was supposed to be about for a teacher in my board of education. In an attempt to secure tenure within the Alberta public schooling system, I had been hiding what I believed about curriculum, teaching, and teenagers for that matter, to please the evaluators. Perhaps I was particularly adept at this way of being in the world. It was reminiscent of my religious upbringing. In fact, I was quite good at hiding my private self and presenting the desired public facade. I even remember telling the mentor that I would keep all of my authentic values about educa-tion "in my back pocket" to be pulled out once I secured tenure. He spoilt this mythology by reminding me that things you put in your back pocket have a way of falling out or being forgotten. For the first time in my teaching career, someone was trying to tap into my professional and intellectual life as a pedagogue; someone was asking me to "compose my life as a teacher." My experience of teaching thus far, while somewhat rewarding interpersonally, that is, I got along well with my students and colleagues, was not a rich or rigorous pursuit.

DEANNE

I remember asking my grade 10 English class to complete their chapter ques-tions as a part of our novel study. I completed chapter questions when I was in high school, and was successful in my studies of English Literature at the university level. So, I reasoned, chapter questions must work. As my students settled into their task, they asked,

"Do we need to answer in complete sentences?"

Yes. You need to practice writing in sentences. This is not Junior High.

Do we need to include the page number?

Yes. You may need to go back to re-read that section of the book later, so note the page number.

Do I need to write in pen or is pencil ok?

In either one...as long as I can read it.

Can we work in partners?

No, I want to see your individual work. I want to see your thinking on this.

Students understand that schooling is about efficiency. These students realized that only a few words are needed to answer the questions that I assigned, and they quickly realized that I was not looking for independent thought, but instead, for rote answers, and so they copied each other's work. As I marked the assignments, I realized that I cared as little about the half-formed answers as the students themselves. I wondered how I would sustain a career filled with such meaningless tasks. I wondered how I had come so far from what I loved about reading novels. I wondered how I could translate my personal, private love of stories into the public world of school.

MAXX

While by most measures, I'd had a successful first year teaching, I just knew that something wasn't right. What was happening in my classroom wasn't resonating with me, it didn't feel true to what I thought was supposed to be happening. I was liked well enough by the students and administration, but I kept thinking that *that* wasn't really enough. I finally figured out that the students and I needed to be gathered around something important and engaging and that the textbook and the photocopied handouts were neither important nor engaging in and of themselves. Soon enough, through the efforts of our mentor and a dozen beginning teachers desiring more, a community began to grow.

DEANNE

We were having some really interesting conversations that seemed to be an extension of some of the ideas that I first encountered as a pre-service teacher in the Master of Teaching program at the University of Calgary . I was thrilled to be able to revisit some of the images of education that I lost sight of when I entered the classroom. I was interested, in the sense of the word that its Latin root indicates, I was *Inter-esse*, I was being between. Between the theoretical language I adopted during my teacher preparation classes, and the daily demands of teaching these students in this high school, I was interested in learning more about the liminal space in which I existed, in which we existed.

MAXX

Our mentor, having discussed the community developing at the high school, invited David Jardine from the University of Calgary into the conversation. Despite his teaching load, in an act of familial generosity, he offered to drive from his westerly house in Bragg Creek to our high school on the easternmost tip of Calgary each week to give a class on the interpretive discourses in education. I remember it clearly: sitting in class and having my comfortable, convenient school-world slip out from underneath me, feeling utter joy at the prospect. In notes that I wrote to Deanne during class, I remember asking her rhetorical questions like, "what did we believe before this opened up?" and "no more faking it, I guess?!" All of a sudden, someone was speaking my private language aloud.

DEANNE

That winter we began what could only be described as, in Pinar's (2004) terms, a "complicated conversation" (185). Studying the history of our profession gave us a shocking awareness of our complicity in the formation of curricular thought in Canada. In the introduction to *A Common Countenance*, Pinar (2008) suggests that "[...] professional preparation requires historical knowledge..." and "what Canadian Curriculum scholars have in common is not the present but the past." As teachers, we have been instituted, set in place, politically, socially, historically, temporally, and pedagogically. We recognized that we were complicit in a systematic, procedural institution that proliferates the status quo. Jardine reminds us that this dominant discourse is often forgetful of others at the margins and their respective discourses. When a young, new teacher such as myself, comes into the system of schooling, we are unaware of the historicity of schooling as a system. We shared the rippling shocks of betrayal, as we recognized that we had mistaken schooling for learning. We began to call our studies metaschooling, school that is about school. We began to recognize that what must be at the heart of education is a rigorous pursuit of what it means to come to understand, and this is the very kind of study that is often drowned out by the loud voices hawking "tips and tricks" to deliver curriculum. To find writers who could articulate this, and to share this revelation with other teachers at our school, was a relief.

MAXX

In the 2006 film *The History Boys*, one of the teachers, Mr. Hector articulates an instance of this feeling,

> The best moments in reading are when you come across something—a thought, a feeling, a way of looking at things—that you'd thought special, particular to you. And here it is, set down by someone else, a person you've never met, maybe even someone long dead. It's as if a hand has come out, and taken yours.

This was my experience listening to Jardine, as we read scholars like Madeleine Grumet, Ted Aoki, Maxine Greene, William Pinar, Hannah Arendt, and then Hans-George Gadamer. It was in this happening that I could more fully understand Heidegger's notion of *aletheia*— where that which has been hidden or covered, is revealed. I felt a provocation to begin examining the commonsense or taken-for-granted understandings of the world and to seek what might otherwise be there, what might be possible. As Evelyn Howe (2008) puts it, "this disclosure, or state of being "not hidden" is *alethia* (truth in the sense both of fact and sincerity) that causes us to appear "lit up", both enlightened and enlightening. It is related both to the authenticity of who we are (*Dasein*) and who we are to, with or for others (*Dasein-mit*)" (n.p. emphasis in original).

DEANNE

It was with a sense of vulnerability that we have begun to allow ourselves to wonder. After years of schooling and hours of conversation, we have come to understand that we still wonder what learning really looks like. In the face of all the things we could do with our students, what *should* we do? If we have been trained to deliver "teacher-proof" curriculum, how can we engage students in intellectually stimulating ways? What is worthwhile?

MAXX

Being able to begin articulating what one believes they *should* be doing, while enlightening, is fraught with challenges associated with being strange or alien to most others. It was a relief for the teachers gathered with Skuce, Jardine and others around a course on Curriculum Studies where we could hear a language that helped us see the possibilities over which we might want to while. However, if as Heidegger argues, language is "the house of being", then language not only has the potential to act, as Gadamer (2004) advocates, as "the medium in which substantive understanding and agreement take place..." (386) but where it can also divide and exclude. It must follow that those who find themselves on the margins of a dominant narrative cannot easily articulate themselves, when language is not available to construct a hermeneutic interpretation of history, politics, gender, and their interplay. In my first year of teaching, I felt absolutely alien in staff and committee meetings. I could not understand why we were dedicating copious amounts of time on, for example, a detailed crafting of rules and regulations about which we neither cared nor in which we believed; what was this about, I wondered? Worse, we spent little to no time on cross-curricular or interdepartmental understandings of our topics and our students. Whose discourse was this that had been adopted? The language of my high school was hard for me to understand, harder still to engage. You can imagine my pleasure then, in our Wednesday evening classes with Jardine, for I was hearing the at once new and yet familiar language of the aforementioned educational philosophers; I heard a language to which I wanted to belong although could not yet speak. This happening allowed me an existence in teaching; it would not be an overstatement to suggest that it saved (composed) my life as a teacher.

DEANNE

Where is the life?

After two years of struggling to prepare meaningful lessons for my students each day, while stifling my own interests in literature in order to present "teachable" materials, I finally allowed myself to utter this question. Where is the teaching life in this profession? Where is *my* life in all of this? As a woman who thought of herself as well educated, creative, and resourceful, why was I only now realizing that I had been utterly schooled? I felt betrayed by my own interest in education, knowing that I was a successful product of a system in which I was complicit, and unaware.

MAXX

While this might have signified the *beginning* of something very important that would change my life in wondrous ways, it mostly felt like the disruptive, frightening *end* of something instead. As Pinar reminds us in the forward to *Sounds of Silence Breaking*, "Reconstructing the public sphere in curriculum and teaching requires reconstructing the private sphere as well" (xiii). The personal, as Miller (2005) stresses, cannot be separated from the professional "Academics," she writes, "need to imagine ways of using experience critically, of using personal writing as an opportunity for a constant reprocessing of identity" (97). Reading the section on Miller's courageous yet seemingly arbitrary "coming out" at a public conference in front of her professional colleagues, reminded me of the anxiety-inducing phenomenon of bringing what is private and personal to the fore. She goes on to defend this choice, stating, "my ongoing work in autobiography thus provided an incentive and a reason, in a conference session, to tell how my life, my 'identities,' and my love exceeded the very academic and social normative discourses and frameworks that tried to contain them" (219). In contemplating the meaning of this anecdote, I remembered such an "excessive moment" from my own experience at the Provoking Curriculum conference in Banff during February of 2007. There we were, Deanne by my side again, thrilled to be among many kin, listening and taking part in conversations about the complicated and contextual in education and the need to de/reconstruct it anew, again and again. Despite the warmth of that kinship, we felt the chill of what embracing this way of being would mean for us. We were beginning to see the cracks, not the good cracks through which light shines into darkness or a plant might push through the asphalt, but the crack that begins as a minor dent in your windshield and before long crosses the expanse, refracting sunlight, blinding you. My understanding of teaching and learning as an epistemological box that I could open, dump into and then close up again before I left school for the day was falling away. It was replaced with the concept of teachers and learners "becoming"; taking up an ontological way of knowing, of becoming what we come to know. In this way, learning demands something of me and teaching demands something of others.

DEANNE

Once we started to understand questions of how, who we were intersected with, what I thought I knew, a mode of being in relation to the school, rather than being governed by the grand narrative of schooling was unavoidable. Curriculum, at least as Grumet (2006) makes clear, is not a one-way trajectory, nor despite its recursiveness, a circle (p. 48). In *Toward A Poor Curriculum*, she

> likened it to a lemniscate, or figure eight, ever enlarging human experience through its extension of both internal and external non ego. What these two terms, taken from Jungian psychology, infer is that at any given point we exist suspended between these two worlds that we know only partially. One is the world external to our consciousness, that popular "outside—world" you've heard so much about, and the other is the world of feelings and thoughts that are suppressed in our development and hence, though internal to us, not available to our conscious thought...So one of the ambitions of *currere* was to provide a method of reflection on educational experience that would

recognize the possibilities and constraints on both inner and outer worlds and enlarge our access to each and both of them. (48)

To begin to speak about curriculum as something that is experienced with students, whose voices are not only helpful, but necessary for theirs and our own learning, is to begin to stake a claim that this way of education isn't one among many "best practices." Therefore, the practice of reflecting on our educational experiences is endemic to learning.

MAXX

Other teachers, unsure of what to make of a community that seemed always in (literal) contradiction, speaking another language, was a source of curiosity at best, and suspicion and distrust at worst. Despite our warm and repeated invitations to all others, recognizing the importance of what Pinar might call "generative tensionality," week after week, no newcomers joined our meetings, or asked us about our work. The only inquiry I ever remember in fact was when a teacher, spotting a couple of us preparing a classroom for class after school, asked us why, if not to become administrators, we were taking a university class in our spare time. Upon hearing our response, that we just wanted to keep reading, writing, and thinking more deeply about teaching and learning, she responded, "Oh, sounds nerdy." Despite the fact that our school board's motto is, "lifelong learning" and "teaching tomorrow's citizens today," the thought that a community of teachers might want to continue to think about what we do in these buildings was foreign, unrecognizable.

DEANNE

It was this sense of suspicion from our colleagues that spurred on slanderous accusations that we were a harem, or cult; why else would a male mentor, or a university professor be so interested in gathering with a group of young, mostly female teachers? Clearly, our arrangement was an uncommon countenance. Truly, we pursued graduate courses and weekly lunch conversations out of necessity. The more we studied, the more necessary a shared cultivation in a critical awareness of schooling became. As we read Pinar (2004), we were struck with the idea of *currere*:

> the Latin infinitive form of curriculum means to run the course, or, in the gerund form, the running of the course-provides a strategy for students of curriculum to study the relations between academic knowledge and life history in the interest of self-understanding and social reconstruction. (35)

I started to revisit my constructed images of education and detach them from "doing school." In this way, teaching has demanded of me something that I never anticipated; this work has demanded that I sift back through my life histories, my stories, to consider who I am, to who I have been in relation to school, and to education. Disrupting a fixed identity is the sometimes painful yet creative purpose of autobiographical research in education.

THE HARVEST

We find ourselves shying away from "conclusions" for they signal endings, closings, and final decisions. Instead, we would like to leave readers with a reminder of what we have harvested: What can we gather as a yield of our work together? We would like to acknowledge not only what we now more deeply understand, but also what questions arise in the wake of those forged paths.

Writing this piece to capture the vicissitudes of studying teaching while engaging in day-to-day praxis, brings to mind a phrase oft repeated by curriculum scholars like David Jardine: in taking up the work interpretively and rigorously, "something gets better, *and* something gets worse."

While there is the liberating and proliferating effect of making public that which was always hidden, it often comes at the cost of harmony and collegiality as colleagues can no longer ignore that which they have to hear and face. While the world of school and classroom becomes immensely more interesting when taken up interpretively, it certainly does not become easier to control, predict or manipulate. This inability, refusal even, to make things easy, in a world that seems interested primarily in efficiency and convenience, is what threatens the dominant narrative of schools. It is for this reason that certain types of teacher work is looked upon with cynicism and distrust. Many teachers can tell you how isolating and stressful this can be. We go to our classrooms and teach our students the best we can, hoping that some of our work can fly "under the radar" of detection of our detractors.

While there is a form of emancipation in knowing and being able to articulate one's historical subjectivity, there is also a weight associated with recognizing one's culpability in the telling and re-telling of an old story that we call public schooling. In this story, as educators we forget ourselves, we forget our lineage, and, divorced from our ancestors, we have nothing to sustain us, save our own natural ability and professional training. If we remain on our own, we become like Icarus who takes flight on wings of feather and wax, flying solo with our ingenuity. Like Icarus, we burn. We may feel the relief of flight, but our idealism outruns our capacity to pursue it, as we fly straight into the burning fire of the sun; teachers often burn themselves out. Therefore, our singularity is often detrimental. Instead, we must be able to remember the historicity of our profession, and enter into the historical conversation around teaching and learning. Here Grumet reminds us that,

> Viewed from this perspective, education emerges as a metaphor for a person's dialogue with the world of his or her experience... To delete dialogue from this concept of educational experience would be to relegate learning to a series of reactive, conditioned behaviours best described as training.

It is this collective forgetfulness of our shared educational heritage that systematically silences certain voices. Propped up on "Monday morning ready" propaganda, we do not have a firm footing in our own history, which could provide powerful images of how teaching and learning could be otherwise. By seeking out other models from our past, we are reminded that the current status quo now institutionalized within public schooling has not always been the case, and should not be allowed to remain past its time.

We hope that the stories we have told and how we have told them are true to a "both/and" way of being. We would argue that "teaching" is actually experienced in the world as complex and devoid of simplistic binaries; it is at once lovely and horrible, frightening and comforting, illuminating and confounding, and in need of both old and new. In our writing, we have tried to emphasize just that ambiguity and unfinishedness by relating our "stories still, in progress" in the hope that other teachers can share their marginalized narratives that are familiar, and disturbingly so. Maxine Greene (1995) proposes,

> Only when the given or taken-for-granted is subject to questioning, only when we take various, sometime unfamiliar perspectives on it, does it show itself as what it is—contingent on many interpretations, many vantage points, unified (if at all) by conformity or by unexamined common sense. Once we can see our givens as contingencies, then we may have an opportunity to posit alternative ways of living and valuing and to make choices. (23)

From this vantage point, we can look to other uncommon countenances, hear other voices, and reconsider possibilities of being otherwise.

REFERENCES

Chambers, Cynthia, Erica Hasebe-Ludt, & Carl Leggo. 2009. *Life Writing and Literary Metissage as an Ethos for Our Times.* New York: Peter Lang.

Gadamer, Hans-Georg. 2004. *Truth and Method.* New York: Continuum.

Greene, Maxine. 1995. *Releasing the Imagination.* San Francisco: Jossey-Bass.

Grumet, Madeleine. 2006. "Where Does the World Go When Schooling Is About Schooling?" *Journal of Curriculum Theorizing* 22 (3): 47–53.

Howe, Evelyn. 2008. "Reflections on dasein-mit: the scholarship of teaching through community engagement". *Synergy* 27 (June), Retrieved October 20, 2009 from http://www.itl.usyd.edu.au/synergy/article.cfm?articleID=324.

Hynter, Nicholas. 2006. *The History Boys*. (Motion picture). United States: Fox Searchlight Pictures.

Miller, Janet. 2005. *Sounds of Silence Breaking*. New York: Peter Lang.

Pinar, William. 2004. *What is Curriculum Theory*. New Jersey: Lawrence Erlbaum Associates, Publishing.

————. 2008. *Introduction to a Common Countenance. Journal of the Canadian Association for Curriculum Studies* 6 (2): 129–155.

AFTERWORD

WILLIAM F. PINAR

To me, an educated person, first and foremost, understands that one's ways of
knowing, thinking, and doing flow from who one is.

Ted T. Aoki (2005 [1987], 365)

"FOR ULUKHAKTOKMIUT, THE PEOPLE OF ULUKHAKTOK," Cynthia Chambers
tells us, "the countenance of the commons lives on in the language, stories,
dances and songs, in clothing and art, in tools and what must be made from
them."[1] That "countenance of the commons," Chambers continues, "lives
on" in *nunakput*, the land, and in *hila*, the "cosmos, atmosphere, oceans and
living beings who dwell in these realms." In "dwelling on the land with all
those other beings where the past becomes present," Chambers explains, the
Innuinait find that "dwelling and wayfinding within *nunakput* is impossible without the commons, without the collective wisdom of those who
had come before, without the smarts and the skills to live in this place."
Chambers concludes:

> What we have in common, the Ulukhaktokmiut elders tell us, is our need to
> live, to make a livelihood that does no harm. What we have in common is our
> need for a curriculum that can help us to do *just* that. (chapter 1)

The concepts Chambers invokes in describing the Innuinait also express, I
suggest, the uncommon countenance of curriculum studies in Canada.

For me, the *commons* is the key concept, as it conveys several crucial elements, not only of Innuinait life, but of universal human life. It is the place,
the land, wherein people dwell.[2] It is not environment (in the sense of an
empty space to be exploited for economic gain), but the *meeting place* of not
only those who are alive today. Rearticulating that "collective wisdom" of
those who have come before, the living seek to dwell in the present without
causing harm. Such collective wisdom produces practical intelligence—sheer

survival requires savvy and skills—enabling the preservation of culture. Culturally specific legacies and universal needs intersect in the emergency of the present, compelling not only the Innuinait to come together, and in the curriculum.

As Chambers' statements suggest, the curriculum can encourage the emergence of intelligence—the "smarts"—that enable people to live in a place, without harm to the place or to themselves or to others. That aspiration is no either-or of course, as the concept of "place" incorporates both itself and those creatures who live within it. Living without doing harm requires practical skills, but even so-called cognitive skills are emplaced and embodied. Orality can communicate the wisdom of the past, rearticulating ancient knowledge in the press of present circumstances, enabling those who inhabit the place in the present to find their ways through the past into the future. Such articulation derives from thought and feeling and instinct preserved through the customs of culture, reconstructed into forms of art that inspirit the world. The systematic preservation of human culture through its reconstruction is undertaken in the curriculum. Through academic study, the past becomes reconstructed in the present for the sake of life now and the life to come.

The curriculum becomes the site wherein the internal complexity of the commons—what Roland Sintos Coloma describes in terms of "heterogeneity, hybridity, multiplicity"—can be recognized. The representation of difference—cultural, linguistic, political, and historical—requires sustained and critical attention to the particularity of place, including its objects, its landscape, and its history. Such attention is not only detached observations, that calm steady gaze we can associate with spiritual reflection but also with science. Such attention also expresses an engagement with what Ted Aoki[3], William E. Doll, Jr. reminds, characterized as "inspiriting the curriculum." The living infuse curriculum, Doll asserts (quoting Aoki 2005 [1987], 365) with the spirit of "dwelling aright in thoughtful living with others." That public compact—"thoughtful living with others"—represents the treaty we make with ourselves, the treaty that some of us are forever breaking, violation requiring reparation (Pinar 2006, 7).

Such "dwelling aright" is, then, simultaneously subjective and social, and it would seem to position ethics—not politics—as central to the commons that is curriculum.[4] "Ethics," Dwayne Donald reminds us, "concerns our basic humanity and our cherished notions of good, responsibility, duty, obligations."[5] Politics privileges power, while ethics affirms our humanity. Power can be productive of course, but whatever its function (often not productive!) politics cannot be expunged from the commons. Ethics can put politics in its place, subservient to (recalling Donald's terms) "good, responsibility, duty, and obligations." With ethics at its center, the commons cannot devolve into a battlefield wherein power rules. Even when it is a site of dissensus (Ziarek 2001, 15), the commons can become the place where even broken treaties can be renegotiated and humanity honored. Ethics, not politics, is the prerequisite to dialogical encounter. As Donald affirms, "the idea of ethical space entertains the possibility of a meeting-place." Meeting makes a space a distinctive place, a commons with an uncommon countenance.

Such meetings are not always momentous. Recall the book club David Lewkowich describes, readers assembling in a Newfoundland pub. That meeting place was no site of life-or-death negotiation, no culture-crushing moment of dispossession and deception. That commons was instead, an occasion of humor as cross-disciplinary communicants hammed it up, while acknowledging that even this meeting place, with apparently so little at stake, was—in Lewkowich's words—"a space of sometimes-discordant and some-times-harmonious textual engagement and conflict—a process of generative and often difficult conversation." Dissensus marks meetings of difference as difficult, but such complicated conversation can occasion generativity, yet another instance of Aoki's (2005 [1986/1991], 161–165) crucial concept of "creative tensionality."[6] Through "the perilous yet liberating nature of social reading," Lewkowich confirms the "relational significance of curriculum." The continuance of the conversation, and not only with those present but also with those in the past, affirms our bond(age), our enmeshment in history, and our dependence on each other in the present.

Those meetings through reading, Lewkowich suggests, were framed by two metaphorical concepts: *poaching* and *landwash*. The latter concept affirms that meeting-through-reading as one of which members "cannot claim sole ownership," recalling traditions (both indigenous and English) of communal access to the land, preserved in the 1217 *Charter of the Forest.* That treaty was broken, Cynthia Chambers reminds us, and the "enclo-sure of the commons" for the "creation of commodities" became the legacy of colonialism in Canada. That legacy is not only legal, but familial, as Chambers' genealogy acknowledges; it is, she writes, "*our* story: the one about the commons, what was shared and what was lost."

While history is not nature (however the two are intertwined: Wapner 2010), that second metaphor—*landwash*—affirms that the margins, how-ever politically vulnerable they are for inhabitants, can also become a space wherein memory is preserved and critique cultivated. For the great Canadian political economist and communications theorist Harold Innis, Watson (2007, 12) reminds, the colonized space was "fundamentally" a "critical one," requiring "a commitment to remaining in the peripheral com-munity.... It was a context in which the personal and the political merged naturally."[7] While certainly geographical,[8] this "colonial space" is also a lived space, wherein the past is preserved and the present reconstructed, what Narcisse Blood, Cynthia Chambers, Dwayne Donald, Erika Hasebe-Ludt, and Ramona Big Head accomplish in their "praxis of *métissage*."[9] As in Chambers' chapter, *métissage*, "as a curricular practice," as conversation among multiple participants, "shows how personal and family stories can be braided in with larger narratives of nation and nationality." Through juxtaposition (Pinar 2009, 154, n. 13), the interrelated dimensions of difference are acknowledged as affinity is sought, not only among peoples (and other living creatures, including bison and magpies) but to places (including the Marias River and the Downtown Eastside of Vancouver), and objects (including one flying rock) as well. Like George Grant[10], this research collective acknowledges "the relationship to oneself first, to one's family, to the community, and to the non-human relations," including historical events, in this case the January 23, 1870 Baker Massacre. Its theatrical remembrance reactivates the past in the present.

Acknowledging "the importance of diverse temporal and spatial relationships," Andrejs Kulnieks, Nicholas Ng-A-Fook, Darren Stanley, and Kelly Young focus upon curricular "language [that] mediates a world full of complex interdisciplinary topographies." And these efforts to understand, they suggest, are "caught up in a larger crisis of perceptual disconnection." Reactivating the past in the present represents one strategy for reconnecting. Autobiographical remembrance becomes, as Ng-A-Fook testifies, yet another "way for reconceptualizing both the content and the purpose of our presence in relation to concepts like environmental sustainability, greenwashing and ecojustice." Such memory work rethinks contemporary curriculum reform—Ng-A-Fook cites the case of Ontario—revealing that, "although somewhat greener, the document in many ways continues to narrate the classical narratives of technological progress with which we 'enlighten' ourselves today." Also disclosed, he notes, is that "a student's 'subjective' presence within their daily activities (within their narrative accounts) is deliberately ignored."

Complexity theory (see Trueit 2012) can also help reorient our perception of a world that would seem to have "come undone," Darren Stanley observes, "where a loss of coherence and meaning has created disconnections across, and between, many different scales of organization." Nature and society can become reconnected when humanity is replaced, within nature, not apart from "it." The "Oral Tradition"—as a living medium of remembrance and expressivity in place—becomes an environmental issue, as Andrejs Kulnieks suggests: "Mythopoetic engagements with place produced, recorded and living in the Oral Tradition can help recover the idea that all places are, to some degree, sacred." Kelly Young reminds us of the "power of language," including how it can function as a "barrier between humans and the natural world," requiring "close analysis" of "root metaphors." Young too critiques the 2007 Ontario curriculum reform as "dominated by a failed science model" and "a commodified approach to environmental education." It is, she concludes, "imperative for us to reconsider the importance of bringing together science, ecojustice education and indigenous environmental studies into a reconceptualist model of environmental education."

The failure of government to incorporate—indeed, forefront—the findings of curriculum research in its policy documents positions children at risk as the enforced curriculum threatens to perpetuate inflated expectations regarding the reciprocity of science, technology, and progress. Failing to acknowledge the subjectivity of students—and of their teachers—disables everyone from reconstructing private passion into public service. This severance of subjectivity from social engagement positions the teacher, as Maxx Lapthorne and Deanne Lomheim Barrett know, as "peering imperiously at her students as she 'delivers' the prescribed government curriculum." The "compositional work" of subjective reconstruction occurred for these two Alberta teachers through the "dialogic space" created during their discussions with David Jardine, Kai Kleinitz, and Tim Skuce at the 4th Biennial Provoking Curriculum Conference.

"When we face each other, and begin to speak our tentative understandings into the topics that so provoke us," Lapthorne and Barrett tell us, "we become composed together, as we rely on each other to fill in the gaps in our memory, and to flesh out the theoretical understandings that we have cultivated, with stories of students who have lived the curriculum." Their statement testifies to the power of orality understood as subjective presence in social experience. This "praxis of *métissage*," as the two colleagues acknowledge, translates "personal, private love of stories into the public world of school." While incorporating the personal and performing the public, the "I" coincides with neither, as Barrett acknowledges: "I was *Inter-esse*, I was being between." That "liminal space" is dialogic, evident in Lapthorne's memory of a meeting with Jardine: "All of a sudden someone was speaking my private language aloud." Such liminal educational experience leaves one questioning and Barrett asks: "In the face of all the things we could do with our students, what *should* we do?" This is the compelling curriculum question—*what knowledge is of most worth?*—that provokes the professional obligation to make curricular judgments about what and how to teach. "What," Barrett emphasizes, "is worthwhile? In the face of all the things we could do with our students, what *should* we do?" Indeed: what knowledge is of most worth?

Animated by ethics and the emergency of the present, that canonical curriculum question inaugurates the curriculum as an ongoing dialogic event.

The judgments teachers and students make, set them on courses of study that can be like journeys.[11] Pat Palulis depicts such an educational journey when she engages us in the story of *Lulie the Iceberg* as "*an act, an event, a happening,*" the telling of which—like the curriculum overall—"*is not yet over.*" Palulis's course becomes "interwoven with the story of the journey of an iceberg," and presented as a "bricolage of recollections." I am struck by the invocation of the iceberg, with its melting and moving not knowable in advance, even if its drift is discernible. Indeed, Palulis depicts her "passage"—and later her teaching—as "driftwork," a concept that associates agency with the currents of the sea, a keenly metaphorical conception that for me is associated not only with place, but with historical moment. In fact, this teacher's passage is multimodal, through time, through space, hidden below the surface, always altering after "affinities and excitations." Referencing "dissident subjectivities," Palulis's passage is also a testimony of teaching in order to open "spaces for difference," wherein one does not travel straight ahead, but swerves. "I find myself seeking these spaces of difference," Palulis tells us. "Sometimes to swerve decisively takes time," she advises. "Your topographies shift. You don't know when it's going to happen." In this driftwork, teachers and students and fictional characters become "adrift in animated conversations," accented in the various "englishes" of children born elsewhere. This is indeed a complicated conversation but there is no puzzle to solve, as the curriculum becomes, for Palulis, "*a mélange of juxtapositions,*" an "intertext" of "site-specific localities." In destabilizing the standardized curriculum, "an architecture of wonder splinters into shards and sets off another pattern of diffractions."

Even outside classrooms, in a "curriculum of the streets," conversation becomes diffracted through "performing identity as a means of survival," the terms by means of which Sharon Anne Cook deciphers photographs of women smoking in Toronto and on Vancouver's Lower East Side. "In this learning site," Cook theorizes, "younger women study the skills, habits and behaviors of the more experienced practitioners and then imitate their 'teachers', often peers, adding to the skill base and making the act their own." Through repetition and the cultivation of habit, these subjects reconstitute themselves: they reconstruct what their lived experience in order to survive. Place, history, and agency intersect in the poses that these women strike, Cook explains: "And the cigarette she holds with such practice in her mouth adds to that general image of worldliness and control as a further construction of the curriculum of the street she wishes to inhabit." In psychoanalytic terms, the cigarette becomes a "transitional object," an expression of free indirect subjectivity, an effort at communication, an opportunity for subjective reconstruction. "The curriculum she accesses," Cook notes, "is one where her cigarette gives her license to express anger amid confusion."

The articulation of anger and confusion seems central to the project of Roland Sintos Coloma. "[M]y research," he tells us, "asks the central question: How do subjects of discrimination turn their grief into grievance?" This is a key question of decolonization, at least for how, as Frantz Fanon[12] conceived the challenge. Context is crucial, and Coloma undertakes a historical and comparative study of Asian Canadians as he investigates both governmental policy and the social activism that it provokes to study "the interplay of race, nation, and citizenship." The very concept of Asian, as Coloma recognizes, can obscure "cultural differences, inter-ethnic conflicts, and colonial trajectories between and within Asian ethnic groups," threatening, in my terms, a "strategically dysfunctional essentialism" (Pinar 2009, 23). Coloma understands:

> How to recognize and value the differences and convergences as well as identify and advocate for ethnic-specific and pan-ethnic concerns is an on-going negotiation among Asian Canadians and a significant issue to address for scholarly, policy, and educational discussions. (chapter 6)

Coloma undertakes the study of "the tension between pan-ethnic and ethnic-specific approaches," including the intersections among class, gender, ability, sexuality, language, spirituality, migration, and generation.

We are not left stranded within the sphere of the abstract, however, as Coloma "foregrounds how unique specificities shed light on multidimensional conditions and broader issues." Here again is the interplay of interpellation and decolonization, as Coloma is committed to challenging "overdeterminations and generalizations" by formulating "an intersectional approach [that] underscores the 'heterogeneity, hybridity, multiplicity' of not only individuals and communities, but also academic fields."[13] As do the other chapters in this important collection, Coloma's chapter demonstrates the heterogeneity, hybridity, and multiplicity of curriculum studies in Canada is a sign of intellectual sophistication and a political opportunity, in Coloma's words, for "imagining and enacting curriculum studies from anti-oppressive perspectives." Such ongoing rethinking, as he knows, "can engender strong affective responses," and so "we need to create spaces for ourselves and students to work through these affective crises." That "space," as David Harvey (2008, 67) reminds, is not "empty, fixed, and abstract," nor does it exist apart from time and place.

Since the end of World War II, Denise Egéa-Kuehne reminds, efforts have been underway in Europe to codify human, including linguistic, rights. Several organizations (among them the United Nations) have sought to preserve heterogeneity, supporting the teaching of "regional" minority languages[14] from preschool through university, and providing access to education in one's own native language. Loss of language, Egéa-Kuehne asserts, represents a loss of "feeling," that culturally distinctive capacity to experience reality. Indeed, she continues, "language is constitutive of reality, experience, and identity." Despite "interdicts," monolingualism is impossible, Egéa-Kuehne concludes—recall the various "englishes" in Palulis's classroom—given the heterogeneity internal to language.

Heterogeneity is not only internal to language but to culture more broadly, and Denise Egéa-Kuehne invokes that aporia[15] in her chapter on multiculturalism. "The challenge is daunting," she acknowledges. How can educators, she asks, "respond to the necessity of respecting, *at the same time*, the particularities of individual differences and singularities *and* the universality of majority law?" In this succinct restatement of the "misleading dichotomy of particularism vs. universalism," Egéa-Kuehne affirms that, "the impossible task of education in the face of diversity is in fact *the very condition* for its possibility." She acknowledges that emphasizing culture threatens agency and responsibility, as "it generally ignores minority students' own responsibility for their academic performance." While understanding and affirming the culture(s) of one's origin and upbringing may constitute universal rights as well as intellectual-affective prerequisites to learning about the cultures of others, cultures of origin can become reified, and its students rendered passive and subservient within it. Only when the heterogeneity inherent in any culture is accented, can appreciation of its vulnerability provoke its preservation *through* reconstruction (Lear 2006, 6). Egéa-Kuehne reminds:

> Yet developing an ability to learn is essentially dependent on developing an ability to reconstruct an understanding of anything other than, different from, learners' prior knowledge and experience of self and the world. Therefore, education means including otherness and multiple, even conflicting voices, thus providing opportunities for critical reflection. Excluding these voices, that is neutralizing education, is tantamount to a decision not to educate. (chapter 5)

Such an "interdiction"—denying the internal heterogeneity of culture—is no less a "silencing" than the refusal to acknowledge the significance of culture in the constitution of subjectivity and society.

What education requires, Egéa-Kuehne argues, is "a paradigm which would enable us *not* to 'go beyond' or *not* to 'bypass' the difficulty of the antinomy universalism/particularism, one which would deconstruct the persistent hierarchy, and empower us to think *from within* such aporias." Such working from within would forefront culture and history in ways that underscore, as Egéa-Kuehne states so succinctly, that "men and women are capable of assuming themselves as both objects and subjects of history, capable of reinventing the world out of an ethical and aesthetic mold of the cultural patterns which exist." It seems to me that Chambers' genealogy—in which autobiography, culture, history, and the natural world are intertwined—provides one striking exemplification of such reconstruction. This "praxis of *métissage*" destabilizes the present not only by juxtaposing difference but by also reactivating the past. The juxtaposition of dissonant domains—the familial, the cultural, and the historical—while historicizing them promises to deflect determinism. Collaborating with others in such a research collective creates a "commons" in which the difference does not become subsumed in the same. That is evident as well in Coloma's affirmation and analysis of "Asian" Canadians, in the juxtaposition of analyses that simultaneously preserve collective identity and acknowledge its incommensurate internal elements. However, addressing the "I" who is at once the one and the many, the same and the other, may, it turns out, require the presence of another creature altogether.

Consider that cat in Kyoto. Wabi Sabi's name puzzled even its owner, who replied to queries regarding it by "an intake of breath," and muttering "that's hard to explain." The cat seems clueless as well. She asks her "animal friends," who refer her to a monkey, "a wise old monkey/living among the pine trees." So Wabi Sabi sets off on a journey (see note 11) from the city to the woods, to Mount Hiei, where she meets the monkey Kosho who, contrary to counsel, cannot tell her the meaning of her name. "That's hard to explain," he (also) says, and advises Wabi Sabi to "Listen. Watch. Feel." Be alive, in other words, pay attention to what happens, and not only to what is around you, but within you. Lived experience, Jackie Seidel and David W. Jardine remind, is experience one "goes through." It is something undergone and perhaps suffered. It implies a "journey." The impetus for such "travel" can be to answer a call, including the call of one's own name. Seidel and Jardine explain: "Names—even the ordinary word "experience"[16], which everyone already understands and whose meaning "goes without saying"—have sometimes hidden or occluded motion and agency, something to show and teach, some path set out that needs to be *taken* in order to be *understood*." Quoting Heidegger, Seidel and Jardine summarize: "Understanding begins when something addresses us."

Wabi Sabi is called into the world to understand its own name, but it is not the cat's question alone that calls the creature to "venture" out: it is the world itself. Seidel and Jardine quote Nishitani: "One sees one's own self in all things, in living things, in hills and rivers, towns and hamlets, tiles and stones, and loves these things 'as oneself.'" No fused identity here however: this is an acknowledgement of the inextricability of self and other, familiarity and difference, the particular and the universal. No static world of binaries, this "impermanence" calls us to the singularity of our subjectivity: "Wabi Sabi herself must go and no one can go for her." Where she goes is into the world in its layered materiality, its historicality.

> This venture that Wabi Sabi takes is intimate to her, how she herself is called and yet, at the same time, it is intergenerational. She herself stands before those who have gone before, traces and tracks of paths through the city, through the woods, up to the old Temple full of the ghosts of those who have gone, and these are her teachers. (chapter 10)

This journey is, Seidel and Jardine point out, pedagogical. Transposed from the forest to the city, it is also a curriculum of the streets, even there, a mythological moment and an intergenerational legacy.

"This intergenerational character of the 'breaking forth' of the name," Seidel and Jardine suggest, "is again found in the language of Gadamer's hermeneutics." They continue: "Becoming experienced (*Erfahrung*) is linked to a journey (*Fahren*) and these are both linked etymologically to those who have traveled here before us, ancestors (*Vorfahren*)." Massacres and suicides reverberate in the sound of the streets, in the hard-to-explain call of names, each event a palimpsest that addresses us, alone and together, in the present, from the past.

Solitude is not being alone of course, but it can secure the silence wherein one can listen to voices futural, past, and present. Non-coincident with itself, solitude affirms the presence of others within oneself, the presence of oneself amid others, a sea of sociality in which driftwork becomes a spatialized, singularized mode of being within the world. "Anthropomorphizing non-human elements," Palulis reminds, "alerts us to... [the] more-than-human world and at the same time makes absent the voices of Arctic peoples." Memories drift into consciousness, massacres, and suicides, traumas that are also testimonies to promises—treaties—unkept, but not forgotten. "It is by opening a space for the affirmation of this promise," Egéa-Kuehne asserts, "of the 'messianic and emancipatory promise,' of the impossible event (the only possible event as event) as a promise, that it will preserve its capital of possibilities, of dynamic ideal in-the-making, to-come." Passage to the future forces a journey through that private past common to us all.

CONCLUSION

Since subjectivity surmounts identity, it is impossible to judge anyone in terms of race, class, gender, or sexuality.

Stefan Jonsson 2000, 264

"The commons is what sustains us all," Cynthia Chambers teaches, "it is the true curriculum, the one that calls us to renew our relationships with one another, that calls us to our commitment to what we have in common, to our stake in the world and its survival." The world that calls to us, and within which our calls are made, occurs across space and through time. Maxx Lapthorne quotes her cinematic colleague Mr. Hector from the 2006 film *The History Boys*. Supplement "reading" with "study" and "teaching," and the intergenerational character of curriculum as *commons*, as meeting place, is communicated, well, corporeally:

> The best moments in reading are when you come across something—a thought, a feeling, a way of looking at things—that you'd thought special, particular to you. And here it is, set down by someone else, a person you've never met, maybe even someone long dead. It's as if a hand has come out, and taken yours.

Perhaps it is Hodge's hand extending itself to ours, the drummer boy, yet another victim of massacre, addressing us now through another.[17]

Not only the dead call us into the world we inhabit today, so do those yet to come. Due to our obsession with the "new," we can forget that the future is already past. As David G. Smith (quoted in the Seidel-Jardine chapter) reminds: "Education seems like a preparation for something that never happens because... it has *already happened*.... There *is* no future because the future *already is*." It is in the past wherein we can find the future.

There are profound differences between fin de siècle Vienna and the postmodern metropolises of contemporary Canada.[18] Robert Musil recalled that Vienna in the first documentary volume of his novel *The Man Without Qualities*. Composed after the collapse of the Hapsburg Empire, that novel, Stefan Jonsson (2000, 1) points out, is no "backward-looking myth but a forward-looking transfiguration of Musil's historical experiences during the 1920s and 1930s." Attuned to the past in his present, Musil was convinced "the post-imperial crisis necessitated a society that would not reduce its subjects to their particular positions in the social hierarchy," and so he used "the fallen empire as a field of experiments for trying out new notions of humanity and society" (2000, 14). Jonsson explains:

> The empire that preceded the war was thus transformed into a past future, an open historical horizon that included the utopian possibility of a supranational and transcultural space, in which the human subject cherished the absence of homogenizing ideologies of nation or culture and recognized the heterogeneity of all identities—an idea that we may associate, not entirely anachronistically, with postcolonial theories of hybridity and *métissage*. (ibid.)

Musil's novel thus anticipates the political and cultural issues present today, in this collection.

The multicultural complexity[19] of Austria at the beginning of the twentieth century stimulated Musil, Jonsson (2000, 264) suggests, to anticipate those concepts of hybridity, border culture, and *métissage* so prominent in late twentieth-century postcolonial theory, including in contemporary curriculum studies in Canada. Some 80 years earlier and in Europe, Musil imagined "a universal or transcultural society," but "its driving force" was not cultural or political, but subjective. More precisely, it is subjectivity noncoincident with culture and politics and with itself (see Pinar 2011, 158)—what Musil imagined as everyone's "tenth character," what Jonsson (2000, 264) terms "the subject's negativity"—that (fortunately) undermines a person's efforts to coincide completely with any identity conferred by culture, politics, or society. Jonsson summarizes:

> At the heart of the Musilian subject, there is a power of distantiation and differentiation that prevents the person from investing too much in his or her identities, and which estranges reality, so that the existing social order comes to appear as just one among an infinite number of possible worlds. (ibid.)

That is the space of subjective freedom prerequisite to the preservation—through reconstruction—of one's culture, one's society, oneself. It is the space academic study can expand and complicate. It is the call of that commons that can be the curriculum.

Passionate engagement in the present draws us into the moment, but it is not there that we can find passage through it. By virtue of the distance that the study of the past can create, we can see the lay of the land. We can listen to those (human and nonhuman) who speak to us, and we can act in their names, through our voices, to reconstruct the commons that is the curriculum. This is genealogical, pedagogical, curricular labor, never alone (even when alone), juxtaposing the familial with the historical, the sea with the land, drifting toward a future we cannot know but where we have been before, if differently. To value "diversity," Denise Egéa-Kuehne understands, means that we teachers

> strive to engage our students in a quest for knowledge which should take them beyond the boundaries of their immediate socio-political contexts, in space and time, and encourage them to take risks in learning and discovering the unfamiliar, the other—within and without themselves—while building a greater sense of responsibility toward themselves and other(s).

Working from within, we can express private passion through public service, that old-fashioned phrase denoting an ethical commitment to the commons. We live in its absence but, as this collection so powerfully testifies, rethinking curriculum studies in Canada as a meeting place requires its reconstruction. After reading this collection, it is clear that that is well underway.

ENDNOTES

1. Unless otherwise specified, all quoted passages come from this collection.
2. Intimacy with the land, with "place" (Kincheloe & Pinar 1991), is not limited to indigenous thought and experience of course, but informs the Canadian experience more generally, as evident, for instance, in the imagination of Canadian landscape painters (and specifically the Group of Seven: see O'Brian and White 2007). For Joe Kincheloe and me working 20 years ago on the American South, "place" was simultaneously a gendered, political, and racialized site of historical experience as well as a geographical region. Today geographical and "natural" elements of "place" are often emphasized, and "nature" is especially relevant in discussions of Canadian conceptions of place. The Canadian attitude toward nature is, Jill Conway (1974, 77) points out, as in "any country built by the exploitation of natural resources, mingled with commercial attitudes." Even with its commodification, nature remains, Conway argues, a "spiritual resource that all the force of modern technology cannot annihilate." In especially indigenous concepts of place, this spiritual aspect remains vibrant.
3. This "elder" of curriculum studies in Canada is acknowledged elsewhere in this collection. "I am called upon to remember my elder as mentor, curriculum scholar Ted T. Aoki," Patricia Palulis testifies, "who teaches us about the metonymic doublings of presence and absence." Dwayne Donald acknowledges Aoki and other key scholars—along with Cree and Blackfoot Elders—as "curriculum forebears." In his thinking about dialogical encounter, David Lewkowich references Aoki's appreciation for the productive nature of "properly tensioned chords" in the curriculum. And Maxx Lapthorne acknowledges Aoki as one of several scholars whose work was formative in her thinking. These references acknowledge the canonical character of Aoki's work in Canadian curriculum studies; his "living pedagogy" lives on, lodged inside the present, enabling scholars to find passages into the future.
4. The two—ethics and politics—are reciprocally related, although not always equally weighted, as we see in this collection. The historical moment, the political situation, the unresolved past and the emergency of the present all invite, if not force, a moving emphasis. Declining to coincide with any of these realities or even with oneself, subjectivity attuned to each can develop discernment and judgment, answering, in curriculum terms, "what knowledge is of most worth?", itself a political as well as ethical question. It is, I submit, the key educational question.
5. Donald continues: "Ethics constitutes the framework of cultural boundaries that we recognize and respect as part of our daily lives." Does ethics coincide with culture? If so, how does it escape conformity? If ethics cannot

exceed culture, how can it become engaged in the renegotiation of treaties of co-existence? Later, Donald construes ethics as non-coincident with place or culture, asserting that ethical space "offers a venue to step out of our allegiances, to detach from the circumscriptive limits of colonial frontier logics, and enact a theory of human relationality that does not require assimilation or deny Indigenous subjectivity." Such a cosmopolitan conception invites a third option, neither assimilation nor affirmation, the path taken by Zitkala-Ša (Pinar 2009, 23–24) for instance, and by Plenty Coups, the great Crow chief who understood, Jonathan Lear (2006, 92) argues, that the cultural devastation he and his people underwent was accompanied by the "collapse of the concepts with which ethical life had hitherto been understood." Such a "subjective catastrophe" (Lear 2006, 96) requires, as Plenty Coups appreciated, subjective and social reconstruction, in Lear's terms "the hope for revival: for coming back to life in a form that is not yet intelligible" (2006, 95). "In this way," Lear (2006, 104) continues, "the Crow hoped for the emergence of a Crow subjectivity that did not yet exist. There would be ways of continuing to form oneself as a Crow subject—ways to flourish as a Crow—even though the traditional forms were doomed. This hope is radical in that it is aiming for a subjectivity that is at once Crow and does not yet exist." In the cataclysm of cultural collapse, Lear (2006, 105) concludes, "the issue of hope becomes crucial for an ethical inquiry into life at the horizons of one's understanding." To erase expectations from present contemplation, I prefer the concept of "resolve" to that of "hope," but Lear's point—that the preservation of culture requires the reconstruction of its key concepts—is a powerful one.

6. "The best hope," Christopher Lasch (1984, 177) concludes, "appears to lie in a creative tension between separation and union, individuation and dependence." That pronouncement only appears universal in its scope, as it is contextualized specifically in Lasch's critique of narcissism in the United States. "Creative tension" can be contextualized across multiple domains, testifying to the inextricable (if often indirect) interrelation between the universal and the particular. "Just as political practice is characterized by the creative tension between the event and agency," Ewa Plonowska Ziarek (2001, 43) suggests, "so too 'sexual experimentation' leads not only to the disruption of the subject but also to reconfiguration of subjective and social forms of life." Pressing against preference and custom in one domain of culture, Ziarek is suggesting, can produce "creative tension" that reconfigures subjective and social life more generally. From the tactile to the auditory but still within the sphere of the sensory, music too—recall that jazz was a memorable reference for Aoki (2005 [1990], 367)—illustrates (as it performs) "creative tensionality," as Cornel West (1993, 105) points out: "I use the term 'jazz' here not so much as a term for a musical art form, as for a mode of being in the world, an improvisational mode of protean, fluid, and flexible dispositions toward reality suspicious of 'either/or' viewpoints, dogmatic pronouncements, or supremacist ideologies.... As with a soloist

in a jazz quintet or band, individuality is promoted in order to sustain and increase the creative tension with the group—a tension that yields higher levels of performance to achieve the aim of the collective project." As West makes clear in that final line, the cultivation of one's individuality is not only an obligation to oneself but to others.

7. Innis declined to abandon the conception of community while seeking to understand the cosmopolitan world emerging around and within him (see Watson 2007, 13). For Innis, Watson (2007, 17) explains, "an individual from the periphery could sustain intense cultural training leading to an indigenous critical perspective without consequent deracination." Such "training" was no uncritical acceptance of contemporary culture, for Innis was convinced that he was facing "the final failure of Western civilization itself" (Watson 2007, 23). His prescience resounds today.

8. One legacy of the Enlightenment, David Harvey (2009, 167) points out, is that "place does indeed appear as something subsequently constructed within a space that is empty, fixed, and abstract." North America was of course not such a space, but already a place, the "permanence" of which, "coupled with stories told about those places, provides a means to perpetuate a cultural identity" (2009, 175). Here Harvey is discussing the power of place in the anthropological research of Keith Basso on the Western Apache, but his point appears pertinent for other cultures as well, and not only indigenous ones.

9. "The value of métissage as a form of curriculum theorizing, especially as it concerns Aboriginal and non-Aboriginal perspectives of Canada and the world," Donald (2004, 25) explains, "is in the ways it can demonstrate interrelatedness." This research collective is enacting postcolonial theories of hybridity and métissage that, as Chambers (2003, 246) described a decade ago, is the "middle or third way" that many Canadian curriculum scholars seem to be calling for. Through their work they are braiding languages and traditions, stories and fragments, desires and repulsions, arguments and conversations, tradition and change, hyphens and slashes, mind and body, earth and spirit, texts and images, local and global, pasts and posts, into a métissage, one that is perhaps 'as Canadian as possible under the circumstances.' It is our way, and it is what we have to offer any inter-national conversation that is curriculum." This distinctively Canadian conception could also be called, after the Cuban poet Nancy Morejon, "transcultracion," as that neologism is, Lionnet (1995, 115) summarizes, also (like the internationalization of curriculum studies) a "process of cultural intercourse and exchange, a circulation of practices that creates a constant interweaving of symbolic forms and empirical activities among different cultures that interact with one another." As Morejon emphasizes, "reciprocal influence is the determining factor here, for no single element superimposes itself on another; on the contrary, each one changes into the other so that both can be transformed in to a third" (quoted in Lionnet 1995, 115). Here, as Lionnet (1995, 115) emphasizes, Morejon is pointing to a "third way, to the métissage of forms

and identities that is the result of cross-cultural encounters, and that forms the basis for their self-portrayals and their representations of cultural diversity." The lasting significance of cross-cultural encounters is evident in John Ralston Saul's inscription of the indigenous at the core of Canadian life (2008).

10. For the great Canadian political philosopher and public intellectual, Potter (2005, xlvii) points out, "what is valuable about particularity is that it provides a path away from the love of the self, toward the love of the good. The essence of particularly is what Grant calls 'the love of one's own,' and it is by loving our own that we move beyond the self and orient ourselves toward the love of something external." See also Kroker 1984, 34.

11. Recall that "travel" is, for Herbert M. Kliebard (2000 [1972], 84) one of the three "metaphorical roots of curriculum design." The other two are "production—the student as "raw material... [to] be transformed into a finished and useful product" and, third, "growth" wherein the curriculum becomes a "greenhouse where students will grown and develop to their fullest potential." (For an important architectural conception of curriculum design, see Grimmett and Halverson 2010.) While Kliebard's juxtaposition stresses their differences over their intersections, indeed their conceivable synergistic capacities. After all, one can "grow" through "travel" and while becoming vocationally competent (e.g. "production").

12. See Pinar 2011, 41–46. Recasting injury into grievance restates (albeit in milder terms) Fanon's specification of self-purification through violence. Violence fails to expunge the internalized other, as Fanon knew. Likewise, does not grievance alone—without subjective reconstruction, without "working through" (Pinar 2011, 211, n. 25) injury, working through that includes self-purification—risk reinscribing colonialist violence by converting colonized subjects to litigants? Does not recasting injury into grievance without subjective reconstruction restate the aggression and conquest that a century earlier (in North America) recast "Asians" as exotic feminized and racialized others (Eng 2001, 17)? Despite its possible cathartic and material effects, does not insisting on official apologies position the government and the non-Asian population as the "host" culture, still conceived as dominant, still capable, by apology, of redressing the past? Without decolonization and the subjective and social reconstruction it requires, does not public grievance threaten to leave the "great white man" in his colonial place of power, at least in the imagination of the grievant? As Coloma appreciates: "one's complicity in processes of exploitation requires a commitment to teaching that pursues self-reflection and to unlearning what one has taken for granted or previously learned as norm."

13. Recall that George Tomkins (1986, 5) emphasized that the Canadian curriculum "was part of an international mainstream from the start, as Canadian educators, like their counterparts in other nations, were influenced by developments beyond their own borders." Unlike (many) other nations, Canada has (officially at least) embraced cultural and national

heterogeneity. So does, this collection makes clear, the academic field of curriculum studies.

14. I am reminded of Pier Paolo Pasolini's resurrection of his mother's regional language—Fruilian—and his detestation of the cultural standardization that the installation of "Italian" threatened. "Pasolini, much later," Rohdie (1995, 28) reports, "recalled his recourse to dialect as a political act within the context of the linguistic policies of fascism. On the other hand, it was a very personal one." We see such interplay between the personal and the political in the protection of place in several essays in this collection.

15. "In modern Greek usage," Bernadette Baker (2009, xi) explains, "aporia (singular aporos) indicate a state of impasse, nonpassage, or logical contradiction that can never be permanently resolved, a state of constant shimmering around a borderline." For Cheah (2006, 100), aporia becomes the provocation of subjective reconstruction: "Put another way, what can we hope to achieve in ourselves through our own makings insofar as we are finite beings, creatures who are given and who come to exist and cease to exist not by our own making? I propose to call this ensemble of problems the aporia of given culture. The aporia is as follows: Culture is supposed to be the realm of human freedom from the given. But because human beings are finite natural creatures, the becoming-objective of culture as the realm of human purposiveness and freedom depends on forces which are radically other and beyond human control. Culture is given out of these forces. Thus, at the same time that cultural activity embodies and performs human freedom from the given, it is also merely given because its power over nature is premised on this gift of the radically other." The reconstruction of determination—whether cultural, economic, or political—specifies the challenge of a subjectively-threaded cosmopolitan education, just as that challenge engaged Marx and Kierkegaard a century and a half ago (see Pinar 2011, 126–140).

16. The concept of "experience," Martin Jay (2005, 5) points out, "has often been used to gesture toward precisely that which exceeds concepts and even language itself." It names, he continues, "the nodal point of the intersection between public language and private subjectivity, between expressible commonalities and the ineffability of the individual interior" (2005, 6–7). And "however much we may construe experience as a personal possession," he adds, "it is inevitably acquired through an encounter with otherness, whether human or not" (2005, 7). Lived experience occurs within alterity; if reconstructed, it can contribute to subjective coherence, a decentered sense of self whose internal heterogeneity and self-conscious temporality does not obscure its continuity nor undermine its capacity for agency.

17. In one poignant tutorial scene in *The History Boys*, Mr. Hector teaches his best student Thomas Hardy's "Drummer Hodge":

> They throw in Drummer Hodge, to rest Uncoffined—just as found:
> His landmark is a kopje-crest That breaks the veldt around: And foreign constellations west Each night above his mound. Young Hodge

the drummer never knew - Fresh from his Wessex home - The meaning of the broad Karoo, The Bush, the dusty loam, And why uprose to nightly view Strange stars amid the gloam. Yet portion of that unknown plain Will Hodge for ever be; His homely Northern breast and brain Grow to some Southern tree, And strange-eyed constellations reign His stars eternally.

18. Fin de siècle Vienna, Janik and Toulmin (1973) point out, was an intellectual hub of continental Europe. There one finds the beginnings of twelve-tone music, "modern" architecture, legal and logical positivism, nonrepresentational painting and psychoanalysis, as well as the revival of interest in Schopenhauer and Kierkegaard. All were taking place simultaneously and they were largely concentrated in Vienna. At the same time the city was described by its own most penetrating social critic—Karl Kraus—as the "proving-Ground for World Destruction" (quoted in Janik and Toulmin, 19). In that last respect, perhaps there is a timeless element to fin-de-siècle Vienna.

19. Austria-Hungary was, Janik and Toulmin, 40) suggest, an ungovernable multiculture of German, Italians, Slovaks, Rumanians, Czechs, Poles, Magyars, Slovenes, Croats, Transylvanian Saxons, and Serbs.

REFERENCES

Aoki, Ted T. 2005 (1986/1991). "Teaching as Indwelling Between Two Curriculum Worlds. " In *Curriculum in a New Key: The Collected Works of Ted T. Aoki*, edited by William F. Pinar and Rita L. Irwin (159–165). Mahwah, NJ: Lawrence Erlbaum.

———. 2005 (1987). "Inspiriting the Curriculum". In *Curriculum in a New Key: The Collected Works of Ted T. Aoki*, edited by William F. Pinar & Rita L. Irwin (357–365). Mahwah, NJ: Lawrence Erlbaum.

———. 2005 (1990]). "*Sonare* and *Videre*: A Story, Three Echoes and a Lingering Note." In *Curriculum in a New Key: The Collected Works of Ted T. Aoki*, edited by William F. Pinar & Rita L. Irwin (367–376). Mahwah, NJ: Lawrence Erlbaum.

Baker. Bernadette. 2009. Introduction to *New Curriculum History*, edited by Bernadette Baker (ix–xxxv). Rotterdam-Boston-Tapei: Sense Publishers.

Chambers, Cynthia. 2003. "As Canadian as Possible under the Circumstances": A View of Contemporary Curriculum Discourses in Canada. In the *International Handbook of Curriculum Research*, edited by William F. Pinar (221–252). Mahwah, NJ: Lawrence Erlbaum.

Cheah, Pheng. 2006. *Inhuman Conditions: On Cosmopolitanism and Human Rights*. Cambridge, MA: Harvard University Press.

Conway, Jill. 1974. "Culture and National Identity." In *National Consciousness and the Curriculum: The Canadian Case*, edited by In Geoffrey Milburn & John Herbert (71–87). Toronto: Ontario Institute for Studies in Education, Department of Curriculum.

Donald, D. 2004. "Edmonton Pentimento: Re-reading History in the Case of the Papaschase Cree." *Journal of the Canadian Association for Curriculum Studies* 2 (1): 21–54.

Eng, David L. 2001. *Racial Castration: Managing Masculinity in Asian America*. Durham, NC: Duke University Press.

Grimmett, Peter P., & Halvorson, Mark. 2010. "From Understanding Curriculum to Creating Curriculum: The Case for the Co-Evolution of Re-Conceptualized Design with Re-Conceptualized Curriculum." *Curriculum Inquiry* 40 (2), 241–262.

Harvey, David. 2009. *Cosmopolitanism and the Geographies of Freedom*. New York: Columbia University Press.

Janik, Allan, & Toulmin, Stephen. 1973. *Wittgenstein's Vienna*. New York: Simon and Schuster.

Jay, Martin. 2005. *Songs of Experience: Modern American and European Variations on a Universal Theme*. Berkeley: University of California Press.

Jonsson, Stefan. 2000. *Subject Without Nation: Robert Musil and the History of Modern Identity*. Durham, NC: Duke University Press.

Kincheloe, Joe L., & Pinar, William F. eds. 1991. *Curriculum as Social Psychoanalysis: The Significance of Place*. Albany: State University of New York Press.

Kliebard, Herbert M. 2000 (1972). "Metaphorical Roots of Curriculum Design." In *Curriculum Theorizing: The Reconceptualization*, edited by William F. Pinar (84–85). Troy, NY: Educator's International Press. (Originally published in Teachers College Record, 72 [3], 403–404, February 1972.

Kroker, Arthur. 1984. *Technology and the Canadian Mind: Innis/McLuhan/Grant*. Montreal: New World Perspectives.

Lasch, Christopher. 1984. *The Minimal Self: Psychic Survival in Troubled Times*. New York: Norton.

Lear, Jonathan. 2006. *Radical Hope: Ethics in the Face of Cultural Devastation*. Cambridge, MA: Harvard University Press.

Lionnet, Françoise. 1995. "'*Logiques Métisses*': Cultural Appropriation and Postcolonial Representations." In *Order and Partialities: Theory, Pedagogy, and the "Postcolonial"* " edited by Kostas Myrsiades & Jerry McGuire (111–136). Albany: State University of New York Press.

O'Brian, John, & White, Peter. eds. 2007. *Beyond Wilderness: The Group of Seven, Canadian Identity, and Contemporary Art*. Montreal and Kingston: McGill-Queen's University Press.

Pinar, William F. 2009. *The Worldliness of a Cosmopolitan Education: Passionate Lives in Public Service*. New York: Routledge.

———. 2011. *The Character of Curriculum Studies: Bildung, Currere, and the Recurring Question of the Subject*. New York: Palgrave Macmillan.

Potter, Andrew. 2005. Introduction to the 40th Anniversary Edition of George P. Grant's *Lament for a Nation* (ix–lxviii). Montreal and Kingston: McGill-Queen's University Press.

Rohdie, Sam. 1995. *The Passion of Pier Paolo Pasolini*. Bloomington, IN: Indiana University Press.

Saul, John Ralston. 2008. *A Fair Country: Telling Truths about Canada*. Toronto: Viking Canada.

Tomkins, George S. 1986. *A Common Countenance: Stability and Change in the Canadian Curriculum*. Scarborough, Ontario: Prentice-Hall.

Trueit, Donna. ed. 2012. *Pragmatism, Postmodernism, Complexity Theory: The Fascinating Imaginative Realm of William E. Doll, Jr.* New York: Routledge.
Wapner, Paul. 2010. *Living Through the End of Nature: The Future of American Environmentalism.* Cambridge, MA: The MIT Press.
Watson, Alexander John. 2007. *Marginal Man: The Dark Vision of Harold Innis.* Toronto: University of Toronto Press.
West, Cornel. 1993. *Race Matters.* Boston: Beacon Press.
Ziarek, Ewa Plonowska. 2001. *An Ethics of Dissensus: Postmodernity, Feminism, and the Politics of Radical Democracy.* Stanford, CA: Stanford University Press.

Contributors

Deanne Lomheim Barrett and Maxx Lapthorne are writers, mothers, and high school teachers at Lester B Pearson High School in Calgary, AB. They have had the good fortune, through their graduate studies, to have worked with some of the best interpretive scholars at the Universities of Calgary and British Columbia. They share an interest in rich conversation, nurturing inquiring minds, pushing the curriculum boundaries, and challenging the dominant narrative in schools.

Ramona Big Head is a PhD student within the Faculty of Education at the University of British Columbia and an instructor at the University of Lethbridge. She is a Blackfoot mother and grandmother. Her Blackfoot name is translated as "Many Sweat Lodge Woman". Her area of research is indigenous theatre and education.

Narcisse Blood is a member of the Blood Tribe (Kainai), located above the Montana, Alberta border. Narcisse is the former Coordinator of a new area of studies for the Red Crow Community College designated as Kainai Studies. Along with this, Narcisse has done a great deal of work in terms of repatriation of ceremonial objects to both Kainai and neighboring tribes with in the Blackfoot confederacy. He and his wife Alvine are involved in traditional societies of the Blood people. With this Narcisse has been a big influence in the development of the current Repatriation Act of The Province of Alberta. In the past Narcisse has served as a member of Blood Tribe Chief and Council for approximately ten and one half years, as well he has had the opportunity to work for the World Council of Indigenous People with such individuals as Marie Marule and George Manual. He has also worked with the National Indian Organization for the Assembly of First Nations. Later choosing to work closer to home, Narcisse became the Vice President of the Indians Association of Alberta with Treaty Seven. Currently, Narcisse also sits on the board for The Nechi Institute in Edmonton, Alberta which is a training center for individuals working in the field of addictions.

Cynthia Chambers is a professor in the Faculty of Education at the University of Lethbridge in southern Alberta. She specializes in Canadian curriculum studies, and teaches courses in language and literacy, Indigenous education, and relational pedagogies. In her research, she practices life writing, *métissage*, as well as relational and community-based approaches to curriculum inquiry.

Roland Sintos Coloma is an assistant professor of Sociology and Equity Studies in Education and the Co-Director of the Centre for Integrative Anti-Racism Studies at the Ontario Institute for Studies in Education of the University of Toronto. His research and teaching focus on history and cultural studies; race, gender, and sexuality; empire, diaspora, and transnationalism; Filipina/o and Asian Canadian studies.

Sharon Anne Cook is a Distinguished University Professor in the Faculty of Education, University of Ottawa. Author or editor of eight books in Education and History as well as about 50 scholarly and professional articles and chapters, her research interests extend to issues of pedagogy, especially related to teaching Peace and Global Education, History, Civics and Health, equity, and gender; and the intersections of the history of women, education, and addictions through visual culture.

Dwayne Donald was born and raised in Edmonton and is a descendent of the Papaschase Cree. He works as an assistant professor in the Faculty of Education at the University of Alberta. The current focus of Dwayne's work is the curricular and pedagogical significance of Indigenous philosophies and ways of knowing.

William E. Doll, Jr. is an Emeritus Professor of Curriculum at Louisiana State University, and Adjunct Professor in the Faculty of Education at the University of Victoria (Canada), and Visiting Professor UBC in Vancouver. In his 55 years of teaching he has taught all grades and most subjects. His books are *A Post-Modern Perspective on Curriculum, Curriculum Visions* (coedited with Noel Gough), and *Chaos, Complexity, Curriculum and Culture* (coedited with Jayne Fleener, Donna Trueit, and John St. Julien). William Doll is a Fulbright Senior Scholar, and in 2005 was awarded the American Educational Research Association's Division B Lifetime Achievement Award. He currently is Associate editor of Complicity, an online journal publishing articles on complexity theory.

Denise Egéa-Kuehne is L.M. "Pat" and Mildred Harrison Endowed Professor and Director of the French Education Project for Research and Teacher Education in the Department of Educational Theory, Policy and Practice at Louisiana State University. Her primary areas of scholarship are theory and philosophy of education, curriculum studies, ethics, and culture and language studies. Her numerous publications include *Derrida & Education* (with Gert Biesta) and *Levinas and Education*, both just republished in paperbacks by Routledge, and more than 100 articles and book chapters. She has delivered over fifty keynotes and guest lectures at universities in the US and across the world, in Bulgaria, Canada, China, Cyprus, England, Finland, France, Malta, New Zealand, Scotland, The Netherlands, Wales. She is a fellow in the Philosophy of Education Society, a member of the John Dewey Society, and has received several awards from the US and from France.

Erika Hasebe-Ludt, PhD, teaches and researches in the Faculty of Education at The University of Lethbridge. Her work in teacher education is in the areas of language and literacy education in connection with curriculum studies, and a focus on narrative inquiry, life writing, and métissage. In addition to various articles in journals and books, she is the coeditor (with Wanda Hurren) of *Curriculum Intertext: Place/Language/Pedagogy* and coauthor (with Cynthia Chambers and Carl Leggo) of *Life Writing and Literary Métissage as an Ethos for Our Times.*

David W. Jardine is a professor of education at the University of Calgary. He is the author of the forthcoming book *Pedagogy Left in Peace.*

Andrejs Kulnieks is assistant professor and program coordinator with the Nipissing University, Schulich School of Education at the Muskoka Campus. His research interests include curriculum theory, language arts, literacies, indigenous knowledge, environmental education, and ecojustice education. Recent publications include: Kulnieks, A., Longboat, D, & Young, K. (2010). *Re-indigenizing Learning: An Eco-hermeneutic Approach to Learning* in *AlterNative: An International Journal of Indigenous People* and Kulnieks, A. Longboat, D, & Young, K. (2011). *Re-indigenizing Canadian Curriculum* in D. Stanley & K. Young (eds.).*Contemporary Studies in Canadian Curriculum.* Calgary, AB: Detselig Enterprises Ltd. He has also published articles with the *Canadian Journal of Environmental Studies,* the *Journal of the Canadian Association of Curriculum Studies,* and the *EcoJustice Review.*

David Lewkowich is a doctoral candidate in McGill University's Faculty of Education. His research interests include young adult literature, reading experience, psychoanalytic theories of learning, and representations of teaching in literature and popular culture. His doctoral research involves an analysis of the cultural and psychic uses of young adult literature.

Nicholas Ng-A-Fook is an associate professor of curriculum theory within the Faculty of Education at the University of Ottawa. He is the acting director of a Canadian Curriculum Theory Project and the Developing A Global Perspective for Educators Program. He is the current co-President of the Canadian Association for Curriculum Studies. He has also published other books like *An Indigenous Curriculum of Place*, and several articles in journals like *Journal of the Canadian Association for Curriculum Studies* (JCACS), *Transnational Curriculum Inquiry* (TCI), and *the Journal of Curriculum Theorizing* (JCT).

Patricia Palulis is an associate professor in the Faculty of Education at the University of Ottawa. She works with language, literacy, literature, culture and spatiality.

William F. Pinar currently holds a Canada Research Chair at the University of British Columbia. He also served as the St. Bernard Parish Alumni Endowed Professor at Louisiana State University, the Frank Talbott Professor at the University of Virginia, and the A. Lindsay O'Connor Professor of American Institutions at Colgate University. He is the author of *The Character of Curriculum Studies* (Palgrave Macmillan, 2011).

Jennifer Rottmann is a PhD candidate within the Faculty of Education at the University of Ottawa. Her research interests include curriculum studies, language and literacy, individual and collective reading experience and narrative inquiry. She has recently published a coauthored article in the *Island Studies Journal* and is a reviewer for the *International Research Journal of Library, Information and Archival Studies*.

Jackie Seidel is an assistant professor and the Director of Field Curriculum in the Faculty of Education at the University of Calgary.

Darren Stanley is associate dean of Graduate Studies, Research and Continuing Education in the Faculty of Education, University of Windsor. His research interests focus on the connections between complex dynamical systems, health and healthy organizations, ecology and ecojustice, and leadership and governance as complex responsive processes. This work has contributed to understanding the underlying conceptual underpinnings, descriptions and images, and pragmatics of living organizations. He has published in the *Journal of Curriculum Theorizing, Complicity: An International Journal of Complexity and Education, Paideusis: Journal for the Canadian Philosophy of Education Society, Educational Insights, Emergence: Complexity and Organization* and *The Innovation Journal: The Public Sector Innovation Journal*.

Kelly Young is an associate professor at Trent University's School of Education and Professional Learning where she teaches English Curriculum methods and foundational courses. Her areas of research include language and literacy, curriculum theorizing, Indigenous knowledges and leadership in ecojustice environmental education. Her research includes two coedited books: *Approaches to Educational Leadership and Practice* (Smale & Young 2007) that challenges contemporary practice in educational leadership, and *Contemporary Studies in Canadian Curriculum: Principles, Portraits and Practices* (Stanley & Young 2011) that includes indigenous and environmental perspectives on Canadian curricula. She has published articles in *Language and Literacy: A Canadian Educational E- Journal (LLRC)*, the *Journal of Curriculum Theorizing* (JCT), the *EcoJustice Review: Educating for the Commons* (EJR), and the *Journal of the Canadian Association for Curriculum Studies* (JCACS).

INDEX

.

CPSIA information can be obtained
at www.ICGtesting.com
Printed in the USA
LVHW080138161222
735343LV00004B/171